Scenic Driving

ARIZONA

Stewart M. Green

FALCON®
HELENA, MONTANA

Falcon® is continually expanding its list of recreational guidebooks. All books include detailed descriptions, accurate maps, and all the information necessary for enjoyable trips. You can order extra copies of this book and get information and prices for other Falcon® guidebooks by writing Falcon, P.O. Box 1718, Helena, MT 59624 or calling toll-free 1-800-582-2665. Also, please ask for a free copy of our current catalog. Visit our website at www.FalconOutdoors.com or contact us by e-mail at falcon@falconguide.com.

Cover photo: Navajo Tribal Park, U.S. 163—Kayenta to Monument Valley scenic drive.
Back cover photo: Arizona 64 scenic drive.
All photos are by Stewart M. Green.

Library of Congress Cataloging-in-Publication Data
Green, Stewart M.
      Scenic driving Arizona / by Stewart Green
            p. cm.
      Rev. ed. of: Arizona scenic drives. c1992
      "A Falcon guide."
      ISBN 1-56044-449-5
      1. Automobile travel—Arizona—Guidebooks.   2. Arizona—Guidebooks.   I. Green, Stewart M. Arizona scenic drives.   II. Title
GV1024.G919   1997
917.910453—dc21
                                                                              96-39245
                                                                              CIP

CAUTION

Outdoor recreational activities are by their very nature potentially hazardous. All participants in such activities must assume the responsibility for their own actions and safety. The information contained in this guidebook cannot replace sound judgment and good decision-making skills, which help reduce risk exposure, nor does the scope of this book allow for disclosure of all the potential hazards and risks involved in such activities.

Learn as much as possible about the outdoor recreational activities you participate in, prepare for the unexpected, and be cautious. The reward will be a safer and more enjoyable experience.

 Text pages printed on recycled paper.

Beauty before me, with it I wander.
Beauty behind me, with it I wander.
Beauty below me, with it I wander.
Beauty above me, with it I wander.
Beauty all around me, with it I wander.
In old age traveling, with it I wander.
On the beautiful trail I am, with it I wander

Dawn Boy's Song on Entering White House
Navajo prayer

ACKNOWLEDGMENTS

This book has its origins in the many trips I took to Arizona as a boy. My family often traveled and camped at the Grand Canyon, Canyon de Chelly, Monument Valley, Hopiland, the vast Navajo Reservation, and Petrified Forest. For that I'm grateful. I still go back to Arizona again and again on pilgrimages. As a photographer I never tire of its beauty and wonder; as a naturalist I enjoy its diversity; as a traveler I rejoice in its soul.

Aldo Leopold, in *Sand County Almanac*, noted that recreational development is "not a job of building roads into lovely country, but of building receptivity into the...human mind." *Scenic Driving Arizona* helps build that receptivity by interpreting and sensitizing travelers to Arizona's geography, natural history, geology, and history. Thanks for that goes first and foremost to Falcon Press. They saw the need and the market for a scenic drives of America series of books. Thanks to publisher Bill Schneider for the continuing opportunity to work with Falcon Press, and kudos for guidebook editor Malcolm Bates who turned a manuscript and pile of photographs into a stunning book.

I appreciate the time National Park, National Forest, and BLM employees gave me in reviewing parts of the manuscript and making suggestions. Thanks to Marti Henderson of CoPubCo for an office space to park my computer and unlimited use of their copy machine and coffee pot. Thanks also to my friends, Dennis and Carol Jackson of Santa Fe, Dave Schultz of Tucson, and Victor Rockwell of Phoenix, for places to unroll a sleeping bag and take a shower. Lastly, a generous thanks to my family—Nancy, Ian, and Brett. This book wouldn't be possible without their love and support.

CONTENTS

Acknowledgments iii
Locator Map vi
Introduction vii
Map Legend xi

The Scenic Drives

1 - Arizona 67: Jacob Lake to Grand Canyon North Rim 1
2 - Oatman Road, Old Route 66 6
3 - Hualapai Mountain Road 11
4 - Arizona 95: Parker to Interstate 40 15
5 - Virgin River Gorge Scenic Drive, Interstate 15 20
6 - Arizona 64: Cameron to Grand Canyon Village 24
7 - U. S. 180: Flagstaff to Valle 30
8 - Sunset Crater & Wupatki Road 35
9 - Arizona Highway 264: Window Rock to Tuba City 40
10 - Canyon de Chelly Rimrock Drives: Navajo Highways 48
11 - Petrified Forest National Park Drive 55
12 - U. S. 60: Globe to Show Low 62
13 - U. S. 60: Miami to Florence Junction 67
14 - The Apache Trail: Arizona Highway 88 71
15 - U. S. 666: The Coronado Trail 79
16 - U. S. 89A: Oak Creek Canyon 86
17 - Perkinsville Road 91
18 - Pearce Ferry Road 96
19 - U. S. 163: Kayenta to Monument Valley 101
20 - Arizona 260:Springerville to Hon Dah 106
21 - Mount Lemmon Highway 111
22 - Gates Pass—Saguaro National Park Drive 118
23 - Arizona Highway 366: The Swift Trail 123
24 - Arizona Highway 186: Willcox to Chiricahua
        National Monument 129

25 - Arizona 82 & 83: Interstate 10 to Nogales 135
26 - U. S. 89: Pinal Pioneer Parkway 140
27 - The Rim Road Forest Road 300 144
28 - Puerto Blanco Drive & Ajo Mountain Drive,
    Organ Pipe National Monument 149
29 - U. S. 95: Yuma to Quartzsite 156

Eroded spires litter the hillside below Massai Point in Chiricahua National Monument. Arizona Highway 186: Willcox to Chiricahua National Monument, page 129.

LOCATOR MAP

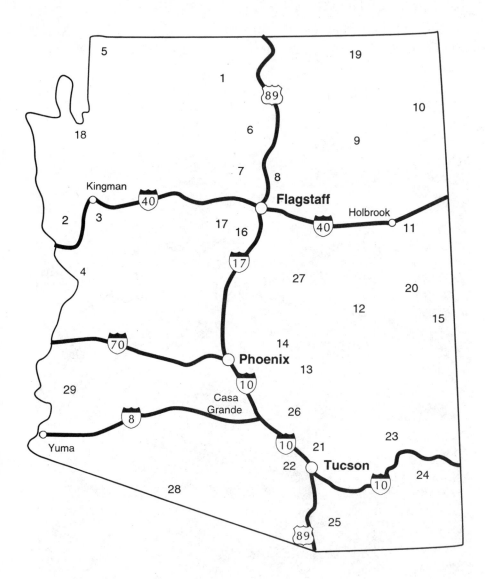

INTRODUCTION

Arizona. There's magic in that word. It conjures up images: ancient Indian cities huddled on the edge of red rock mesas; deep canyons filled with immense silences; sandstone ramparts suffused with the rising sun's golden glow; armies of strange, candelabra-shaped cacti that march across stony bajadas. It's a powerful landscape. One with an ethereal, timeless beauty, one that gets inside you and won't let go.

Arizona, then, begins with the land. It dominates the state, dictating where its cities are built, its rivers flow, and its highways run. It's a land of extreme contrasts and diversity: sere desert plains and lush spring-fed gardens; lofty snowcapped peaks and gorges chiseled by flash floods; windswept sand dunes and grassy prairies dotted with grazing cattle. Arizona, with 113,510 square miles, is divided by geographers into two main physiographic regions—the Colorado Plateau and the Basin and Range Province. A third transition zone, the Mogollon Rim, is sometimes added.

The Colorado Plateau, encompassing the upper two-fifths of the state, is a rugged land of sweeping sagebrush plains, towering cliffs, and deep canyons. Bare-bones sandstone, rubbed raw by swirling winds and quick thunderstorm runoff, characterizes the plateau. Some of Arizona's grandest scenery, including the Grand Canyon, Monument Valley, and Canyon de Chelly, is sculpted from the plateau's colorful stratum. Each sandstone formation—Kaibab, Coconino, Moenkopi, Chinle, Wingate, Kayenta, Navajo, DeChelly and others—tells a different story, its mute layers testimony to the earth's ceaseless changes. Here hides evidence of emerald tides washing on ancient beaches, meandering rivers that coil across forested deltas, vast dune fields shaped by prehistoric winds, and long-extinct life that dominated lost worlds. Volcanic peaks, like the San Francisco Mountains, dot the plateau.

The Basin and Range Province, spreading across southern and western Arizona, is just that—a region of broad basins flanked by ragged mountain ranges that tower above the desert like sky islands. This area, characterized by myriad species of cacti, houses Arizona's largest cities, rich agricultural lands, and untouched swaths of pristine Sonoran Desert at Organ Pipe Cactus National Monument and Kofa National Wildlife Refuge.

The Mogollon Rim divides the Colorado Plateau from the Basin and Range, winding for 200 miles across the state's mid-section like a twisted spine. The rim is a series of great escarpments and mountain ranges, like the volcanic White Mountains and the gaudy cliffs at Oak Creek Canyon. The rim also forms a transition zone between the two provinces with plants and animals from each mingling in a biological melting pot.

Arizona's diverse topography harbors equally diverse plant and animal communities. Desert shrub, including saguaro, creosote, sagebrush, and saltbush, covers forty percent of the state. Conifer forests, like the world's

Coatis are common mammals found along southern Arizona's scenic drives.

largest ponderosa pine forest on the Mogollon Rim, coats ten percent, while pinyon pine, juniper, and oak woodlands spread over twenty-five percent of Arizona. Grasslands make up the remaining twenty-five percent.

A large variety of animals and birds from the Rocky Mountain, Great Basin, and northern Mexican ecological communities live here, including black bear, bighorn sheep, rare Sonoran pronghorn, coati, javelina, and mountain lion. The state's habitats shelter many rattlesnake species, Gila monsters, tropical birds like the coppery-tailed trogon and thick-billed parrot, the six-foot-long Colorado squawfish, and the tiny desert pupfish, a minnow that survives water temperatures in excess of 100 degrees.

Arizona offers a breathtaking selection of scenic attractions, historic points of interest, awesome scenery, and adventuresome recreation. The state boasts twenty-two national parklands, including famed Grand Canyon National Park, Canyon de Chelly National Monument, Coronado National

Memorial, and Lake Mead National Recreation Area. Six national forests and twenty-three Indian reservations, including the almost 9 million-acre Navajo Reservation, spread across Arizona. Rafters thrill to some of the nation's premier whitewater in the Grand Canyon. Fishermen and boaters find watery playgrounds, like Lake Roosevelt and Lake Mead, scattered across the state. Rock climbers discover vertical challenges on Mt. Lemmon's sun-baked granite. The snowy backcountry attracts both skiers and snowmobilers. Thousands of miles of trails and roads lace Arizona, many following ancient

Canyon Lake, on the Apache Trail, is a favorite lake for boating and fishing.

Indian paths, pioneer wagon roads, and emigration routes.

Scenic Driving Arizona allows travelers to explore and discover Arizona's unique spirit of place. Over 1,400 miles of paved and unpaved roads and highways on twenty-nine different scenic drives introduce visitors and residents alike to the diversity and wonder that is Arizona. The drives showcase Arizona's beauty, sampling its famous wonders and finding its hidden corners.

These Arizona highways cross lava flows at Sunset Crater, traverse the South Rim of the Grand Canyon, pass Hopi villages perched on mesa-tops, twist along the historic Coronado Trail, explore the cacti gardens and jagged mountains at Organ Pipe Cactus National Monument, and climb the lofty sky islands of Mt. Graham and Mt. Lemmon. Travelers find waterfalls, Anasazi petroglyphs, ghost towns, abandoned gold mines, petrified logs, dormant volcanos, wind-ruffled pine forests, and stately stands of saguaro.

The thirty-nine scenic drives highlighted here are not by any stretch of the imagination the only scenic drives in Arizona. Almost every stretch of blacktop has some redeeming quality or feature. Some readers may disagree with the selections, feeling an exceptional drive was omitted. And they're right. Few of these selections can be classified as backroads, most are paved two-lane highways. After you've driven these roads, there are others that beckon, leading to secret, off-the-beaten-track places. It's best you discover them yourself. These adventurous backroads include the Ruby Road, Bradshaw Mountain Road, Peach Springs Canyon Road, the old Safford to Clifton highway, El Camino del Diablo, Schnebly Hill Road, and state route 288 through Pleasant Valley. These roads are rough, unpaved, and may require four-wheel-drive vehicles. Be prepared when driving Arizona's scenic highways. Make sure your vehicle is in good working condition. It's a good idea to top off the gas tank before setting off. Know your vehicle and its limits. Above all use common sense. Don't enter washes with running water. Watch for blind curves, steep grades, narrow roads, and slick gravel surfaces. Pull well off the highway for views and sightseeing. Stay on designated roads. Off-road driving on fragile desert soils can leave irrepairable damage. Summer temperatures in the desert regularly climb above 100 degrees. Carry plenty of water for yourself and your car. Five gallons is not too much.

Most of the drives cross public land. Respect private property, livestock fences, and mining claims. Federal laws protect all archaeological and historic antiquities on public land, including Indian ruins and artifacts, fossilized bone and wood, and historic sites. Put out all campfires. Try to camp at a previously used site, it minimizes impact. And pack out trash.

The best roads are those that lead you on, that give you that urge to keep going, to see what's around the next bend. Follow Arizona's highways and watch the landscape reveal itself in snatches. Mountain ranges rise up and recede, canyon depths yawn beyond the guardrail. The spirit lifts as the road rises. Go and immerse yourself in Arizona. It will amaze and astound you. The land will get inside you, and it won't let go.

MAP LEGEND

Scenic Drive (paved)		Interstate	(00)
Scenic Drive (gravel)		U. S. Highway State or Other	(00)
Interstate			
Paved Roads		Principal Road	(375)
Unpaved Roads		Forest Road	[0000]
Points of Interest	6	Pass or Saddle	
Hiking Trail		Mountain	
Overlook	▣	Crater	
Mine		River, Creek, Drainage	
Ski Area			
Picnic Area	🏕	Lakes	
Campground	▲	Dry Lake	
Building	■	Meadow or Swamp	
National Forest Boundary		Springs	
Wilderness Boundary		National Parks	
Indian Reservation		Recreation Areas, State Parks, National Monuments	
State Boundary			

Saguaros line the Gates Pass-Saguaro National Monument Scenic Drive on the west side of the rugged Tucson Mountains.

General description: A forty-four-mile-long, paved scenic drive that traverses the forested Kaibab Plateau to Bright Angel Point on the North Rim of Grand Canyon National Park.

Special attractions: Grand Canyon National Park, Point Imperial, Cape Royal, Bright Angel Point, scenic views, hiking, camping, picnicking, photography, backpacking, wildlife, Kaibab National Forest.

Location: Northern Arizona. Jacob Lake on U.S. 89A, lies thirty miles east of Fredonia and eighty miles west of Page.

Drive route number: Arizona Highway 67.

Travel season: Mid-May until December 1, weather permitting. All the North Rim facilities, including lodges and campgrounds, close in late October, with the park remaining open for day-use only until December 1 or heavy snows close the road.

Camping: The National Park Service's North Rim Campground has eighty-two sites. Reservations are necessary in summer. To make reservations call or write DESTINET, P.O. Box 85705, San Diego, CA 92138-5705, (800) 365-2267. Reservations can be made for no more than eight weeks in advance. DeMotte Park Campground, with twenty-five sites, lies in Kaibab National Forest five miles north of the park. Jacob Lake Campground in Jacob Lake has fifty sites. Primitive camping is permitted in Kaibab National Forest.

Services: North Rim services include showers, laundry, groceries, gas, lodging, and restaurants. Gas is available just north of the park as well. All services are available in Jacob Lake on a limited basis.

Nearby attractions: Marble Canyon, Lake Powell, Lees Ferry, Pipe Spring National Monument, Zion National Park, Coral Pink Sand Dunes State Park (Utah), Arizona Strip.

For more information: Grand Canyon National Park, P.O. Box 129, Grand Canyon, AZ 86023. (520) 638-7888. Forest Service Visitor Center, Kaibab National Forest, 200 W. Railroad Ave., Williams, AZ 86046 (520) 635-4061.

The drive: Arizona Highway 67 traverses south from Jacob Lake across the high, lonely Kaibab Plateau, traveling through stately pine forests, past groves of quaking aspen, and over wide grassy meadows. John Wesley Powell, the famed explorer of the Colorado River and the Grand Canyon, wrote that the Kaibab Plateau "is covered with a beautiful forest, and in the forest charming parks are found....In winter deep snows lie here, but the plateau has four months of the sweetest summer man has every known." This pleasant, paved, forty-four-mile-long drive ends at Grand Canyon Lodge near Bright Angel Point on North Rim of the Grand Canyon National Park. The view from here is spectacular, one of the best in the park.

The highway opens in mid-May after the last snow drifts have melted away. The lodges and campground in the national park close in late October, although the road remains open for day use only until the end of November or heavy snowstorms close the road. Visitors should expect cool temperatures on the plateau and canyon rim, where elevations range between 8,000 and 9,000 feet. Expect daily highs between the forties and seventies, and frosty temperatures at night, even in summer. Heavy thunderstorms commonly occur on July and August afternoons. Winters are severe. Anyone venturing in by skis or snowmobile should be prepared for subfreezing temperatures and frequent snowfall. The long distance from Jacob Lake, coupled with snowfall that regularly exceeds twenty-five feet, makes plowing the highway prohibitively expensive and impractical.

The scenic drive begins in Jacob Lake at the intersection of U.S. Highway 89A and Arizona Highway 67. Jacob Hamblin, a Mormon explorer, lent his name to shallow Jacob Lake. During the 1850s through the 1870s he poked around northern Arizona, looking for townsites for prospective Mormon settlements. Hamblin, also a missionary among the Hopi and Navajo, negotiated several treatys with local Indians. Jacob Lake, at 7,900 feet, is a small service community with gas, groceries, lodging, and restaurant available. At the intersection of the highways is Jacob Lake Campground, a fifty-site National Forest campground. There are several hiking trails nearby. Ask at the Forest Service visitor center in Jacob Lake for more information. Just south of town on the drive is an R.V. park.

The road heads south from Jacob Lake, a winding corridor that slices through a dense forest of 100-foot-high ponderosa pines. Occasional groves of white-barked quaking aspen and small grassy meadows border the highway. The drive is a designated National Forest Scenic Byway and an Arizona State Scenic Parkway. The Kaibab Plateau Trail, a section of the Arizona Trail, parallels the highway. The Arizona Trail is a proposed path from Mexico to Utah. The road also follows the old five-day stagecoach route early Grand Canyon visitors took to the North Rim.

The Kaibab Plateau, a great uplifted monocline called Kaibab or "Mountain lying down" by the Piute Indians, is capped by the gray-white Kaibab limestone that is well-exposed along the rim of the Grand Canyon. The limestone, full of tiny fossils, was deposited 25 million years ago in a warm, shallow sea. Few streams or lakes appear atop the plateau because of poor surface drainage. Most water flows through underground passageways, before bursting forth as giant springs like Thunder River and Roaring Springs below the Grand Canyon's rim.

The canyon's north rim lies 1,000 feet higher than the Coconino Plateau and the South Rim. The North Rim, less than ten miles from its southern counterpart, embraces different ecosystems in its Canadian life zone. The north rim receives twenty-eight inches of rainfall annually, twice the amount on the south rim. The landscape along the scenic drive as it traverses the Kaibab Plateau is characterized by two distinct coniferous forests—the ponderosa pine near Jacob Lake and the Englemann and blue spruce, and Douglas fir forest.

This is a land that teems with a diversity of life. Wildflowers—goldenrod,

Visitors enjoy the view south from Bright Angel Point on the North Rim of Grand Canyon National Park.

sunflower, aster, columbine, and Kaibab paintbrush—carpet road-side meadows in summer. Autumn brings the flutter of aspen leaves falling to the ground like freshly minted gold coins. Animals, including over fifty mammal species and ninety bird species, inhabit the forest. DeMotte Park, just before the park boundary, and other grassy areas are good places to spot mule deer, Merriam's turkey, blue grouse, occasional mountain lions, and the Kaibab squirrel.

The Kaibab squirrel is perhaps the plateau's most famous resident. The Kaibab squirrel is closely related to the Abert squirrel on the south rim, in fact they were once the same species. Now the Grand Canyon separates the two species, both of which rely on the ponderosa pine as a year-round food source. The squirrels, trapped in their respective forests, evolved into different species with different characteristics. The Kaibab squirrel is found only on the Kaibab Plateau and nearby Mt. Trumbull. A walk in the woods along the drive usually yields a squirrel sighting. Look for a large, handsome squirrel with a dark body and magnificent white tail.

DeMotte Park, a large meadow rimmed by forest, lies twenty-five miles south of Jacob Lake. A twenty-five-site U.S. Forest Service campground lies just west of the highway at 8,750 feet elevation. A roadside stop also has a lodge, restaurant, gas, and groceries. Forest Road 422 heads west from here, leading to branch dirt roads that dead-end at remote, spectacular Grand Canyon overlooks including Fire Point, Timp Point, Parissawampitts Point, and Crazy Jug Point. Forest Roads 610 and 611 head east from the drive just south of DeMotte Park. These end at points that overlook Marble Canyon and the Vermillion Cliffs. Check at the National Forest info station in Jacob Lake for road conditions.

The drive continues south and enters Grand Canyon National Park. The highway winds through shallow canyons, past lush forests, and humpbacked ridges. The road makes an abrupt bowknot bend, passes the eighty-two-site National Park campground, and ends at a large parking lot by historic Grand Canyon Lodge. A short .5-mile walk on a paved trail leads to 8,153-foot Bright Angel Point.

This airy overlook is a fitting end to a great Arizona road trip. It's a mild shock to step from the serene, shadowy forest to the brink of the arid, dazzling Grand Canyon. Sharp cliffs stairstep down from the rim, ending in boulder-choked canyons and rounded platforms, before more cliffs drop away to the hidden Colorado River. Buttes, spires, buttresses, ampitheaters, temples, mesas, and gargoyles, all painted in a stone rainbow of color, fill the abyss. Ten miles across the void, sits the south rim and the Coconino Plateau, and beyond tower the sacred San Francisco Peaks, the eroded remains of a once mighty stratovolcano.

Facilities and services on the North Rim, besides camping, include lodging, dining, tours, interpretative activities, showers, trail rides, a general store, laudromat, and gasoline. Campground reservations are recommended in the summer months. The dirt roads that lead to remote overlooks make good mountain bike rides. Many excellent hiking trails, including the ten-mile Widforss Trail, thread along the canyon rim. The fourteen-mile-long North Kaibab Trail drops down to the river.

An excellent side trip heads east just north of Bright Angel Point and travels eight miles to Point Imperial, the highest point on either rim, and twenty miles to Cape Royal and its scenic views of the eastern Grand Canyon. An Anasazi Indian ruin sits along the road near Walhalla Overlook.

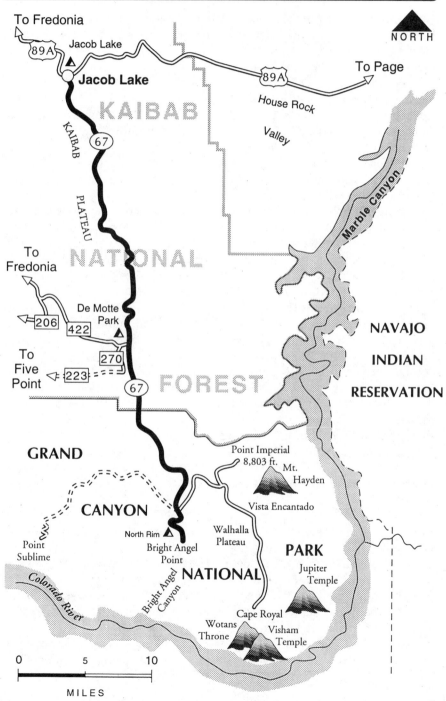

To Fredonia

89A Jacob Lake

Jacob Lake

KAIBAB

KAIBAB

67

PLATEAU

NATIONAL

To Fredonia

De Motte Park

206 422

To Five Point

270

223

67

FOREST

To Page

House Rock

Valley

Marble Canyon

NORTH

NAVAJO

INDIAN

RESERVATION

GRAND

CANYON

Point Sublime

North Rim

Bright Angel Point

NATIONAL

Colorado River

Bright Angel Canyon

Point Imperial 8,803 ft.

Mt. Hayden

Vista Encantado

Walhalla Plateau

PARK

Jupiter Temple

Cape Royal

Wotans Throne

Visham Temple

0   5   10

MILES

5

General description: This forty-seven-mile-long road climbs from the broad Sacramento Valley just south of Kingman over Sitgreaves Pass in the jagged Black Mountains to the old gold mining camp of Oatman. The drive then runs south to Golden Shores just north of Topock.

Special attractions: Oatman, Goldroad, old mines, hiking, wildlife, scenic views, Havasu National Wildlife Refuge.

Location: Far western Arizona. The drive runs between Kingman and Golden Shores just north of Interstate 40's Exit 1 at the California border.

Drive route name: Oatman Road, Old Route 66.

Travel season: Year-round. The road is mostly dry except for occasional winter rainstorms and summer cloudbursts. A dusting of snow might fall a few times each winter atop the mountains.

Camping: No public campgrounds along the drive. Ed's Camp offers a rustic RV campground, otherwise there are campgrounds in Kingman and Bullhead City. Hualapai Mountain Park south of Kingman has a campground atop the Hualapai Mountains. Primitive camping is allowed on BLM lands along the drive. Check with the BLM office in Kingman (602) 757-3161 for information. Katherine Landing Campground, with 173 sites, in Lake Mead National Recreation Area lies just north of Bullhead City.

Services: All services are available in Kingman and Bullhead City. Limited services are found in Golden Shores, Oatman, and Ed's Camp. Fill your gas tank before driving the road.

Nearby attractions: Kingman, Hualapai Mountain Park, Hualapai Mountains Back Country Byway, Lake Havasu, Lake Mead National Recreation Area, Grand Canyon Caverns, Chloride, Bullhead City, Laughlin, Lake Mohave, East Mojave National Scenic Area.

For more information: BLM Kingman Field Office, 2475 Beverly Ave., Kingman, AZ 86401, (520) 757-3161. Kingman Chamber of Commerce, 333 W. Andy Devine, P.O. Box 1150, Kingman, AZ 86402, (520) 753-6106. Oatman-Goldroad Chamber of Commerce, P.O. Box 422, Oatman, AZ 86433, (520) 768-4871.

The drive: The Oatman Road traverses a forty-seven-mile section of beloved Old Route 66, a 2,400-mile-long highway that linked Chicago's Lake Michigan with the Pacific Ocean's billowing surf at road's end in Los Angeles. For some fifty years, from the mid-1920s through the mid-1970s when parts of five different interstate highways replaced it, Route 66 was America's national road. The highway, crossing eight states, crept through so many small towns it became known as the Main Street of America.

Through Arizona, Route 66 traversed a railroad corridor surveyed by Lieutenant Edward F. Beale and his exotic caravan of soldiers, camels, and

The Oatman Road, Old Route 66, meanders through the scenic Black Mountains.

Arabian camel drivers in 1857. Beale predicted his route, later followed by the Atchison, Topeka & Santa Fe Railroad and Route 66, would "inevitably become the great emigrant road to California." In the early 1930s Route 66 did indeed become a major emigrant road, what novelist John Steinbeck called in *The Grapes of Wrath* the "mother road, the road of flight," when as many as 500,000 dispossessed, jobless refugees from Oklahoma, Texas, and Arkansas escaped the Dust Bowl and the Great Depression's poverty by migrating west along the highway to California, the land of dreams and plenty.

The Oatman Road scenic drive follows one of the last and best preserved stretches of Route 66 from Exit 44 on Interstate 40 just south of Kingman to Golden Shores four miles north of Exit 1 on Interstate 40. The section from Oatman to Golden Shores is deteriorating, with some pavement sections ripped up and graveled. The road, built for leisurely driving, takes a couple hours to drive. Allow more time to explore Oatman and the ruins at Goldroad. The road offers spectacular overlooks, old mine ruins, wild burros and bighorn sheep, and hiking access to the mostly wild Black Range.

Weather atop the drive is pleasant year-round, although summer can be very hot. Bullhead City, about fifteen miles northwest of Oatman, is one of the nation's hottest towns, with temperatures regularly climbing above 110 degrees. Oatman and the higher Black Mountains are cooler, but expect summer highs in the nineties and 100s. Spring, winter, and fall are mild, with daily highs ranging from fifty to ninety degrees. Rainfall is infrequent, and snow might dust the range's highest peaks two or three times a winter.

The Oatman Road scenic drive begins just south of Kingman at Exit 44 on Interstate 40. The road, passing occasional homes and ranchettes, heads straight southwest across the Sacramento Valley, a broad basin between the Hualapai Mountains to the east and the Black Mountains to the west. The valley's bedrock floor hides beneath thousands of feet of gravel, sand, and silt washed down from the mountains. After a few miles the road crosses sandy Sacramento Wash, a dry arroyo that drains the wide valley, before climbing up a bajada or alluvial outwash apron east of the Black Mountains.

After about twelve miles the highway crosses Meadow Creek and turns west up its wide valley into the Black Mountains. Thimble Butte, a 4,062-foot-high volcanic neck, lifts its castellated ramparts to the north. The Black Mountains, one of Arizona's longest ranges, measures over 100 miles from its northernmost reach at Lake Mead to its southern tip at Interstate 40. The range is a jumbled chaos of volcanic rocks deposited by violent volcanic eruptions in Cretaceous and Tertiary times between 50 and 100 million years ago. The sharp, toothed peaks, like Thimble Butte, that stud the range along the highway are the petrified inner conduits of long extinct volcanoes that once belched fire and ash. Horizontal-lying lava flows, some as young as two million years, top the mountains and form bands of dark basalt cliffs along the range crest.

The road passes Ed's Camp a few miles west up Meadow Creek. This tree-shaded stop, nestled in the scrubby hills alongside the highway, is one of the last intact self-contained Route 66 Roadhouses. The camp, established by the late Ed Egerton, boomed in the 1930s and '40s when streams of travelers wound their way over the Black Mountains. At Ed's Camp they could stop, gas up, top their water jugs, gather information on road hazards and detours ahead, or rest up for the rigors of driving across the broiling California desert. Egerton's yard was filled with belongings that travelers pawned for an extra dollar's worth of gas to bring them closer to the Pacific shore. Here too, nervous lowlanders could hire a local to drive the family sedan over the steep, spiraling road where abrupt dropoffs bordered the outside lanes and grades reached seventeen percent. Today Ed's Camp offers several RV campsites, a small store, and a fire agate mine. The highway twists and switchbacks west, steadily climbing past low lava-capped hills sparsely covered with Joshua trees, scrubby junipers, ocotillos, creosote bushes, prickly pear cacti, and teddy bear cholla cacti. A few miles higher the road crosses the range

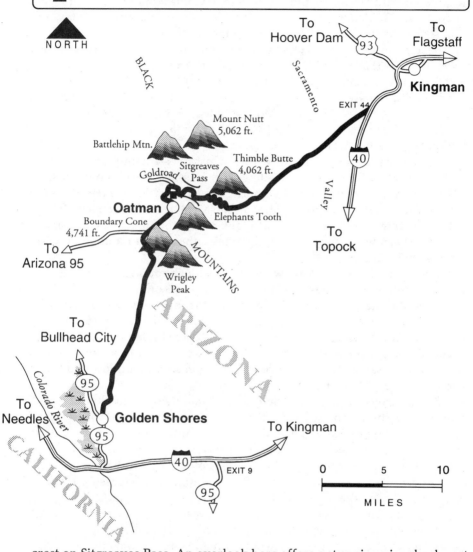

2   OATMAN ROAD—OLD ROUTE 66

NORTH

BLACK

To Hoover Dam

93

To Flagstaff

Sacramento

Kingman

EXIT 44

40

Mount Nutt
5,062 ft.

Battlehip Mtn.

Sitgreaves
Pass

Thimble Butte
4,062 ft.

Goldroad

Oatman

Boundary Cone
4,741 ft.

Elephants Tooth

Valley

To
Topock

To
Arizona 95

MOUNTAINS

Wrigley
Peak

ARIZONA

To
Bullhead City

Colorado River

95

To
Needles

95

Golden Shores

To Kingman

40

EXIT 9

95

CALIFORNIA

0   5   10

MILES

crest on Sitgreaves Pass. An overlook here offers a stunning view back east to the ragged, forested Hualapai Mountains and the Sacramento Valley.

Another fine view unfolds from a point just west of the summit. The road loops below, the spiny ridges of the Black Mountains march northward, the turquoise ribbon of the Colorado River glistens in its deep valley, and distant, hazy California mountain ranges poke above the dry barrenness.

The narrow highway drops steeply beyond the viewpoint, switchbacking down steep mountainsides strewn with broken volcanic crags. Some of these switchbacks and roadcuts were excavated seventy years ago by Chinese laborers. Many of the switchbacks are adorned by original, dry-laid, rock retaining walls.

Further down, on a pinched corner, lies a few crumpled walls and weathered foundations that mark the site of Goldroad, the area's first gold boom town. Gold was discovered in the Black Mountains in the 1860s, but rich strikes in the Cerbat Mountains to the northeast emptied the area of prospectors. In 1902, however, Jose Jenerez and his grubstake partner struck a wealthy lode that assayed at forty ounces to the ton. They sold the mine for $50,000 a few months later. A town named Goldroad grew up around the diggings and housed hundreds of miners. By the time the richest ore was exhausted in 1931, the Goldroad lode yielded $7.3 million dollars of low-grade ore. The town was razed in 1949 to save on taxes. Under Arizona law, buildings, whether in use or not, are taxed—a law which has led to the needless destruction of many of Arizona's historic structures.

The road continues winding downhill, passing steep mountainsides littered with mine tailings and weathered headframes. After a few miles the drive swings south and enters Oatman. The town nestles in shallow valleys among knobby hills on the west flank of the Black Mountains. The Elephant's Tooth, a sharp white quartz peak, dominates the abrupt mountain escarpment above Oatman.

Oatman got its start in 1902 when Ben Taddock found a vein of gold. In the next three years the Vivian Mine yielded over $3 million in gold, and the rush was on. The town that grew up around the mine was called Vivian. In 1909 it was renamed Oatman, supposedly for Olive Oatman, a girl kidnapped by Indians in 1851 and later sold as a slave to Mojave Indians on the Colorado River. During its prosperous heyday the town boasted two banks, seven hotels, twenty saloons, a stock exchange, the Mohave and Milltown Railroad, and almost 20,000 residents.

Mining thrived until 1942 when the federal government shut down all working gold mines for the war effort. The Oatman mines, at the center of Arizona's richest gold district, yielded over $36 million in ore. Overnight the town's population was decimated. After the war, labor costs rose and mining the gold became too expensive. The crowning blow came in 1952 when Route 66 was rerouted south around the Black Mountains, bypassing Oatman altogether. Today the town subsists on a growing tourist trade. It's a good place to stop and wander. The setting is spectacular and numerous old buildings survive including the false-fronted Lee Lumber Company, the Glory Hole Antique Shop, and the old Oatman Hotel, now converted into a small museum.

The road runs southwest from Oatman, passing scrubby volcanic peaks pockmocked with abandoned mines, including the fabulously wealthy Tom Reed Mine and the Gold Dust and White Chief mines. After two miles a junction is reached. The drive turns left or south on Old Route 66. Arizona Highway 95, just south of Bullhead City, lies twelve miles down the other fork.

The drive swings around prominent 4,741-foot-high Boundary Cone south of the junction and rolls over a wide, spreading bajada of coarse gravel that slopes west to the Colorado River. Sections of the old highway blacktop have eroded away on this segment and are replaced by gravel. This seventeen-mile leg glides southwest to Golden Shores, dipping through shallow arroyos, crossing greasewood-covered gravel terraces, and curving around low hills.

Golden Shores, a small resort community at the drive's end, lies alongside Topock Marsh and Havasu National Wildlife Refuge. The shimmering thread of the Colorado River runs just west of the marsh. Topock, a Mojave Indian word meaning "water crossing," and Interstate 40 sit four miles south of Golden Shores.

3 HUALAPAI MOUNTAIN ROAD

General description: A sixteen-mile-long paved and gravel road that climbs from Kingman to the crest of the rugged Hualapai Mountains in west-central Arizona.

Special attractions: Hualapai Mountain Park, camping, picnicking, hiking, rock climbing, birdwatching, Wild Cow Springs Recreation Site.

Location: West-central Arizona. South of Kingman and Interstate 40.

Drive route names: Hualapai Mountain Road and Hualapai Ridge Road (BLM Road 2123).

Travel season: Year-round. The gravel section of the road beyond Hualapai Mountain Park can be blocked with snow in the winter.

Camping: An eighty-one-site campground is in Hualapai Mountain Park, with restrooms, grills, and eleven sites with full hook-ups. Wild Cow Springs, a primitive BLM campground, has campsites and restrooms. Bring your own water.

Services: All services are available in Kingman.

Nearby attractions: Hualapai Mountains Back Country Byway, Kingman, Oatman, Havasu National Wildlife Refuge, Grand Canyon Caverns, Old Route 66, Lake Mead National Recreation Area.

For more information: BLM, Kingman Field Office, 2475 Beverly Avenue, Kingman, AZ 86401. (520) 757-3161. Kingman Chamber of Commerce, P.O. Box 1150, Kingman, AZ 86402, (520) 753-6106.

The drive: The Hualapai Mountains, the highest range in western Arizona, lifts its craggy summits high over hot desert valleys. From Interstate 40 they shimmer in summer like a mirage on the horizon. Bullhead City, Needles, and Lake Havasu City, less than forty miles to the west, are regularly the nation's official hot spot. But climb 5,000 feet up the Hualapai Mountain Road from Kingman, and the summer temperature averages a cool seventy-eight degrees.

The paved twelve-mile-long Hualapai Mountain Road climbs up to popular 2,320-acre Hualapai Mountain Park, a Mohave County parkland.

The Hualapai Mountain Road twists away below the range crest to Wild Cow Springs.

Drivers can continue four more miles on the Hualapai Ridge Road, an unpaved, mostly one-lane road that ends at the Bureau of Land Management's Wild Cow Springs Recreation Site, before turning around and retracing their steps. Those with four-wheel drive vehicles can continue south another twenty-one miles along the range crest to scenic Boriana Canyon. This entire route, from Kingman to Boriana Canyon and Yucca is the BLM's forty-five-mile-long Hualapai Mountains Back Country Byway. Summer visitors can expect pleasantly warm temperatures with daily highs between seventy and eighty-five degrees. Expect hot temperatures in the desert near Kingman. Nights are generally cool. Spring and fall are warm, with temperatures in the forties to seventies in the higher elevations, and fifties to nineties lower down. Winters are cold up in the park. Snow and rain closes the gravel section of the drive, although the Hualapai Mountain Road is passable. Annual precipitation above 6,000 feet ranges between eighteen and twenty inches.

The scenic drive begins in Kingman, off Interstate 40, at the intersection of Andy Devine Avenue and Stockton Hill Road. Kingman, the seat of Mohave County, began as a railroad stop in 1883 and was named for Lewis

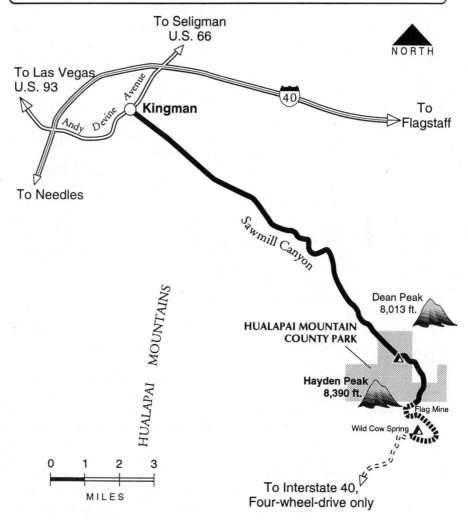

To Seligman
U.S. 66

NORTH

To Las Vegas
U.S. 93

Andy Devine Avenue

Kingman

40

To
Flagstaff

To Needles

Sawmill Canyon

HUALAPAI MOUNTAINS

Dean Peak
8,013 ft.

HUALAPAI MOUNTAIN
COUNTY PARK

Hayden Peak
8,390 ft.

Flag Mine

Wild Cow Spring

0   1   2   3

MILES

To Interstate 40,
Four-wheel-drive only

Kingman, an engineer. The Hualapai Mountain Road heads southeast from Kingman and enters Sawmill Canyon. Climbing quickly, the drive passes from Mojave desert scrub into a dense pinyon pine and juniper forest that sprawls across the lower mountain slopes. Pinyon-juniper forest is excellent animal habitat, particularly for mule deer which use it for shelter and forage in the cold winter months.

After ten miles, the drive reaches Hualapai Mountain Park spread across a high saddle between 8,013-foot Dean Peak and 8,390-foot Hayden Peak. The range's high point, 8,417-foot Hualapai Peak, lies just south of the park. Granite crags and boulders jut boldly above the dense ponderosa pine and oak woodland that coats the steep mountainsides. Groves of wind-ruffled quaking aspen and white fir grow high atop the range crest.

The Hualapais, composed of ancient Precambrian schist, gneiss, and granite, are famed for their many rocks and minerals, including one of the world's purest mica deposits. Gold, silver, and tungsten have all been extracted from the range. The mountains are named for the Hualapai (pronounced wall-a-pie) Indians, meaning "people of the tall pines," a Yuman tribe that once lived in the broad valleys below the range and along the lower Colorado River. The tribe was relocated northwest in 1870 to their present reservation bordering Grand Canyon National Park.

The Hualapai Mountains sit at an ecological crossroads. To the west along the Colorado River and extending into California lies the Mojave Desert with its characteristic Joshua trees and basin-and-range topography. Southward into Mexico stretches the Sonoran Desert and its many species of cacti and colorful floral displays. And to the northeast lies the Great Basin Desert and the Colorado Plateau. Here, in the Hualapai Mountains, these three great deserts meet and mingle. Stately saguaro cacti in Arizona's northernmost stand and ocotillo grow along the range's southern margin. Joshua tree forests spread along wide bajadas or outwash plains beneath the range's western escarpment. The pinyon pine and juniper woodland on the mountain slopes are part of a typical Great Basin ecosystem.

This remote range also harbors a unique and rich variety of wildlife. Over eighty bird species, including hawks, owls, warblers, Gambel quail, whip-poorwills, hummingbirds, and flycatchers, live here. Mammals include the only elk herd in western Arizona and mule deer, mountain lion, bobcat, coyote, rabbits, raccoons, squirrels, and skunks. The endangered Hualapai Mexican vole inhabits Antelope Wash below Wild Cow Spring. The rare rosy boa, Sonoran mountain kingsnake, western blackheaded rattlesnake, Arizona black rattlesnake, and blacktailed rattlesnake are some of the fifteen reptile species in the range.

The Hualapai Mountain Park is a great place to explore the range and discover some of its secrets. The park has a large eighty-one-site campground, rental cabins, a small visitor center, and picnic facilities. A fifteen-mile trail system winds through the park, including a great trail that climbs two miles from the campground to the lofty summit of Hayden Peak. The unobstructed view from the summit includes the Black Mountains, the Aquarius Mountains, and the plateaus above the western Grand Canyon. Hualapai Peak can be climbed via the Aspen Springs Trail and the Potato Patch Loop Trail.

Beyond the park, the drive follows Hualapai Ridge Road (BLM Road 2123), a narrow track that winds across steep hillsides and dips in and out of narrow canyons below the range crest. Gambel oak, manzanita, juniper, mountain mahogany, walnut trees, and ponderosa pine grow on the slopes. After four miles, Wild Cow Springs Recreation Site is reached. This primitive campground has campsites, pit toilets, grills, and tables. Bring your own water, none is available here. The campground is also the end of the road for passenger cars. Turn around and head back—the scenery is just as nice the second time.

General description: This fifty-seven-mile scenic drive parallels the scenic east bank of the Colorado River from Parker through Lake Havasu City to Interstate 40 nine miles east of the California border.

Special attractions: Buckskin Mountain State Park, Lake Havasu State Park, Havasu National Wildlife Refuge, Topock Gorge, Lake Havasu City, London Bridge, camping, hiking, fishing, boating, waterskiing, canoeing, wildlife observation.

Location: Far western Arizona. The road follows the Colorado River between Parker and Interstate 40.

Drive route number: Arizona Highway 95.

Travel season: Year-round. Spring, fall, and winter are ideal times to drive the highway and visit Lake Havasu. Temperatures generally average between sixty and ninety, with occasional light rain in winter. Summers are scorching hot. Lake Havasu City's daily May high is ninety-five degrees, with July's average reaching 108 degrees. September cools down to 102 degrees. Summer offers the lake's best fishing.

Camping: La Paz County Park and Buckskin Mountain State Park north of Parker have campgrounds with hook-ups and showers. La Paz has 600 sites and Buckskin Mountain eighty-three, with twenty-seven additional sites in its River Island Unit. Empire Landing, eight miles north of Parker on the California side of the river, has a campground with a beach. Lake Havasu State Park boasts five campgrounds, although two are boat-only access. The Pittsburg Point Unit, on the west side of London Bridge, offers 1,150 sites. The Cattail Cove Unit and Sand Point Marina, both fifteen miles south of Lake Havasu City off AZ 95, have forty and 177 sites respectively. Private campgrounds and RV parks are found in both Parker and Lake Havasu City.

Services: All services are available in Parker and Lake Havasu City.

Nearby attractions: Oatman, Hualapai Mountain Park, Kingman, Hualapai Back Country Byway, Alamo Lake State Park, Kofa Mountains, Kofa National Wildlife Refuge, Quartzsite, Bullhead City, Lake Mojave, Lake Mead National Recreation Area.

For more information: Lake Havasu Area Visitor and Convention Bureau, 314 London Bridge Rd., Lake Havasu City, AZ 86403, (520) 453-3444. BLM Havasu Resource Area, 2610 Sweetwater, Lake Havasu City, AZ 86403, (520) 505-1200.

The drive: The fifty-seven-mile-long Arizona 95 drive parallels the scenic lower Colorado River from Parker to Interstate 40. The road unfolds through spectacular desert terrain—the river gorge lined with ancient volcanic rocks, cactus-studded mountains that lift craggy summits into the brilliant sky, and Lake Havasu shining like a watery jewel against a tawny desert carpet. The land here is elemental. It's been lifted, heaved, twisted, and faulted, and then rubbed down to bare-bones rock and left exposed to the sun, wind, and sky.

The paved, two-lane highway is best driven in spring, fall, and winter. Daily temperature highs range between sixty and ninety during these months, although winter days can be cooler. Parker's average January high is a pleasant sixty-seven degrees. Light rain occasionally falls. Summers are blistering hot. July, the hottest month, averages 108 degrees daily in Lake Havasu City. On July 7, 1905 Parker recorded the state's all-time high of 127 degrees. Expect summer highs to be at least in the low 100s. Localized thunderstorms drop heavy rains in late summer.

The drive begins in Parker, a 420-foot-high town lying on the Colorado River's east bank just across from California. The town, named for U.S. Commissioner of Indian Affairs General Eli Parker, was founded in 1865 and lay four miles south of its present location. In 1905 the Arizona and California Railroad laid track to the north, and the town moved up river alongside the railroad. Parker, surrounded by the Mojave and Chemehuevi Indian tribes' Colorado River Indian Reservation, is the gateway to southern Lake Havasu. To start the drive, turn north in downtown Parker on Arizona 95.

The highway, heading north, crosses the Bouse Formation, a layer of limestone, siltstone, and mudstone over 2,000 feet thick. The formation, deposited about 5 million years, was laid down on the Gulf of California's floor when it reached this far north. Ubiquitous creosote bushes are widely spaced on the dry desert floor.

After a few miles the road enters rough, barren hills between the river and the Buckskin Mountains. This range trends northwest across the river as the Whipple Mountains in California. The highway, between two and four lanes in this stretch, is flanked by outcrops and roadcuts of ancient Precambrian gneiss that composes the Buckskin Mountains' core. Towering volcanic crags scatter across the mountains east of the drive, forming high cliffs and buttresses. The Whipple Mountains to the highway's west in California form a foreboding wall broken by spires, buttes, mesas, and mountains.

The Buckskin Mountains have been thoroughly prospected since 1864 when a rich copper discovery, the Planet Mine, was made. Several ghost towns are found on its backroads. The best preserved is Swansea, a company town founded to smelter the area's copper in 1909. The townsite is marked by the brick smelter's ruins, a few crumbling buildings, foundations, and tailings from the mill and mine.

The highway section from Parker to Parker Dam is called the Parker Strip. Numerous motels, resorts, and campgrounds lie along the Colorado River on both the Arizona and California shores. La Paz County Park, eight miles north of Parker, offers 600 campsites, picnic areas, showers, tennis courts, a swimming beach, boat ramp, and eighteen-hole Emerald Canyon Golf Course. Three miles north sits 1,676-acre Buckskin Mountain State Park, a popular destination for campers, hikers, waterskiers, and fishermen. Just upriver is the park's River Island Unit, with camping, picnicking, and river access. The glassy river on the Parker Strip is actually Lake Moovalya, a

London Bridge in Lake Havasu City, on Arizona 95, is one of Arizona's most popular visitor attractions.

reservoir formed by Headgate Rock Dam at Parker. Moovalya is a Chemehuevi Indian word meaning "blue water."

The turnoff to Parker Dam is at Mile 15 from Parker. The dam, reputed to be the world's deepest, reaches down through 235 feet of river-bottom gravel to its bedrock anchor. Only the top eighty-five feet of the 385-foot concrete dam rises above the river. The dam forming forty-five-mile-long, 25,000-acre Lake Havasu, stores water that is diverted to southern California via the 392-mile-long Colorado River Aqueduct. Parker Dam was completed in 1938. Visitors can inspect the dam and power plant on a free, self-guided tour.

Past the dam, the highway swings east for a couple miles and crosses the Bill Williams River branch of Lake Havasu. The river, originating in the mountains near Prescott, is named for early 19th century trapper and guide Bill Williams. He was described as, "Long, sinewy and bony, with a chin and nose almost meeting, he was the typical plainsman of the dime novel....His buckskin suit was bedaubed with grease until it had the appearance of polished leather; his feet were never encased in anything but moccasins, and his buckskin trousers had the traditional fringe on the outer seam." The

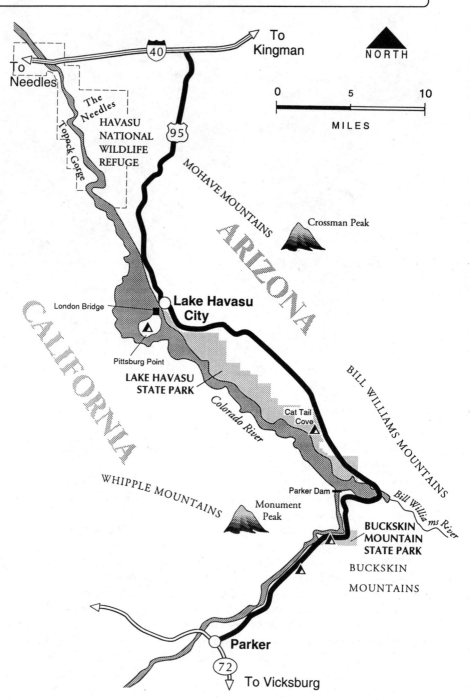

To
Kingman

NORTH

0   5   10

M I L E S

To
Needles

The
Needles

HAVASU
NATIONAL
WILDLIFE
REFUGE

Topock Gorge

MOHAVE MOUNTAINS

ARIZONA

Crossman Peak

London Bridge — **Lake Havasu City**

Pittsburg Point

CALIFORNIA

LAKE HAVASU STATE PARK

Colorado River

Cat Tail Cove

BILL WILLIAMS MOUNTAINS

WHIPPLE MOUNTAINS

Monument Peak

Parker Dam

Bill Williams River

BUCKSKIN MOUNTAIN STATE PARK

BUCKSKIN MOUNTAINS

Parker

72

To Vicksburg

marshy wetlands along the river upstream from the bridge provides great bird habitat and is protected in the south section of Havasu National Wildlife Refuge. A pulloff on the north side of the bridge offers picturesque views of the river and the basalt-rimmed Buckskin Mountains beyond.

The highway runs northwest from the bridge and skirts the western edge of the Bill Williams Mountains and the Aubrey Hills. A turnoff to Lake Havasu State Park lies six miles north of the Bill Williams River. A spur road leads one mile down to the Cattail Cove Unit, with forty campsites, and Sand Point Marina, with a concession-operated 177-site campground. The Aubrey Hills are protected as a 6,000-acre bighorn sheep sanctuary in the state park.

Lake Havasu State Park, Arizona's largest state parkland, is twenty-five miles long and encompasses over 15,000 acres. The park stretches along the lake's eastern shore from near Parker Dam to just north of Lake Havasu City. The lake, a popular year-round destination for boaters, waterskiers, and fishermen, is stocked with bluegill, crappie, large-mouth bass, and catfish. It is a well-known striped bass fishery, with the stripers ranging from five pounds to over fifty.

The drive drops down into the Chemehuevi Valley and Lake Havasu City on thick gravel terraces deposited by the ancestral Colorado River. Lake Havasu City began in 1964 with twenty-four square miles of desert adjoining the lake and a dream. California industrialist Robert McCulloch, who bought the land for $75 an acre, teamed up with Texan C.V. Wood to create a new city out of the barrenness. What really put the new town on the map and brought attention, money, and tourists was their purchase of the London Bridge in 1968. The bridge, bought for $2.46 million, was disassembled, shipped by sea and land, and its 10,275 blocks rebuilt above a lake channel. The bridge, dedicated in 1971, is Arizona's second most popular attraction next to the Grand Canyon. Lake Havasu City, with a population of 20,000, is now a complete resort community. Numerous hotels, restaurants, and campgrounds scatter across town. Visitor activities include fishing, golfing, houseboating, waterskiing, and boat tours on the lake.

The drive runs north across alluvial gravels deposited by the Colorado River and after a few miles bends northeast and climbs into the rugged Mojave Mountains. Towering volcanic necks, the inner conduits of long-extinct volcanoes, punctuate the landscape. Dikes, formed when molten magma seeped into cracks and fissures, radiate from the rocky peaks. Creosote, ocotillo, cactus, and wildflowers including brittlebush spread over the dry mountains and washes. About ten miles north of Lake Havasu City the road crests the range and drops for five miles down a broad, gravel apron to Sacramento Wash and Interstate 40.

Kingman lies thirty-five miles northeast up the interstate, while Topock and the California border sit a scant nine miles west. Topock is the setting-off point for an excellent seventeen-mile-long canoe trip down Topock Gorge in Havasu National Wildlife Refuge. The Black Mountains, traversed by the Oatman-Old Highway 66 scenic drive, lift their cliffed ramparts north of the highway's end.

5 VIRGIN RIVER GORGE SCENIC DRIVE
Interstate 15

General description: The Virgin River Gorge drive, following Interstate 15 for twenty miles across the corner of northwestern Arizona, slices through a scenic desert canyon.

Special attractions: Scenic views, camping, hiking, rock climbing, desert wildlife, Joshua tree forests, Virgin River Gorge Recreation Area (BLM).

Location: Far northwestern Arizona. Interstate 15 travels twenty-nine miles across Arizona, between St. George, Utah and Las Vegas, Nevada. The fourteen-mile-long gorge begins three miles south of the Utah border and ends twelve miles east of Nevada.

Scenic route number: Interstate 15.

Travel season: Year-round. Spring and fall, with pleasant temperatures ranging from fifty to ninety degrees, are ideal for visiting the gorge. Be prepared for daily summer temperatures to exceed 100 degrees. Carry plenty of water when hiking. The gorge's low elevations guarantee mild winter weather and little snowfall.

Camping: The BLM runs a 114-site campground with shaded tables, restrooms, and water at the Virgin River Gorge Recreation Area just off the Interstate. Commercial campgrounds are in nearby St. George, Utah.

Services: All services are available at St. George, Utah and Mesquite, Nevada.

Nearby attractions: Lake Mead National Recreation Area, Zion National Park, Grand Canyon National Park, Pipe Spring National Monument, Gold Butte Back Country Byway, Beaver Dam Mountains Wilderness Area, Paiute Wilderness Area, Snow Canyon State Park, Las Vegas.

For more information: BLM, Arizona Strip District Office, 390 N. 3050 E., St. George, UT 84770, (801) 673-3545.

The drive: The Virgin River Gorge Scenic Drive follows Interstate 15 for fourteen miles through a deep, rugged canyon in Arizona's far northwestern corner. The four-lane highway traverses a rough land rich in wildlife, solitude, and scenery. Most folks whiz through the gorge in their air-conditioned, mile-a-minute automobiles en route to the glitter of Los Angles and Las Vegas, while a few travelers slow down and explore the gorge, finding Joshua tree forests, mountain lion tracks etched in the river's muddy bank, and a stillness broken only by the distant hum of highway traffic.

The Arizona segment of Interstate 15, when dedicated in 1973, was one of the most expensive projects in the interstate highway system. The twenty road miles from the Utah border to the Littlefield interchange cost over $48 million in 1973 dollars. The twisting highway pushes through towering road cuts, especially in the lower gorge. The Virgin River was rechanneled twelve times in the gorge. There are numerous pull-outs along the highway where

Fleet-footed pronghorn antelope grace the roadsides of many northern Arizona scenic drives.

visitors can safely park for sightseeing, hiking, or climbing.

The gorge highway is open year-round. Fall and spring, with moderate temperatures, are perhaps the best time to explore the area. Winters are mild and generally warm, with little snowfall clinging to the canyon sides. Summer is hot, expect daily temperatures over 100 degrees every day. Few clouds or showers bring respite from the heat. Carry water, especially if you plan on hiking, and a hat.

The scenic drive begins three miles south of the Utah border, just outside St. George. The drive begins by dropping into a side canyon of the Virgin River Gorge. Cliff bands of sandstone and limestone stairstep upward from the highway. The highway reaches the river after a couple of miles. The isolated upper gorge is reached by walking upstream from here, following cow trails on the stony banks above the river.

The Virgin River, named the Rio Virgin in 1776 by Padre Silvestre Escalante during his search for a route between Santa Fe and California, begins at an elevation of about 9,000 feet on the forested flanks of the Markagunt Plateau north of Zion National Park in southeastern Utah. The river, gathering tributaries and power, slices down through soft Navajo sandstone in Zion, creating the park's deep, narrow canyons. In Zion, the Virgin drops as much as eighty feet per mile, a fall ten times greater than that of the Colorado River in Grand Canyon National Park. Beyond Zion, the river flows southwest past St. George, down the abrupt Virgin River Gorge, meanders across a dry plain in Nevada, and empties into an arm of Lake Mead.

The Virgin River and the highway, upon reaching the main gorge, twist

21

sinuously downstream, past water-worn boulders that litter the river bed. Thick stands of tamarisk trees, an Asian-imported shrub, Arizona ash trees, and occasional cottonwoods and willows line the cobbled shore. The arid mountainsides above the river are dominated by scattered Joshua tree forests. The Joshua tree, named by early Mormons for the plant's uplifted arms in supplication resembling the Biblical Joshua, is a relative of the yucca and a member of the lily family. The trees thrive on the gorge's warm south-facing slopes, where sufficient moisture exists. In spring, wildflowers like globemallow, marigold, and sand verbena carpet the mountainsides with colorful blossoms above the road.

The Virgin River Gorge Recreation Area, run by the Bureau of Land Management, and the Cedar Pocket Rest Area lies halfway through the gorge at Milepost 18. Head south from the exit to the recreation area. The 114-site campground has two loops; one on a bench above the river and the other close to the river. The campground features water, restrooms, and tables with ramadas. An overnight fee is charged at the year-round facility. The recreation area, at 2,700 feet, makes a great place to stop and explore the gorge.

A short trail leaves the upper campground loop and drops down to the muddy river. The riverbed is a good starting point to explore the area's natural diversity. An excellent cross-country hike through a Joshua tree forest begins on the north side of the highway interchange and enters the rugged 19,600-acre Beaver Dam Mountains Wilderness Area. Another longer hike leaves the south side of the campground and follows rough Sullivan Canyon past Atkin Spring to the lofty summit of 8,012-foot Mt. Bangs in the 84,700-acre Paiute Wilderness Area. The hike is twelve miles one-way.

The Beaver Dam Mountains, Virgin Mountains, and Black Rock Mountains, flanking the scenic highway, straddle the Basin and Range and Colorado Plateau geologic provinces as well as the Great Basin and Mojave deserts. Plants and animals representative of both deserts intermingle here—Joshua trees and sagebrush, desert tortoise and collared lizard. Over 250 wildlife species live here, including turkey vultures, prairie falcons, golden eagles, great horned owls, killdeer, rattlesnakes, deer, and desert bighorn sheep transplanted in 1981 from the Kingman area.

The river gorge has long been a scenic corridor for travelers. The earliest human evidence is a 10,000-year-old Clovis projectile point found at the campground. Later occupants include the Anasazi Indians who built granaries in the canyon and a twenty-one-pithouse village just outside the gorge at the Littlefield bridge. They deserted the area by 1150. The Old Spanish Trail, first traversed by Escalante and Dominguez in 1776, brought trade caravans packing wool blankets through the gorge to trade in California for horses and mules. Jedediah Smith, the famed American mountain man and trapper, led the first American party through the Virgin River Gorge in 1826.

Beyond the recreation area, the gorge narrows and deepens. The rock strata on the west side of the mountain range dips steeply to the west. The highway fills the canyon bottom. The muddy river, hemmed in by cliffs,

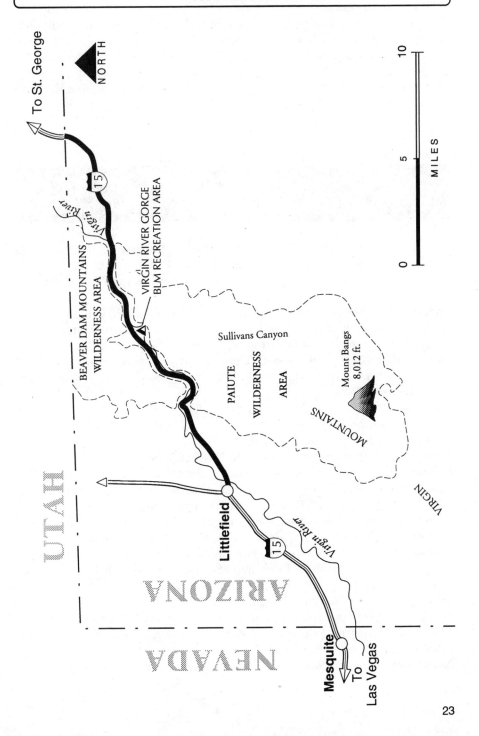

winds beneath highway bridges. Limestone crags as high as 500 feet soar above the road. Excellent climbing on the steep, pocketed rock walls increasingly attracts climbers to test their skills. Several pulloffs allow access to the crags.

Abruptly the gorge ends. The tilted rock layers of the mountain wall plunge into a wide, sloping plain and the river gently meanders southwest toward Lake Mead. After three miles the interstate passes Littlefield, Arizona's most remote town. No roads within Arizona lead to Littlefield. This is a good turn-around point for those who want to travel back up the gorge to St. George. The Nevada border and Mesquite lie another eight miles west on the highway.

6 ARIZONA 64
Cameron to Grand Canyon Village

General description: A fifty-seven-mile-long paved drive that climbs from Cameron up the eastern flank of the Kaibab Plateau to Grand Canyon National Park. The drive follows the canyon's South Rim to Grand Canyon Village.

Special attractions: Grand Canyon National Park, Little Colorado River Gorge, camping, hiking, scenic views, Navajo Reservation, visitor center, interpretative programs, photography, Kaibab National Forest.

Location: North-central Arizona. The drive begins at Cameron on U.S. 89, fifty-two miles north of Flagstaff, and ends at Grand Canyon Village on the canyon's South Rim.

Drive Route Number: Arizona Highway 64.

Travel Season: Year-round. Winter snows can be heavy along the rim road, but the road is plowed and sanded.

Camping: Mather Campground, with 320 sites in seven loops, is at Grand Canyon Village. Reservations are necessary during the busy summer months. Reservations are made through MISTIX, P.O. Box 850-705, San Diego, CA 92138-5705, (800) 365-2267. Reservations can be made no more than eight weeks in advance. From December 1 through March 1 Mather Campground operates on a first-come, first-served basis. Desert View Campground, thirty-two miles west of Cameron in the national park, has fifty sites. This campground is generally quieter than Mather, and is on a first-come basis. Primitive camping is allowed in Kaibab National Forest. Showers are available at Grand Canyon Village.

Services: All services are available at Grand Canyon Village and Flagstaff. Gas and groceries are available at Desert View. Limited services, including gas and lodging, are in Cameron.

Nearby attractions: Navajo Reservation, Hopi Reservation, San Francisco

Marvelous vistas of the majestic Grand Canyon are found along Arizona 64 as it winds along the canyon's South Rim.

Peaks, Sunset Crater National Monument, Wupatki National Monument, Marble Canyon, Flagstaff.

For more information: Grand Canyon National Park, P.O. Box 129, Grand Canyon, AZ 86023, (520) 638-7888.

The drive: Arizona Highway 64, a fifty-seven-mile-long road between Cameron and Grand Canyon Village, parallels the spectacular Little Colorado River Gorge and the awesome South Rim of Grand Canyon National Park. The scenic route traverses some of Arizona's best country and offers superlative views. This land casts its own special spell on visitors. Out here, under the hot summer sun, there is a sense of limitless space. Distant mirages shimmer and dance in the dry heat on the Marble Platform. Cloud shadows blotch the sweeping edge of the Coconino Plateau. And the Grand Canyon itself stuns the first-time viewer into silence. Its buttes, temples, escarpments, cliffs, buttresses, and chasms march across the horizon in varying shades of red.

The eighteen-mile-wide, 227-mile-long Grand Canyon has always had the ability to surprise and intrigue. Naturalist Joseph Wood Krutch writes, "At first glance the spectacle seems too strange to be real. Because one has never seen anything like it, because one has nothing to compare it with, it stuns the eye but cannot really hold the attention...For a time it is too much like a scale model or an optical illusion." President Teddy Roosevelt called it "the one great sight which every American...should see." Naturalist John Burroughs said the canyon was "The world's most wonderful spectacle, ever changing, alive with a million moods." But all visitors have not been so entranced by the canyon. After his 1858 exploration, U.S. Army Lt. Joseph Ives deemed the region "altogether worthless...Ours has been the first, and will doubtless be the last, party of whites to visit this profitless locality...intended by nature to be forever unvisited and undisturbed."

The scenic drive is open year round. Summer visitors can expect daily highs between seventy and ninety degrees. Nights are cool. Heavy thunderstorms typically occur on July and August afternoons on the canyon's south rim. Autumns are cool and dry, with highs between fifty and seventy. Winters are cold and windy. Heavy snowfall piles up in the higher elevations, while the desert around Cameron receives little snow. The road is plowed and maintained during the winter. Spring brings cool and often windy weather.

The drive begins on the Navajo Reservation two miles south of Cameron on U.S. 89 or fifty-two miles north of Flagstaff, by turning west on Arizona Highway 64. Cameron, at 4,200 feet, was named for Ralph Cameron, a trailbuilder and miner in the region and one of Arizona's first senators. Originally a trading post for the Navajos, Cameron was first called Tanner's Crossing after Mormon pioneer Seth Tanner. The old Mormon trail crossed the Little Colorado River just north of the town, one of the few safe hardrock passages across the treacherous quicksand riverbed.

The road rolls west over the Moenkopi Formation, its chocolate-colored layers of sandstone, mudstone, and shale broken into shallow canyons and ridges. The Moenkopi, deposited in the Triassic Period some 20 million years ago as part of a wide mudflat over which the sea advanced and retreated, is well known for its dinosaur tracks. Many in the Cameron area were left by the four-legged *Chirotherium*. Occasional Navajo hogans nestle among the outcrops, and sheep and goats browse on the sparse grass.

After six miles, the highway swings under Coconino Point and the spectacular East Kaibab Monocline, an uplift that forms the Coconino Plateau on the South Rim of the Grand Canyon and the Kaibab Plateau on the canyon's North Rim. A monocline is a fold that connects flat-lying rocks at an upper level with flat-lying rocks at a lower level. The sharply dipping rock layers here nose-dive about 2,000 feet from the Coconino Plateau above to the highway. The route runs northwest under the towering escarpment, and reaches the gorge of the Little Colorado River after nine miles. The Little

Colorado, called *Tol Chaco* or "red water" by the Navajo, begins high on 11,470-foot Mt. Baldy in eastern Arizona's White Mountains and twists some 350 miles to its confluence with the Colorado River in the Grand Canyon. The ruddy river, draining over 20,000 square miles, usually runs intermittently or not at all except after punishing summer thunderstorms or heavy runoff.

Short roads lead to two overlooks off the highway that offer dramatic views of the narrow Little Colorado River Gorge. Carved over 1,000 feet deep into the flat, barren Marble Platform, the empty chasm falls steeply away from the Kaibab limestone cliffs that line the canyon rim. Below are massive walls of Coconino sandstone, and below that runs the thin braided thread of water. Stand on the canyon rim and a deafening silence filters up from the depths, a silence born of time and the flowing river. Be cautious on the gorge rim and watch children. Some of the viewpoints are unfenced and have loose rock. Booths selling souvenirs and jewelry made by Navajo artisans are at both overlooks.

The Little Colorado River Gorge slices deeply into the Marble Platform along the Arizona 64 drive.

Past the second overlook, the road begins climbing the flank of the East Kaibab Monocline to the top of the Coconino Plateau. The Little Colorado Gorge and the tawny Marble Platform spread out beyond the highway. After a couple miles the road enters a scrubby pinyon pine and juniper forest and Kaibab National Forest. Eight miles later the road climbs into Grand Canyon National Park, passes the entrance station, and comes to 7,438-foot-high Desert View, the easternmost overlook on the canyon's south rim. Services available at Desert View include gas, food, a restaurant, and a fifty-site campground.

Desert View is a good beginning of the Grand Canyon for visitors. The views are immense and spectacular, some of the best in the national park. The Marble Platform spreads east, fading into the distant Hopi Mesas, Black Mesa, and to the northeast towers Shinumo Alter and the rounded dome of Navajo Mountain. Northward, the Colorado River runs down precipitous Marble Gorge from Lake Powell, tiers of cliffs towering above the river. And below the rimrock lies the canyon abyss, a mighty statement to the relentless power of the river.

The Grand Canyon is perhaps the world's greatest example of erosion, as well as an open book documenting almost half the earth's history—almost two billion years—in its horizontal rock pages. Here, in each different stratum, lies evidence of the constantly changing earth—the uplift and erosion of great mountain ranges, the land's inundation by vast seas, great sand dunes spread by stiff winds, belching volcanos and lava flows, and the grand evolution of life itself.

Beyond Desert View, the scenic drive follows the twenty-five-mile-long East Rim Drive to Grand Canyon Village in the heart of the national park. The drive passes numerous overlooks—Navajo Point, Lipan Point, Moran Point, Grandview Point, and Yaki Point—that offer tremendous views into the canyon. The Tanner, Hance, Grandview, and South Kaibab trails all begin along the drive. The road dips and winds through shallow washes and grassy glades, and past scrubby pinyon pine and juniper woodlands and dense ponderosa pine forests. A diverse selection of wildlife inhabits the national park, including seventy mammal species, 250 bird species, twenty-five reptile species, five fish species, and five amphibian species. Tusayan Ruin, an Anasazi Indian pueblo occupied about 1185 A.D., lies about three miles west of Desert View. A museum by the site displays exhibits on the Indians in the canyon area.

The scenic drive ends at Grand Canyon Village, the park headquarters. All services are available here, including food, restaurants, showers, park information, lodging, and 320-site Mather Campground. Reservations, through MISTIX, are necessary in summer. The last overlook before the village is Mather Point. Only one-fourth of the entire Grand Canyon can be seen here. The point is named for Stephen Mather, the first director of the National Park Service in 1916. Eight-mile-long West Rim Drive travels west of the village, ending at Hermits Rest. Due to congestion, the road is closed in summer with a free shuttle bus to ferry passengers.

6

ARIZONA 64: CAMERON TO GRAND CANYON VILLAGE

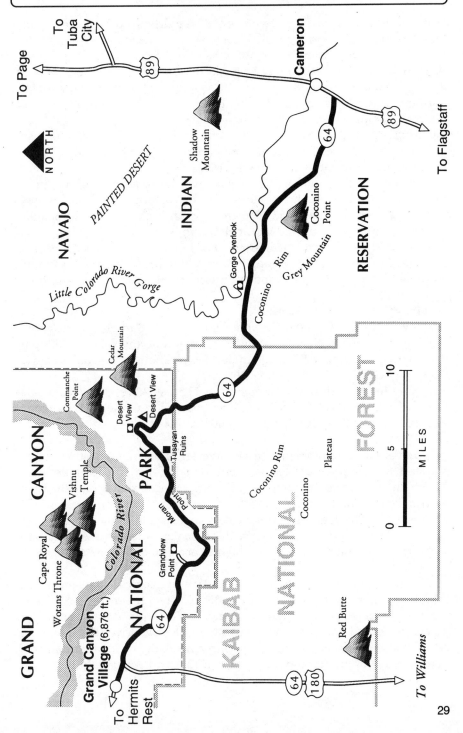

General description: This fifty-one-mile-long drive, a designated Arizona Scenic Road, passes through thick forests, open meadowlands, and sagebrush flats on the western slope of the San Francisco Peaks.

Special attractions: San Francisco Peaks, Kachina Peaks Wilderness Area, Kendrick Mountain Wilderness Area, Coconino National Forest, Flagstaff, Museum of Northern Arizona, Fairfield Snowbowl, Flagstaff Nordic Center, camping, hiking, cross-country skiing, scenic views.

Location: Central Arizona. U.S. 180 runs northwest from Flagstaff and Interstate 40 to Valle. The Grand Canyon lies thirty miles north of Valle.

Drive route number: U.S. Highway 180.

Travel season: Year-round. The highway is dry through most of the spring, summer, and fall. Expect heavy summer thunderstorms in July and August. Winters are snowy. The road is usually icy or snowpacked. It's a good idea to carry chains, a shovel, and warm clothes in winter.

Camping: Primitive camping in Coconino National Forest on side roads off the highway. No established campgrounds along the scenic drive. Camping is available at Bonito Campground by Sunset Crater and in the national forest southeast of Flagstaff.

Services: All services in Flagstaff.

Nearby attractions: Grand Canyon National Park, Sunset Crater National Monument, Wupatki National Monument, Walnut Canyon National Monument, Oak Creek Canyon, Navajo Indian Reservation, Little Colorado River Gorge and Grand Falls, Mogollon Rim.

For more information: Coconino National Forest, 2323 E. Greenlaw Lane, Flagstaff, AZ 86001, (520) 527-3600. Flagstaff Visitor Center, 1 E. Route 66, Flagstaff, AZ 86001, (520) 774-9541, (800) 842-7293.

The drive: The U.S. 180 scenic drive travels fifty-one miles northwest from Flagstaff around the forested western flank of majestic San Francisco Mountain, passing numerous small volcanos, before crossing onto the broad Kaibab Plateau and ending at Valle at the road's junction with Arizona Highway 64. The highway offers access to Fairfield Snow Bowl, one of Arizona's best ski areas, and the Kachina Peaks Wilderness Area, a large wilderness that embraces Arizona's highest peaks and the state's only alpine vegetation zone.

The highway, an officially designated Arizona scenic road, is open year-round. Summer and fall are the best times to travel the road. The days are warm, with highs between sixty and eighty. Thick pine forests broken by aspen groves and flower-strewn meadows border the drive. The mountains attract bad weather and average about thirty inches of precipitation annually. Expect heavy afternoon thunderstorms in July and August. Spring can be pleasant, but days are often cool and blustery. Winter brings a blanket of snow that muffles the land. The highway can be icy and snowpacked. Plan accordingly by carrying chains, a shovel, and warm clothes.

The drive begins in downtown Flagstaff at the junction of Interstate 40 Business Loop, U.S. 89, and U.S. 180. Head northwest on U.S. 180 on Fort Valley Road. Flagstaff, northern Arizona's largest town, nestles against the southern slopes of San Francisco Mountain. The area was first settled by Thomas F. McMillan in 1876. That same year a group of Boston settlers camped here and on July 4th stripped a tall pine of its branches and tied a flag onto the giant flagstaff, giving the town its name. The Atlantic and Pacific Railroad arrived in 1882 and with it the town grew as a center for lumbering and ranching.

Today, Flagstaff is home to Northern Arizona University, Lowell Observatory, Pioneer Historical Museum, and the Museum of Northern Arizona. The Museum of Northern Arizona, on U.S. 180 on Flagstaff's northern outskirts, is a gem. It offers excellent displays of southwestern natural history, archaeology, and Indian art. Flagstaff has all services for travelers.

The highway heads northwest through ponderosa pines and open meadowlands. In Fort Valley, seven miles from Flagstaff, Forest Road 516, Snow Bowl Road, turns north and climbs seven miles up to Fairfield Snow Bowl ski area. The area, with thirty-two runs, offers some of Arizona's best skiing. The Agassiz Skyride operates in summer and carries visitors from 9,500 feet to 11,600 feet. For those who would rather hike to Arizona's rooftop, the nine-mile round-trip Kachina Peaks Trail begins at the ski area and climbs up to the 12,670-foot summit of Humphreys Peak, Arizona's highest point.

Mule deer browse among aspens along U.S. 180.

The San Francisco Mountains, the remnant of a giant stratovolcano, tower over U.S. 180 northwest of Flagstaff.

The view from the mountaintop is breathtaking. The Grand Canyon and the forested Kaibab Plateau stretch across the north; rounded Navajo Mountain lies 125 miles to the northwest; Dinetah, the arid Navajo homeland, rolls out to the east; and to the southeast glimmer the snowcapped summits of the distant White Mountains. Be prepared for alpine conditions when hiking. Severe lightning storms occur in July and August. Hikers must stay on designated trails above timberline to protect the fragile alpine tundra. The 1,200-acre tundra zone atop the mountains has been isolated from other alpine plants long enough that several unique species have evolved. Heavy foot traffic imperils their survival, leading to the closure of Mt. Agassiz and a ban on indiscriminate hiking.

San Francisco Mountain is actually the centerpiece of the San Francisco Volcanic Field, a 2-million-acre area covered with lava flows and over 400 cinder cones. The mountain, a cluster of four peaks, was once a massive, symmetrical stratovolcano that looked like Japan's Mt. Fujiyama. The volcano grew from eruptions that began 2.8 million years ago and ended about 200,000 years ago. Geologists estimate the mountain's height reached 15,600 feet. Later, a violent, sideways, Mt. St. Helens-type explosion blasted out the mountain's northeast side and formed its present shape. Glaciation smoothed the mountain's rough contours. The volcanic field is still active. Sunset Crater, on the field's east edge, erupted a scant 1,000 years ago.

The peaks are sacred to the Hopi and Navajo Indians, who have long lived in the dusty desert below them. The Hopi call them *Nuvatukya'ovi*, or "Place of Snow on the Very Top," and believe they are the home of the kachinas and the source of rain for their crops. The Navajo named them *Dok'o'sliid* or "Sacred Mountain of the West," and say they were fastened to the Earth by a sunbeam. The mountain's Anglo name was given by Franciscan padres who explored through here in 1629. Because of their religious significance and unique biological communities, the San Francisco Peaks were preserved in

To Grand Canyon

NORTH

180

Valle

64

180

To Williams

Red Mountain
7,965 ft.

COCONINO

NATIONAL

Slate Mountain
8,215 ft.

Saddle Mountain

KAIBAB

Kendrick Peak
10,418 ft.

KENDRICK

PARK

White Horse Hills

To
U. S. 89

NATIONAL

418

180

Arizona
Snow Bowl

Humphrey's Peak
12,670 ft.

FOREST

Agassiz Peak

FOREST

516

KACHINA
WILDERNESS
AREA

To
Cameron

To
Williams

OBSERVATORY
MESA

180

40

89

To
Holbrook

Flagstaff

40

17

To Phoenix

0   5   10

MILES

the 18,200-acre Kachina Peaks Wilderness Area in 1984.

The highway runs north alongside the western slope of the San Francisco Peaks, passing through thick stands of ponderosa pine. Occasional groves of quaking aspen and open meadows scatter along the roadside. The Flagstaff Nordic Center, fifteen miles from Flagstaff, offers thirty kilometers of groomed cross-country ski trails from beginner to expert. The road runs across Kendrick Park, a broad, grassy valley studded with grazing cattle. Numerous wild animals live in the dense forest and grasslands, including mule deer, coyote, mountain lion, black bear, elk, Merriam's turkeys, and herds of pronghorn antelope. Kendrick Park Picnic Area, with five sites, makes a good lunch stop in the woods on the north side of the open park. Kendrick Mountain Wilderness Area, dominated by 10,418-foot Kendrick Mountain, lies west of the park.

The drive bends northwest, traveling across old lava flows and past Slate Mountain and Red Mountain, two small volcanos. A three-mile trail begins two miles west of U.S. 180 on Forest Road 191 and winds up to Slate Mountain's 8,215-foot-high summit. Red Mountain lies another five miles up the road. Erosion has carved out the inside of this small cinder cone, leaving a maze of narrow canyons. A trail ascends to the 7,965-foot top on the cone's southeast flank. Both peaks offer marvelous views of the San Francisco Peaks and the surrounding volcanic field.

Past Red Mountain the highway begins losing elevation. It leaves the cool ponderosa forest behind and enters a scrubby pinyon pine and juniper

Sunset Crater Volcano National Monument spreads out below O'Leary Peak in early evening.

woodland. The road crosses progressively older lava flows, coated with grass, sagebrush, and lichen, before dropping onto the undulating Coconino Plateau. The plateau surface, forming the south rim of the Grand Canyon 30 miles to the north, is floored by Kaibab Limestone. Moving away from the mountains, the climate becomes drier and an open sagebrush savannah dominates the land. The San Francisco Peaks tower above the highway to the southeast, their snowy summits glimmering like alabaster towers. After fifty-one miles, the highway joins Arizona 64 at Valle and turns north to Grand Canyon National Park. Williams lies twenty-eight miles south on Arizona 64.

8 SUNSET CRATER & WUPATKI ROAD

General description: This thirty-five-mile-long loop drive passes a spectacular volcanoscape at Sunset Crater Volcano National Monument and explores ancient Anasazi and Sinagua ruins at Wupatki National Monument in north-central Arizona.

Special attractions: Sunset Crater Volcano National Monument, Wupatki National Monument, cinder cones, lava flows, lava tube cave, visitor centers, camping, hiking, picnicking, Indian ruins, scenic views.

Location: North-central Arizona. The drive begins on U.S. 89 ten miles north of Flagstaff and ends on U.S. 89 twenty-five miles north of Flagstaff. The drive is easily accessible from Interstate 40.

Drive route number and name: Forest Service Road 545. Wupatki-Sunset Crater Loop Road.

Travel season: The paved drive is open year-round, but is subject to temporary closure during winter storms.

Camping: Bonita Campground, across from the Sunset Crater Visitor Center, contains forty-four sites without trailer hook-ups. The campground is administered by Coconino National Forest. It is open from mid-May through early fall on a first-come, first-served basis. Nightly campfire programs are conducted from June through August. There is no backcountry camping allowed in either national monument. Additional campgrounds are found in Flagstaff and Coconino National Forest.

Services: All services in Flagstaff, including gas, groceries, and a wide variety of accommodations.

Nearby attractions: Grand Canyon National Park, San Francisco Peaks, Museum of Northern Arizona, Flagstaff, Navajo Indian Reservation, Little Colorado River Gorge, Grand Falls of the Little Colorado River, Walnut Canyon National Monument, Oak Creek Canyon, Sedona, Meteor Crater.

For more information: Superintendent, Wupatki and Sunset Crater National Monuments, 2717 N. Steves Blvd., Suite 3, Flagstaff, AZ 86004, (520) 556-7042. Coconino National Forest, 2323 E. Greenlaw La., Flagstaff, AZ

86001, (520) 527-3600. Flagstaff Visitor Center, 1 E. Route 66, Flagstaff, AZ 86001, (520) 774-9541, (800) 842-7293.

The drive: The Sunset Crater-Wupatki road makes a thirty-five-mile-long open loop drive through a recent volcanic field at Sunset Crater Volcano National Monument and past the ruined villages of ancient Indians who lived here almost one thousand years ago in Wupatki National Monument. This is a country of distant vistas and dry sunlight; of summer lightning and rain veils over far-off mesas and mountains; of ponderosa pine forests and sun-hammered sagebrush flats.

The scenic drive connects at both its north and south ends with U.S. 89. The Sunset Crater entrance is ten miles north of Flagstaff. The Wupatki turnoff is twenty-five miles north of Flagstaff. The paved road, open year-round, is accessible to all types of vehicles and has frequent turnouts and light traffic.

Summer visitors to Sunset Crater, at 7,000 feet, can expect generally mild temperatures, with highs ranging from the seventies to the nineties. Wupatki, at 4,800 feet, is hot in summer with highs frequently above 100 degrees. Afternoon thunderstorms are common in the higher elevations during July and August. Winters are cold with plentiful snow at Sunset Crater. Wupatki's winters are warmer and drier. Sunset Crater's annual precipitation averages twenty-two inches, while Wupatki is considerably drier with just over eight inches falling every year.

The drive begins by turning east off U.S. 89 ten miles north of Flagstaff. The road, for the first three miles, drops down through an open ponderosa pine forest into spacious Bonito Park, a wide sagebrush- and grass-covered clearing. Westward towers the San Francisco Peaks, the remains of what was once a strato volcano that towered as high as 15,000 feet before its collapse some 500,000 years ago. Geologists say the peaks possibly formed after a violent Mt. St. Helens-type sideways explosion blasted out its northeast flank. Humphreys Peak, the tallest peak at 12,633 feet, is Arizona's highest point. The San Francisco Peaks are also the nucleus of the San Francisco Volcanic Field, a 2,200-square-mile area that is covered with ashfall, lava flows, and over 400 cinder cones. The field, currently dormant, has been active over the last two million years.

Past the lava flow, the road swings along the base of Sunset Crater and traverses through the Cinder Hills, a somber black landscape studded with occasional ponderosa pines. The pines find moisture by spreading their roots out just below the ground's surface. This shallow root system makes them vulnerable to blowdown by strong winds. Other plants growing on the cinders and lava include quaking aspen, Apache plume, mullein, rabbitbrush, red gilia, Indian paintbrush, and pink penstemon, a flower unique to the San Francisco Volcanic Field.

Past Sunset Crater and the Cinder Hills, the drive turns northeast. Here, at seven miles, a right turn on Forest Road 244 leads to Grand Falls, a spectacular 185-foot-high waterfall on the Little Colorado River. The muddy

Wupatki Ruin, on the Sunset Crater-Wupatki drive, was occupied by the Anasazi almost 1,000 years ago.

falls formed when lava from Merriam Crater blocked the river channel. The river generally flows only in spring and after torrential thunderstorms.

Painted Desert Vista is encountered a few miles further on. The wide view encompasses the colorful strata of the Painted Desert and the vast valley of the Little Colorado River. Beyond, to the east, lie the Hopi Mesas. To the north, on a clear day, bulges rounded Navajo Mountain. The Painted Desert is famed for the red, purple, grey, and blue-tinted Chinle Formation, and the wealth of dinosaur tracks found in the chocolate-colored Moenkopi sandstone. Five picnic sites are found at the viewpoint. Northeast of Painted Desert Vista lies Strawberry Crater Wilderness Area, while across the road is Kana'a Lava Flow and Black Bottom Crater.

As the road drops northward, the land becomes drier. A pinyon pine and juniper woodland replaces the ponderosa pine forest. As the drive swings below Woodhouse Mesa and enters Wupatki National Monument, the Great Basin desert scrub habitat replaces the pinyon and juniper trees. This dry landscape is characterized by the grey sheen of sagebrush. Another common shrub is fourwing saltbush, a browse plant used by the Indians as a flour ground from its dried seeds. Other plants include yucca, Mormon tea, snakeweed, globe mallow, jimson weed, and Peeble's bluestar, a rare flower found only in the Little Colorado valley.

Wupatki National Monument, a 35,253-acre parkland, protects about 2,500 archaeological sites left by at least two separate Indian cultures that inhabited the area: the Kayenta Anasazi and the Sinagua. The Anasazi built many of the pueblos in the northern part of the monument, including Lomaki and Crack-in-the-Rock Pueblo, as well as leaving most of the petroglyphs that mark their passing. Visitors should remember that it is illegal to keep any archeological find, including potshards and arrowheads, that are found at

Wupatki. Entry into the monument's backcountry is by permit only. Hikers without a permit must stay on established trails at Wupatki, Wukoki, Citadel, and Lomaki ruins.

The Sinagua, a Spanish term for "without water," moved into the area after the violent explosions at Sunset Crater forced them from their farmlands in the valleys around the volcano. After the eruption, they found that they could grow their beans, corn, and squash in areas that were previously too dry for farming. The thin ash layer deposited from the volcanic eruptions provided a mulch that reduced the evaporation rate of the area's meager rainfall. This new fertility of the Little Colorado River region set off a land rush, drawing Indians from different cultural traditions.

From the late 1000s to 1200, a period of just over 100 years, the Wupatki area flourished as a cultural crossroads. As many as 4,000 Indians inhabited the area, sharing new farming and construction methods, learning pottery and basketry techniques, trading goods from Mexico, and intermarrying. But by 1200 A.D. the building ended, and the area was abandoned by 1250, possibly due to the dispersal of the ash, depleted natural resources, and a drought beginning in 1215.

The first ruin found on the drive is Wukoki, a well-preserved masonry pueblo perched atop an island of Moenkopi sandstone. It is reached by a 2.5-mile gravel road. Just past the turn to Wukoki lies the monument's visitor center and largest ruin, Wupatki, a Hopi word that means "tall house." Wupatki was three stories high, contained about 100 rooms, and housed between 100 and 200 people. One of the site's most interesting features is the Ball Court, an oval masonry ring that indicates cultural connections with southern Arizona and Mexico. Next to the court is a natural blowhole. The underlying Kaibab limestone here is full of fissures that create a natural barometer. Air blows out the hole with considerable force when the below-ground air pressure is greater than that above-ground. The visitor center, at 4,900 feet, has exhibits detailing the archaeology and natural history of the monument.

The road heads northwest across Deadman Wash and the broad Wupatki Basin before climbing south around 5,589-foot Doney Mountain, an ancient volcanic crater. The peak is named for homesteader Ben Doney, who searched all over the Wupatki country for the Lost Padre Mine. The Doney Picnic Area is on the mountain's west side. A short trail starts at the picnic area and ends atop Doney Mountain.

Continuing west, the drive crosses Antelope Prairie, a rolling grassland studded with occasional junipers. An archaeological survey here yielded ninety to 100 sites per square mile. Alert visitors will see fleet-footed pronghorn antelope grazing on the open grasslands, as well as blacktail jackrabbits, coyotes, bobcats, red-tailed hawks, and soaring turkey vultures.

Near the end of the drive lie Citadel, Nalakihu, and Lomaki ruins. Citadel Ruin, built atop a lava-rimmed butte, is perhaps the most impressive. It was two stories high, contained about thirty rooms, and commanded a lofty view over the surrounding country. Below it are farming terraces. Citadel Sink, a 173-

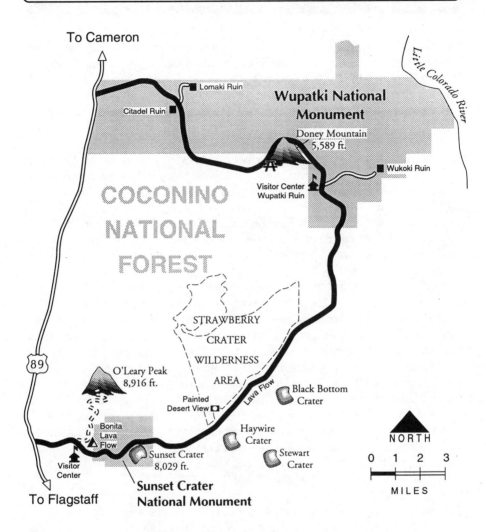

To Cameron

Lomaki Ruin

Wupatki National
Monument

Citadel Ruin

Doney Mountain
5,589 ft.

Wukoki Ruin

COCONINO

NATIONAL

FOREST

Visitor Center
Wupatki Ruin

Little Colorado River

STRAWBERRY
CRATER
WILDERNESS
AREA

O'Leary Peak
8,916 ft.

89

Painted
Desert View

Lava Flow

Black Bottom
Crater

Bonita
Lava
Flow

Haywire
Crater

Visitor
Center

Sunset Crater
8,029 ft.

Stewart
Crater

NORTH

0   1   2   3

MILES

To Flagstaff

**Sunset Crater
National Monument**

foot-deep natural sinkhole in the Kaibab limestone, sits near Citadel Ruin.

A short spur road leads to Lomaki Ruin, the last stop on the scenic drive. Lomaki, Hopi for "beautiful house," lies at the end of a .25-mile trail. This two-story, nine-room village is well-preserved. Other small ruins scatter along sharp, rocky headlands nearby, holding their secrets and mysteries under the fallen rubble of ten centuries. The drive continues west over the grassland, offering fine views of the San Francisco Peaks to the south, rounded cinder cones to the west, and the sere Little Colorado River basin to the northeast. The road ends on U.S. 89 twenty-five miles north of Flagstaff.

9 ARIZONA HIGHWAY 264
Window Rock to Tuba City

General description: A 169-mile-long paved highway in northeastern Arizona that traverses both the Navajo and Hopi reservations between Window Rock, capital of the Navajo Nation, and Tuba City.

Special attractions: Window Rock Tribal Park, Navajo Tribal Museum, Kinlichee Navajo Tribal Park, Hubbell Trading Post National Historic Site, Hopi Reservation, Walpi, Second Mesa, Hopi Cultural Center, Third Mesa, Coal Canyon, sightseeing, scenic views, Indian dances.

Location: Northeastern Arizona. Arizona 264 begins at Window Rock on the New Mexico border and runs across the Navajo and Hopi reservations to Tuba City, just east of the Grand Canyon.

Drive route number: Arizona Highway 264.

Travel season: Year-round. Summer and fall are the best times to drive the highway, with warm days and clear skies. Afternoon thunderstorms are common in late summer. Winters are cold, but generally dry. Spring days are often windy and cool.

Camping: There are not a lot of campgrounds along the highway. Camping is permitted at Tse Bonito Tribal Park and Window Rock Tribal Park in Window Rock. Summit Campground is nine miles west of Window Rock atop a 7,750-foot pass. Keams Canyon has a commercial campground. The only camping on the Hopi Reservation is at the Hopi Cultural Center on Second Mesa.

Services: All services are available in Window Rock, Keams Canyon, the Hopi Mesas, and Tuba City. Limited services are available in Ganado.

Nearby attractions: Canyon de Chelly National Monument, Petrified Forest National Park, Navajo National Monument, Grand Canyon National Park.

For more information: Hopi Tribal Headquarters, Box 123, Kykotsmovi, AZ 86039, (520) 734-2415. Navajo Parks Department, Box 9000, Window Rock, AZ 86515, (520) 871-6647. Hubbell Trading Post National Historic Site, P.O. Box 150, Ganado, AZ 86505, (520) 755-3475.

The drive: Arizona Highway 264 stretches 169 miles across both the vast 14,000,000-acre Navajo Indian Reservation and the ancient homeland of the Hopi Indians in northeastern Arizona. This scenic drive traverses an arid, lonely land that unfolds like a giant colorful Navajo rug patterned with rock-rimmed mesas, wide dusty valleys, broken badlands, and sculptured sandstone buttes. It is also a land rich in history and prehistory, with ancient villages, sacred mountains, and a 19th century trading post.

The highway crosses the heart of Dinetah, the West Virginia-sized Navajo Nation that sprawls across parts of Arizona, New Mexico, and Utah. It is a place that is both beautiful and severe with its rigorous climate and austere landscape. It is a place that also gives a sense of identidy and a system of values to its inhabitants—the *Dine'*, the people we call Navajo.

Yuccas scatter across snow-covered ground on the Navajo Reservation on Arizona 264.

When the Navajo were first created, according to myths, their land was marked by four sacred mountains in the four directions—Blanca Peak and Mount Taylor in New Mexico, the La Plata Mountains in Colorado, and the San Francisco Peaks in central Arizona. The Navajo were semi-nomadic wanderers, relatives of the Canadian Athapascans and the Apaches, who arrived in the Southwest between 1300 and 1500 A.D. The Zuni Indians called the newcomers Apaches de Navahu, meaning "Enemies of the arroyo with the cultivated fields," and shortened to Navajo. They learned pottery, agriculture, and weaving from their Pueblo neighbors, and later became skilled horsemen and sheperds with stock obtained from the Spanish. The Navajo were granted their vast reservation in 1868 and have grown into the nation's largest Indian tribe. In 1972 the Navajo Nation was formed when the United States government turned control of the reservation over to the tribe.

Arizona 264 is open year-round. Summer and autumn are the best times to drive it. Summer days can be warm, with highs reaching 100 degrees, but temperatures are generally moderate. Expect afternoon thunderstorms, especially in July and August. Autumn brings clear, warm days and chilly nights. Winters are cold and often snowy. Spring days are warm and windy, with occasional snowfalls. The gravel side roads often become muddy and impassable after snow or rain.

The drive begins on the New Mexico border in Window Rock, the capital and administrative center of the Navajo Nation. The Navajo Council House, shaped like a giant ceremonial hogan, is the meeting place of elected tribal delegates who govern the reservation. The town, at 6,750 feet high, also boasts the Navajo Zoological Park and the Navajo Tribal Museum, which offers a good introduction to Navajo culture and history. Nearby are Tse Bonito and Window Rock tribal parks. Complete services, including gas, shopping, restaurants, lodging, and camping are found in Window Rock.

The highway climbs west from Window Rock up the sloping apron of the Defiance Plateau and after nine miles reaches a 7,750-foot pass atop the ponderosa pine-covered tableland. Here Summit Campground offers camping and picnicking in the cool forest, and a welcome respite from summer heat. Heading west the blacktop traverses the gently dipping western slope of the Defiance Plateau, a 100-mile-long anticline that parallels the New Mexico border. As the road drops it enters a thick pinyon pine and juniper forest that slowly changes into a broad sagebrush-coated plateau. Kinlichee Ruin or "Red House," a seventy-five-room Anasazi pueblo and Navajo tribal park, sits two miles north of the highway. The turnoff is twelve miles west of the summit at Cross Canyon Trading Post. A small primitive campground is nearby.

Almost twenty miles from the summit the drive enters Ganado, a small town named for Ganado Mucho or "Many Cattle," a Navajo chief who befriended trader John Lorenzo Hubbell. Just west of Ganado, among the cottonwoods along dry Pueblo Colorado Wash, lies Hubbell Trading Post National Historic Site, Arizona's most famous trading post. The post, still open for business, gives a glimpse back to the time when this was still raw, unsettled country.

The post, established by Hubbell in 1876, did a brisk business with the Navajos, selling calico, yarn, dye, axes, tools, wagons, harnesses, food, and other essentials. Calico cost ten cents a yard, a pound of coffee was twenty-five cents, a 100-pound sack of flour cost $5.50, and a Stetson hat was $4.50. The post was built like a hacienda forming a large square, with stables, corrals, warehouses, an office, the store, and a guest hogan for visiting Navajos. Hubbell, one of the first traders to see the commercial possibilities of Indian art, encouraged local silversmiths and weavers to trade their work. The site, operated by the National Park Service, has a visitor center, gift shop, and offers tours of the post. Weavers and silversmiths often demonstrate their craft in the Visitor Center.

Five miles west of Ganado the highway enters the southern edge of Beautiful Valley, a broad valley between high mesas and shaped by Chinle Wash. Here is the road's intersection with U.S. Highway 191 which runs north to Canyon de Chelly and the Utah border. The drive continues west along the southern fringe of Beautiful Valley. There are expansive views

Hubbell Trading Post National Historic Site preserves an authentic Navajo trading post along the Arizona 264 scenic drive.

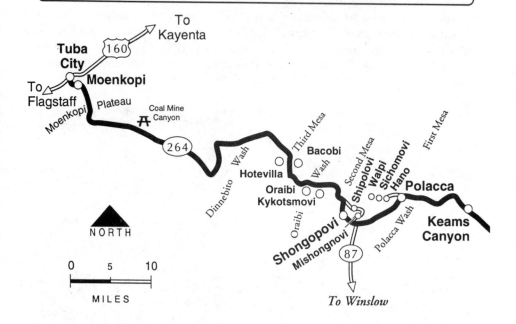

9 ARIZONA HIGHWAY 264 WINDOW ROCK TO TUBA CITY

To Kayenta

Tuba City — 160

Moenkopi

To Flagstaff

Moenkopi Plateau

Coal Mine Canyon

264

Dinnebito Wash

Third Mesa Wash

Bacobi

Hotevilla

Oraibi
Kykotsmovi

Oraibi Wash

Second Mesa

Shipolovi
Walpi
Sichomovi
Hano

Polacca

First Mesa

Keams Canyon

Shongopovi
Mishongnovi

87

Polacca Wash

To Winslow

NORTH

0   5   10
MILES

north to the Chuska Mountains and Black Mesa. After a few miles the highway climbs onto high sagebrush-covered mesas, before dropping into scenic Steamboat Canyon. Sandstone cliffs line the canyon walls above grazing cattle and horses, and octagonal hogans. Steamboat Rock lies midway through the canyon, a sandstone ship in a sea of sage.

Beyond Steamboat Canyon, the highway dips and rolls over mesatops and through valleys and boulder-choked canyons. After twenty-two miles the road drops sharply into Keams Canyon, the easternmost community on the Hopi Reservation. The town and the canyon are named for trader Thomas Keam. His trading post was established in 1872. All services, including a campground with water, are available here. Two miles up the canyon is Inscription Rock, with pioneer scout Kit Carson's signature engraved on it.

The abandoned ruins of Awatovi lie three miles south of town on Antelope Mesa above dry Jeddito Wash. This large pueblo site, covering twenty-three acres, was occupied by the Hopi until 1700. Spanish Franciscan padres built a mission here in 1629 to convert the Hopi to Christianity. Fearful that the new religion would damage their culture, the Hopi destroyed the church and murdered the priests during the Pueblo Revolt on 1680. The mission was reestablished, but again destroyed in 1700. This time the Hopi massacred all

44

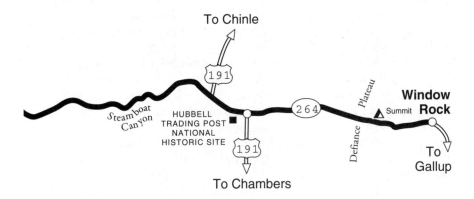

NORTH

0   5   10

MILES

To Chinle

191

Steamboat Canyon

HUBBELL TRADING POST NATIONAL HISTORIC SITE

191

To Chambers

264

Plateau

Defiance

Summit

Window Rock

To Gallup

reestablished, but again destroyed in 1700. This time the Hopi massacred all the village men, and resettled the women and children in other Hopi villages. Permission to visit the site must be obtained from Hopi Tribal Headquarters.

The drive heads west from Keams Canyon down a widening canyon rimmed by broken cliff bands. After a few miles the highway crosses broad Polacca Wash and reaches the First Mesa. The Hopi villages spread across three lofty mesas that reach finger-like southwest from Black Mesa. The towns, perched on the edge of these mesa citadels, are ancient. Some, like Old Oraibi, have been continuously occupied since 1100 A.D.—the oldest inhabited village in America. The Hopi are believed to have descended from the prehistoric Anasazi Indians that built the marvelous cliff cities at Mesa Verde and near Kayenta.

The Hopi, never conquered by the Spanish or Anglo cultures, are a proud, traditional people. Use respect when visiting the Hopi villages and lands. Photography is mostly forbidden in the towns, particularly during religious ceremonies. Most of the ceremonies and dances take place between the Winter Solstice and the time when crops are harvested in late summer. During the dances benevolent spirits, the Kachinas, are summoned from their homes in the San Francisco Peaks seventy-five miles to the west to bring dates and locations, on dances is available at the Hopi Cultural Center on Second Mesa.

Nine of the twelve Hopi villages sit atop the three mesas. One exception is Polacca, below First Mesa on the west side of Polacca Wash. Turn in Polacca and climb one mile west up a spur road to a parking area atop First Mesa. Three villages—Hano, Sichomovi, and Walpi—sit on the narrow, rock-rimmed mesatop. Hano and Sichomovi are almost indistinguishable, lying alongside each other. Hano, however, is not a Hopi village, but rather a Tewa settlement transplanted from the Rio Grande region after the unsuccessful Pueblo Revolt in 1680. The Tewa have kept their own language and ceremonies through the ensuing centuries.

Walpi, perhaps the most famous Hopi village, perches on the narrow tip of First Mesa 600 feet above the dry, windswept washes below. Tiers of sandstone cliffs line the mesa, and jumbled boulders litter steep talus slopes below. The views are marvelous here. On a clear day all of Hopi land stretches away from Walpi—the sacred San Francisco Peaks pierce the southwest horizon, and to the south tower the volcanic Hopi Buttes. Approaching Walpi from Sichomovi, the mesa neck narrows to only fifteen feet. This traditional village, inhabited for over 300 years, is now home to about thirty residents. Visitors are welcome to browse through Walpi, but photography, tape and video recording, and sketching are prohibited.

The Second Mesa lies seven miles west of Polacca across a barren valley, broken occasionally by Hopi fields still farmed in the old way. Three villages—Shongopavi, Shipaulovi, and Mishongnovi—are on Second Mesa. Shongopavi, the largest village with over 700 residents, was one of the first pueblos established on the mesas. Shipaulovi and Mishongnovi are reached by a paved spur road that climbs steeply up from Arizona 264. Also atop Second Mesa is the Hopi Cultural Center with a museum, motel, gift shop, and restaurant that serves traditional Hopi food. Camping is available next to the center.

The drive heads northwest, dropping down the flank of Second Mesa and crossing deeply eroded Oraibi Wash, its sandy banks lined with cottonwood, tamarisk, and Russian olive trees. On the west side of the wash lies Kykotsmovi, the headquarters for the Hopi Tribal Council. The town was founded by Christian converts and Hopis from Oraibi who had cooperated with the U.S. government. The highway climbs abruptly up Third Mesa, passing a small picnic area with shaded ramadas and tables. The Third Mesa, far away from the Anglo influence of Keams Canyon, houses the most traditional Hopi.

Oraibi clings to the southeastern edge of Third Mesa, its worn cluster of stone houses huddled on the mesa's rim. The village, North America's oldest continuously inhabited town, dates to the 1100s. That was a period when the Hopi ancestors were still living in Mesa Verde's cliffed cities and farming the fertile lands around Sunset Crater. Oraibi, at the turn of the 20th century, housed almost 1,000 Hopi. Dissension between traditional and progressive Hopi led to a split, with those wanting to retain the old customs and remain isolated from the white culture leaving and establishing Hotevilla and Bacavi, the two other villages on Third Mesa, in 1906 and 1909.

Hotevilla is the most traditional village. It was founded in 1906 after splitting from Oraibi. Village leader Yukiuma, head of the Fire Clan, refused to send children to the new government school at Keams Canyon. The U.S. cavalry arrested Hotevilla's leaders, forcibly removed the village children, and sent them to school. Oraibi and Hotevilla have maintained the split to the present day. Bacavi, across the highway from Hotevilla, was established in 1909 after several Hotevilla families moved back to Oraibi but left because of smouldering resentment and witchcraft accusations. The three villages on Third Mesa are often closed to visitors; respect their privacy and traditions.

The highway drops down a steep canyon on the western flank of Third Mesa. A pullout allows views of Hotevilla to the west. The village lines the mesa rim. Below are terraced gardens irrigated with nearby spring water. The road heads northwest across sandy Dinnebito Wash and climbs onto Howell Mesa.

From here to Tuba City, thirty miles northwest, the land is a high, barren steppe, broken only by scattered grass, sagebrush, rock outcrops, and occasional scrubby juniper trees. The sky dominates this land, the Moenkopi Plateau, with wispy cirrus clouds high overhead or thunderstorms trailing curtains of rain across distant mesas. This uniform stretch of road has a wonderful feeling of space, timelessness, and freedom.

As the highway crosses the Moenkopi Plateau, a turnoff fifteen miles from Tuba City at a windmill and Coal Mine Mesa sign leads north to a scenic overlook above Coal Canyon. This lovely canyon, hidden from the nearby highway, is a colorful badlands seamed by bands of coal. Both the Hopi and Navajo have long mined the soft bituminous coal found here in this land of few trees. Hopi legend says the ghost of an Oraibi woman who fell to her death in 1872 from the cliffs stalks the canyon on moonlit nights. The white, diaphanous figure can be seen in a side-canyon near the overlook. The scientific explanation is that the ghost is actually a phosphorescent pinnacle. It releases vapors that linger into the night and creates the shimmering apparition. A primitive campground sits on the canyon rim.

The drive continues west across the plateau, then swings north and drops down a gradual sandy gradient to Moenkopi, the westernmost Hopi village. Moenkopi, meaning "Place of Running Water," was started by Chief Tuba of Oraibi in 1870 so Third Mesa farmers could irrigate their fields with water from year-round springs. The Indians would often run the sixty-two miles from Oraibi to Moenkopi to tend their crops. The village, with its green fields and fruit trees, is on the Navajo reservation.

The highway and scenic drive ends two miles later at U.S. 160 in Tuba City, named for Hopi headman Tuba, or Toova. The town, now an administrative and trading center for the Navajo, was founded in 1878 by Mormon farmers. Tuba City has lots of amenities for travelers, including gas, lodging, and restaurants. In October, visitors can enjoy the Western Navajo Fair with a rodeo, arts and crafts, and dances.

10 CANYON DE CHELLY RIMROCK DRIVES
Navajo Highways 64 and 7

General description: Two Navajo highways, totaling forty-three miles, that follow the lofty rims of Canyon de Chelly and Canyon del Muerto in Canyon de Chelly National Monument in northeastern Arizona.

Special attractions: Canyon de Chelly National Monument, Anasazi ruins, White House Ruin, hiking, outstanding views, rock art, Spider Rock.

Location: Northeastern Arizona. The drives begin at the Canyon de Chelly National Monument Visitor Center just east of Chinle and about three miles east of U.S. 191.

Drive route numbers: Navajo Highways 64 and Navajo Highway and National Park Service Road 7.

Travel season: Year-round. Spring, summer, and fall are pleasant, with summer highs in the low 90s. Winters are cool but dry.

Camping: Cottonwood Campground, near the monument headquarters, is open year-round. The no-fee area has restrooms, picnic tables, dump station, and water. Avoid leaving valuables in an unattended campsite.

Services: All services are available in Chinle, including motels, restaurants, groceries, and gas. The famous Thunderbird Lodge is next to the park campground.

Nearby attractions: Navajo Indian Reservation, Four Corners Monument, Window Rock, Hopi Indian Reservation, Navajo National Monument, Monument Valley, Shiprock, Hubbell Trading Post National Historic Site.

For more information: Superintendent, Canyon de Chelly National Monument, P.O. Box 588, Chinle, AZ 86503, (520) 674-5500.

The drive: The Canyon de Chelly rimrock drives follow two Navajo highways along the lofty cliff edges of Canyon del Muerto and Canyon de Chelly in northeastern Arizona's Canyon de Chelly National Monument. The two paved routes, totaling forty-three miles, stop at numerous spectacular viewpoints above the canyon, offering vistas of streaked sandstone walls, ancient Anasazi Indian ruins, and Navajo hogans and fields. The name De Chelly is thought to be a Spanish corruption of the Navajo word *Tsegi*, meaning "rock canyon." The words are now pronounced in English as "d'shay."

Canyon de Chelly National Monument, an 83,840-acre parkland on the Defiance Plateau, is administered by the National Park Service in conjunction with the Navajo tribe, which owns the land. Travel in the monument is limited to the two rim drives and a short trail to respect the privacy of the Navajos still living in the canyons and to protect the many fragile ruins. Visitors who want a closer look at the canyons and their ruins can hire Navajo guides through the monument's visitor center to hike, horseback ride, or four-wheel up the canyons. Thunderbird Lodge, near monument headquar-

Spider Rock, the world's tallest free-standing spire, sits below the rimrock in Canyon de Chelly National Monument.

ters, offers half- and full-day commercial trips during good weather.

The rim drives are open year-round, with each season bringing a distinctive mood to the canyons. In spring, snowmelt from the Chuska Mountains floods Rio de Chelly and wildflowers bloom atop the canyon rims. Summers are pleasant, with daily highs in the nineties and afternoon thunderstorms in July and August. Autumn is an ideal time to visit the monument. The cooler days are colored by golden cottonwoods along the dry washes and clear expanses of blue sky. Winters are chilly, with highs in the forties. Chinle averages six inches of snow each winter, but it only lingers on the cool north-facing slopes.

Both rim drives begin at the monument visitor center, just east of Chinle. The visitor center offers a good introduction to Canyon de Chelly National

Monument, with museum displays on the area's archeology and natural history. Guided hikes and talks are held through the summer. A hogan, the traditional east-facing Navajo home, sits nearby. Hogans, circular domed structures made of mud and logs, are used not only for everyday living by Navajos but for ceremonial uses as well. Almost every Navajo family either still lives in a hogan or has one next to their modern house. Hogans, used by the many Navajos who farm in Canyon de Chelly National Monument, scatter across the canyon floors.

Cottonwood Campground lies just south of the visitor center. This free, year-round campground has restrooms, picnic tables, a dump station, and water. Campfire programs are presented from May through September. Visitors can also stay at the historic Thunderbird Lodge just south of the campground. The lodge was originally a trading post built in 1902 by Sam Day. It later expanded into a hotel to accommodate the visitors who flocked to see the nearby cliff dwellings and canyons.

The South Rim Drive, following Navajo Route 7, begins just past the visitor center. The road dips down and crosses the Rio de Chelly in a dense cottonwood forest. Turn south here for access to the campground and Thunderbird Lodge. The drive climbs steadily up the gentle western slope of the humpbacked Defiance Plateau, a 100-mile-long uplift that began rising some 50 million years ago. As the land slowly rose, meandering streams draining the Chuska Mountains to the east maintained their winding courses, incising these steep-walled canyons in the plateau's flank over the last three million years.

The first overlook, reached after two miles, is a good stop for examining the canyon's rock formations. The main cliff-forming rock is De Chelly sandstone, a formation deposited 230 million years ago as an immense field of sand dunes. It also forms the monumental buttes and mesas of Monument Valley in northern Arizona. Some 50 million years later the Shinarump conglomerate, a coarse, erosion-resistant layer, was deposited atop the De Chelly sandstone by sand and gravel-laden streams that drained surrounding highlands.

Tsegi Overlook, .5 mile farther on, offers spacious views of the canyon. Rio de Chelly, its shallow water gleaming in the sunlight, swings across the wide canyon below, past cottonwood groves and plowed fields. The Navajo farms in the canyons are occupied in the warmer months. Main crops include corn and squash, as well as peaches and apples from orchards. South of the overlook, small sand dunes nestle against rock outcrops.

The next stop, Junction Overlook, provides a spectacular view of the junction, or confluence, of Canyon de Chelly and its main tributary, Canyon del Muerto, Spanish for "Canyon of the Dead." Discerning eyes can find, in a shallow cave in the far canyon wall, the well-preserved walls of fifteen-room Junction Ruin. Down canyon is First Ruin, a ten-room dwelling first described in 1882.

A short spur road another two miles up the drive leads to White House Overlook. The vista from this overlook is thrilling, one of the best in the

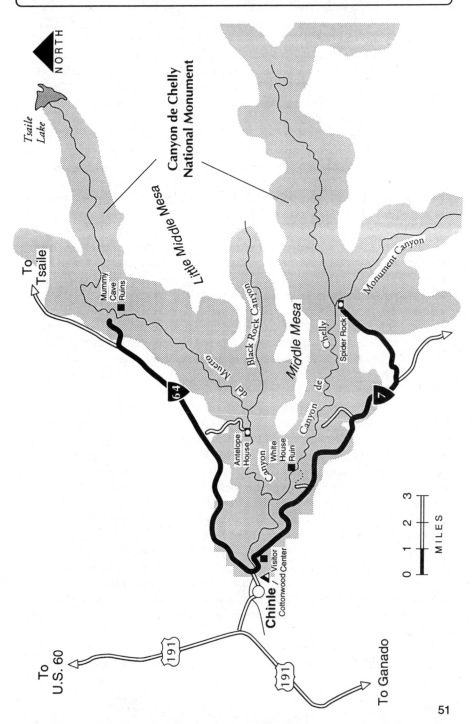

NORTH

Tsaile Lake

Canyon de Chelly National Monument

Little Middle Mesa

To Tsaile

Mummy Cave Ruins

del Muerto

Black Rock Canyon

Middle Mesa

Monument Canyon

Spider Rock

Canyon de Chelly

64

7

Antelope House

Canyon

White House Ruin

0 1 2 3
MILES

Chinle
Visitor Center
Cottonwood Center

191

191

To U.S. 60

To Ganado

51

monument. Towering pink cliffs, streaked by black desert varnish and broken by cracks, ledges, and overhangs, hem in the twisting thread of Rio de Chelly. White House Ruin, nestled in a dark alcove fifty feet above the cottonwoods, is dwarfed by the canyon's monumental majesty. White House Ruins Trail, a 2.5-mile round trip hike, drops 600 feet from the overlook to the ruin below. This is the only self-guided trail in the monument. Allow at least two hours to hike it, and carry water in summer.

White House Ruin, a multi-storied pueblo, was occupied, like most of the other canyon ruins, between A.D. 1050 and 1300 by the Anasazi Indians. The Navajo word Anasazi means "the ancient ones." The Navajos also called them the Swallow People, likening them to the cliff swallows that build their adobe nests in the canyon walls.

The monument's four canyons—Canyon de Chelly, Canyon del Muerto, Black Rock Canyon, and Monument Canyon—sheltered and nourished the Anasazi for over 1,000 years and later served as a mountain stronghold for the Navajos in their fight against first the Spanish and later the American governments. The Basketmakers, the area's first permanent inhabitants, left their trademark basketry and the remains of semi-subterranean, circular pithouses in the canyons beginning about A.D. 350. Over the following centuries, the Basketmaker Anasazi adopted new ideas, including the bow and arrow, the cultivation of corn, beans, and squash, pottery, and above-ground pueblos, that created a prosperous culture that reached a zenith in Canyon de Chelly by A.D. 1100.

Over the next 200 years the Anasazi flourished here, building large communal houses below the canyon cliffs. Then, in the thirteenth century, the Anasazi departed this homeland, leaving their once bustling cities to the owls, bats, and lizards. This abandonment of not only Canyon de Chelly, but the entire Four Corners region, was probably due to a prolonged drought coupled with resource depletion and farmland erosion.

For over 400 years Canyon de Chelly lay empty, until the late 1700s when an Indian group calling themselves *Dine* or "the people" drifted into this redrock country. Today, these Athapascan newcomers, originally from the boreal forests of Canada, form the Navajo Tribe. The Navajos quickly settled into the fertile canyons, grazing horses and sheep on the grassy meadows. They also used the canyons as a base for raiding nearby settlements, bringing the wrath of the United States Army on them.

In 1863 Kit Carson was given the unenviable job of defeating the proud and spirited Navajos and in January, 1864 he began the invasion of Canyon de Chelly. Marching the length of the canyon, his troops destroyed cornfields, orchards, and hogans. Without food or shelter, the Navajos surrendered and began the "Long Walk" 300 miles eastward to Fort Sumner in New Mexico. For four years the 8,000 exiled Navajos lived on the dry, treeless plains near Fort Sumner, before the U.S. government allowed them to return to their Arizona homeland.

The drive continues east, slowly climbing through scattered pinyon pine and juniper, for five miles to the turnoff for Sliding Rock Overlook. Sliding

Rock Ruin, perched on a sloping sandstone ledge, lies across the canyon. The Anasazi built retaining walls to keep the pueblo from sliding into the canyon.

The last overlook and the end of the drive is Spider Rock Overlook, eleven miles east of Sliding Rock Overlook. A short trail leads to the canyon edge, here reaching depths of 1,000 feet. Spider Rock, the world's tallest free-standing spire at 800 feet high, sits at the junction of Canyon de Chelly and Monument Canyon below the overlook.

Spider Rock, called *Tse Na'ashje'ii* by the Navajo, is home to *Na'ashje'ii Asdzaa* or Spider Woman, an important deity in the Navajo pantheon. One local legend says the Spider Woman captures misbehaving children from nearby hogans and carries them back to the top of Spider Rock, leaving their white bones to bleach atop the spire in the sun.

The paved South Rim Drive officially ends at Spider Rock. Navajo Route 7, however, continues southeast toward Window Rock. A short spur off the graded road leads to an overlook of Three Turkey Ruin, a well-preserved dwelling in Three Turkey Canyon south of Canyon de Chelly. Return via the South Rim Drive to the visitor center to continue the scenic route up the North Rim Drive.

The twenty-one-mile-long North Rim Drive, following Navajo Route 64, begins east of the Visitor Center. It crosses a bridge and begins climbing gentle slickrock benches on the western slope of the Defiance Plateau. The first turnoff, reached after five miles, leads to Ledge Ruin Overlook. A short trail winds over bedrock to the viewpoint on the north rim of Canyon del Muerto. A towering cliff shelters thirty- to fifty-room Ledge Ruin. The deep canyon, flanked by streaked walls, lies west of the overlook. Beyond the canyon stretches green Chinle Valley and a high, forested mesa.

A few miles up the drive is the turnoff to Antelope House Overlook. A short trail leads from the parking area to two overlooks. The first one offers dizzying views down to the junction of Canyon del Muerto and Black Rock Canyon. Above the junction is the Navajo Fortress, a natural rock fort that sheltered Navajos from attack by Spanish and American forces.

The other viewpoint looks down on Antelope House Ruin, a ninety-one-room site damaged by stream erosion. An overhanging wall of salmon-colored De Chelly sandstone rears over the silent city. The Navajos call this site *Jadi' Dayijeehi*, or "Running Antelope" for the stylish antelope painting on the cliff face beside the ruin. The art is thought to be the work of Navajo artist Dibe Yazhi who lived in the canyon in the 1830s. Other incomparable galleries of rock art created by both Anasazi and Navajo are scattered along Canyon del Muerto's cliffs.

Mummy Cave Overlook lies off a spur road near the drive's end. This viewpoint looks down on Mummy Cave, perhaps the most beautiful ruin in the monument. The dwelling, built on a rock pedestal under a huge overhanging cliff, boasted over seventy rooms. It and the canyon were named for two human burials found weathering out of the trash mound below the ruin during the 1880s. The Navajo name for the site is *Tse'yaa Kini* or "House Under the Rock." Archaeologists say the cave is one of the oldest

A sandstone cliff sweeps above White House Ruin in Canyon de Chelly National Monument.

continuously occupied sites in the Southwest, with habitation lasting over 1,000 years. First, the basketmakers dug their pithouses in the cave's soft floor, and later the Pueblos built the stone houses that still stand.

Another road leads from Mummy Cave to the Massacre Cave Overlook. This shallow alcove below the canyon rim was given its bloody name after a Spanish war party led by Lieutenant Antonio Narbona attacked Navajos taking refuge on the boulder-strewn ledge in 1805. Narbona reported 115 Navajo dead and thirty-three prisoners in his report to the governor of Santa Fe. He also substantiated his account with a package containing the ears of eighty-four warriors. The Navajo account differs markedly, claiming that the Spanish massacred mostly women, children, and old people because the men were away hunting. The cave walls still bear marks where rifle shots from the rim near today's overlook ricocheted off the sandstone.

The scenic drive ends at Massacre Cave high atop the Defiance Plateau. Visitors can continue up Navajo Route 64, across sagebrush-covered swales and over low ridges coated with pinyon pine and juniper to Tsaile. On the Tsaile campus of Navajo Community College is Hatathali Museum. South of Tsaile lies Wheatfields Lake with a campground and good fishing.

11 PETRIFIED FOREST NATIONAL PARK DRIVE

General description: This twenty-eight-mile scenic drive in eastern Arizona traverses Petrified Forest National Park, an eroded landscape of twisted gullies and low mesas that preserves the petrified logs of a 225-million-year-old forest.

Special attractions: Petrified logs, fossils, Painted Desert, Anasazi ruins, petroglyphs, hiking trails, backpacking, scenic views, visitor center, Rainbow Forest Museum.

Location: East-central Arizona. The northern access to the drive is at Exit 311 on Interstate 40, twenty-five miles east of Holbrook. The southern access is nineteen miles west of Holbrook on U.S. 180. An entrance fee is required to enter the park.

Drive route name: Petrified Forest Scenic Drive.

Travel season: Year-round. Spring and autumn temperatures are generally pleasant, ranging between fifty and ninety. Summers can be hot, expect daily highs over ninety degrees. Carry water and wear a hat when hiking in summer. Winters are cold and dry, although snow occasionally closes the road.

Camping: There are no campgrounds in the park. Wilderness backpack camping is allowed; obtain a free permit and more information at the park's visitor center and museum. There are private campgrounds, with full hookup, in Holbrook.

Services: All services are available in Holbrook, including motels, campgrounds, groceries, and gas.

Nearby attractions: Hopi Indian Reservation, Navajo Nation, Canyon de Chelly National Monument, Hubbell Trading Post National Historic Site, Lyman Lake State Park, Mogollon Rim, White Mountains, Homolovi Ruins State Park.

For more information: Superintendent, Petrified Forest National Park, AZ 86028, (520) 524-6228.

The drive: The twenty-eight-mile-long Petrified Forest scenic drive crosses an undulating plain broken by pale-tinted buttes, eroded mesas, and wide tawny grasslands in hourglass-shaped Petrified Forest National Park in east-central Arizona. The park lies on the edge of the Painted Desert, a long, colorful badlands that stretches from the Petrified Forest to the Grand Canyon along the Little Colorado River. It's a desolate landscape, weathered by dry heat and torrential rain. Its appearance, however, is deceptive, for buried in this colorful wasteland lies a hidden 225-million-year-old forest.

At that time, during the Triassic Period, Arizona was in the tropics some 1,700 miles to the south and part of Pangea, a super-continent. The climate was warm and wet. Sluggish streams and rivers meandered northwest across

Hikers climb Teepee Butte above the Petrified Forest National Park scenic drive.

a wide floodplain toward a sea. Silt, sand, mud, and volcanic ash from nearby highlands washed downstream past dense tropical forests.

The forest was much different from today's woodlands. The trees, mostly cone-bearing conifers distantly related to the Araucarias in today's Southern Hemisphere, towered 200 feet over the lush forest floor. Dense ferns and fifty-foot-tall horsetails clotted the riverbanks. It was a green and brown world. Flowering plants had not yet evolved. There were no birds, mammals, grasses, or butterflies. It was also a dangerous world. Giant metaposaurs, six- to ten-foot-long amphibians, and twenty-foot-long, crocodile-shaped phytosaurs splashed through the streams in search of fish and small prey, while *Postosuchus*, the largest carnivorous reptile, prowled the forest. This is the forest that lies hidden at Petrified Forest National Park. All it takes is observation and imagination to bring it back to life.

The drive begins at Exit 311 on Interstate 40, twenty-five miles east of Holbrook. The park is a fee area. The paved road is open daily year-round, although severe winter weather may temporarily close it. There are numerous pullouts and scenic overlooks along the road for sightseeing and hiking. There is no camping in the park, other than back-country camping. Get a permit at the visitor center or museum.

The park, open year-round, averages 5,400 feet in elevation. Each season in this high desert brings a distinct voice to the land's annual rhythm. Summer is a good time to visit. Expect hot days, with highs up in the nineties, and afternoon thunderstorms. Fall days are pleasant, with just a hint of coolness in the air. Winters are cold and breezy on this high plain. Occasional snowstorms coat the land in a white mantle. The days are generally clear with highs in the thirties and forties. Spring often brings windy weather that sweeps brown dust clouds over the land. Be prepared for cool weather and even late snow. Wildflowers carpet the desert in May and June.

The Painted Desert Visitor Center, just off Interstate 40, is the first stop on the drive. A small museum introduces visitors to the national park and its geologic and natural wonders. A short park orientation film is also shown. The museum shop sells books, maps, and posters. Nearby is a service station, restaurant, and gift shop.

The drive, for the first five miles, swings along the edge of a high mesa above the Painted Desert. Marvelous views unfold from each of this road section's eight designated overlooks—Tiponi Point, Tawa Point, Kachina Point, Chinde Point, Pintado Point, Nizhoni Point, Whipple Point, and Lacey Point. This is a land of long views. The forest-clad Defiance Plateau rims the northeast horizon. Pilot Rock, the park's high point at 6,235 feet, lifts its dark, eroded ridges above the badlands north of Pintado Point. Northwest lie the volcanic Hopi Buttes; to the west, 100 miles away, stands the ragged profile of the San Francisco Peaks; and below the southern sky stretches the White Mountains, their snowcapped summits gleaming like whitewashed towers.

Below the lofty, windswept viewpoints lies a wide expanse of roughly carved, barren badlands—the 43,030-acre Painted Desert Wilderness Area. The colorful Chinle Formation forms this section of the Painted Desert. The multicolored shades—muave, purple, red, brown, gray, and green—change with the sunlight between dawn and dusk. The colors of the formation, deposited as mud and silt along stream floodplains, are due to iron oxides in the soil. A trail at Kachina Point drops steeply down into the Painted Desert. At the bottom, hikers are free to walk anywhere. Also at Kachina Point is the Painted Desert Inn, a classic adobe structure that is a National Historic Landmark. Chinde Point has a picnic area with water and restrooms.

After five miles, the road swings south, crosses Interstate 40, and begins dropping toward the Puerco River across a rolling land covered with sagebrush, saltbrush, sunflowers, and Apache plume. The wide, sandy valley of the Puerco has long been a corridor for travelers. First the Indians and then the Spanish used this easy passage.

Later the United States, after winning northern Arizona in the Mexican War in 1848, surveyed the area for railroad and wagon routes to California. In 1853, Lt. Amiel Whipple explored the region. He noted in his journal,

"Quite a forest of petrified trees was discovered today, prostrate and partly buried in deposits of red marl." The Santa Fe Railroad came through northern Arizona in 1882, bringing settlers and a string of supply towns—Holbrook, Winslow, Flagstaff, and Kingman. During the 1890s entrepreneurs ravaged the fossil forest, carting off thousands of tons of wood and dynamiting logs in search of exquisite crystals. Outrage over the depredations led to the creation of Petrified Forest National Monument in 1906. Congress established the national park in 1962.

West of the road at the Puerco River is the ghost town site of Adamanna, an 1890s railroad stop named after early rancher Adam Hanna. This was the jumping off point for tours into what was then called "Chalcedony Park." Just beyond the river bridge lies Puerco Ruin, a large Anasazi Indian site with seventy-five rooms that may have housed as many as fifty people. The site had two occupations—from A.D. 1100 to 1200, and A.D. 1300 to 1400. The Anasazi grew corn, beans, and squash along the river floodplain, made colorful pottery and delicate baskets, and etched galleries of rock art on rock walls throughout the park. A paved path winds through the ruin. Because the area is heavily used, stay on the trail to avoid damaging the site. Look for many petroglyphs on the rocks below the site.

Past Puerco Ruin, the road climbs onto a narrow mesa. A short spur leads west to Newspaper Rock, a spectacular gallery of Anasazi rock art. The rock, an upright, flat-faced sandstone slab, lies at the bottom of a cliff. An overlook provides views of the petroglyphs below. Binoculars bring their detail closer. The petroglyphs, pecked into the dark, varnished rock surface, astound the imagination. Handprints, deer, lions, snakes, animal tracks, lizards, kachina faces, a sun and moon, and Kokopelli, the hump-backed flute player, jam the rock face. What does this art mean? It's a question that has long plagued archaeologists. Is it mere doodling, the depiction of myths and legends, the story of clan wanderings, a kind of hunting magic, a solar calender, or some of each? Whatever the answer is, it evades us. Better to simply appreciate the art and the glimpse it gives into the ancient Anasazi soul.

The drive runs southeast, enters a barren badlands, and passes The Tepees. These sharp, teepee-shaped buttes rise out of the ground like the buried ruins of a prehistoric city. Beyond The Teepees the road swings onto a broad grassy plain. Fleet pronghorn antelope, coyotes, jackrabbits, cottontail rabbits, and occasional hawks are seen along the drive.

The three-mile-long Blue Mesa spur road turns east on the grassland and climbs onto Blue Mesa, one of the park's most spectacular sections. The road, making a loop atop the mesa, offers great views of the eroded mesa and lots of petrified logs. Pedestal logs perch on the rounded haystacks, low hills with steep sides. An excellent one-mile loop trail drops from the mesa-top into the colored badlands of bentonite, a soft, easily-eroded clay. Flecks of petrified wood scatter everywhere, while thick tree trunks lie on the bottom of steep ravines. The Navajos say the logs are the bones of *Yietso*, an ancient monster slain by ancestral Navajos. Blue Mesa is a good place to observe the process of petrification and the subsequent erosion that uncovered the petrified forest.

A tumble of petrified logs in an arroyo on Blue Mesa along the Petrified Forest National Park scenic drive.

Most of the petrified trees, relatives of the modern Norfolk pine, in the national park were washed down from nearby highlands by floods some 225 million years ago. Swift river currents broke the bark and branches off the trees, before burying them in silt and mud in backwaters and lagoons. Groundwater, seeping through the silt, deposited silica minerals within the tree's cellular structure. Eventually the wood became petrified, preserving

PETRIFIED FOREST
NATIONAL PARK DRIVE

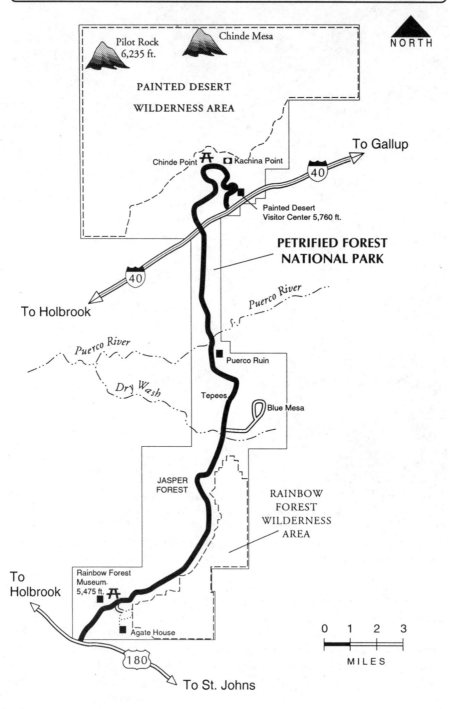

NORTH

Pilot Rock
6,235 ft.

Chinde Mesa

PAINTED DESERT

WILDERNESS AREA

To Gallup

Chinde Point   Kachina Point

40

Painted Desert
Visitor Center 5,760 ft.

PETRIFIED FOREST
NATIONAL PARK

40

To Holbrook

Puerco River

Puerco River

Puerco Ruin

Dry Wash

Tepees

Blue Mesa

JASPER
FOREST

RAINBOW
FOREST
WILDERNESS
AREA

Rainbow Forest
Museum.
5,475 ft.

To
Holbrook

Agate House

0   1   2   3

MILES

180

To St. Johns

for millions of years the beauty, strength, texture, and life of the once great forest. Uplift and erosion, beginning 60 million years ago, stripped the land of its protective rock layers above the Chinle Formation and exposed the long-buried petrified logs.

The next stop on the drive is at Agate Bridge, a 100-foot-long log spanning a forty-foot-wide wash. Erosion of the soft clay layers underneath left the log suspended over the ravine. Concrete pilings help preserve the bridge. In 1886, local cowboy Tom Paine won a $10 wager by riding his horse across the hard agate.

Both the Jasper Forest and Crystal Forest pulloffs offer views of the scattered remnants of petrified logs. A short .8-mile-long loop trail threads through Crystal Forest, a dense accumulation of petrified wood. This area was subject to severe exploitation as 19th century profiteers dynamited many logs in search of semi-precious stones such as smoky quartz and purple amethyst crystals. Many of the massive logs were reduced to the scattered piles of chips seen today.

Remember as you roam through Petrified Forest National Park that while you are welcome to pick up and examine fossils and petrified wood, it is illegal to take anything as a souvenir. If every one of the almost one million park visitors took one piece every year, the beauty and enjoyment of the park would be rapidly diminished. Petrified wood gathered outside the park is sold by park concessions and at roadside shops for as little as a quarter apiece. Help preserve the park by leaving it as you found it—on the ground. The Flattops parking area allows access to the narrow 7,240-acre Rainbow Forest Wilderness Area along the park's southeastern boundary. This pristine wilderness is a great area to explore by either day-hiking or backpacking. Just obtain a free permit for overnight camping and set out. The walking is easy across the spacious land and chances are you will be alone. Very few visitors use the park's backcountry. A good trek, if you have a shuttle, is to start at Agate Bridge and hike to the Long Logs.

The Long Logs and Agate House trails both begin near the park's southern boundary. The Long Logs Trail, a .5-mile, paved loop walk, passes through the largest concentration of petrified wood in the park. Many of the park's longest intact logs are found along the trail, including one measuring 116 feet long. Agate House Trail, a half-mile path, ends at an amazing eight-room pueblo ruin perched atop a rounded knoll. The isolated, one-story structure was built entirely of petrified wood and adobe about A.D. 1100.

The last stop on the scenic drive is at the Rainbow Forest Museum and the Giant Logs Trail. The museum exhibits depict how the trees became petrified and the life of the ancient forest. The .5-mile Giant Logs Trail, beginning behind the museum, leads past many logs including "Old Faithful," a massive trunk that measures nine and a half feet at its base. A short distance past the museum, the drive ends on U.S. 180. Holbrook lies nineteen miles to the west, while St. Johns is thirty-nine miles east. Visitors entering the park from U.S. 180 should reverse the drive, beginning at the Rainbow Forest Museum and ending at the Painted Desert Visitor Center on the Interstate.

General description: An eighty-seven-mile-long highway that crosses the heart of the precipitous Salt River Canyon between Globe and Show Low.
Special attractions: Salt River Canyon, scenic views, camping, hiking, fishing, rafting, White Mountain Apache Indian Reservation, San Carlos Indian Reservation, Tonto National Forest, Globe, Show Low.
Location: East-central Arizona. The scenic drive travels from Globe, eighty-seven miles east of Phoenix on U.S. 60, to Show Low atop the Mogollon Rim.
Drive route numbers: U.S. Highway 60, Arizona Highway 77.
Travel season: Year-round. The road is dry most of the year, although icy and snowcapped conditions can occur on the higher elevations near Show Low and south of the river canyon.
Camping: Jones Water Campground, a National Forest site seventeen miles from Globe, lies alongside the highway. It has twelve sites. Seneca Lake, an Apache tribal park, sits just over the road thirty-three miles north of Globe. Primitive camping is available near the Salt River bridge.
Services: All services are available in Globe and Show Low. Limited services, including gas, are available at the Salt River bridge.
Nearby attractions: Mogollon Rim, White Mountains, Sunrise Ski Area, Kinisba Ruins, Besh-ba-gowah Ruins, Tonto National Monument, Roosevelt Lake, Salt River Canyon Wilderness Area, Superstition Wilderness Area.
For more information: Tonto National Forest, 2324 E. McDowell Road, P.O. Box 5348, Phoenix, AZ 85010, (602) 225-5200. White Mountain Apache Game and Fish Dept., P.O. Box 220, Whiteriver, AZ 85941, (520) 338-4385. San Carlos Tribal Office, P.O. Box O, San Carlos, AZ 85550, (520) 475-2361. Show Low Chamber of Commerce, P.O. Box 1083, Show Low, AZ 85901, (520) 537-2326. Greater Globe/Miami Chamber of Commerce, P.O. Box 2539, Globe, AZ 85502, (520) 425-4495.

The drive: The eighty-seven-mile-long Globe to Show Low scenic drive follows U.S. 60, one of America's first coast-to-coast highways, north from Globe through the isolated mesas of the Apache Range, across the precipitous Salt River Canyon, and onto the forested Mogollon Rim to Show Low. The road traverses a wide variety of topography, climates, and plant communities. It crosses the transition zone from the Colorado Plateau in northern Arizona to the searing deserts of the south. The canyon bottom, at 3,000 feet, basks in a moderate year-round climate with prickly pear cacti, sotol yuccas, agaves, and palm trees, while ponderosa pine woodlands at 6,331-foot-high Show Low are buried under thick blankets of winter snow. The usually busy highway links Interstate 40 with Phoenix and Tucson. Plenty of pullouts and scenic views allow travelers to enjoy the drive's diversity.

The road is open year-round, although heavy snow might occasionally close the upper sections. Winter temperatures are cool at the lower elevations

U. S. 60 traverses the spectacular Salt River Gorge.

and cold on the rim. Summers are cool atop the rim near Show Low, but temperatures often climb to 100 degrees in the canyon bottom and near Globe. Afternoon thundershowers occur almost daily in July and August somewhere along the route. Spring days are delightful along the road. It can be freezing in Show Low, but short-sleeve weather in the canyon.

The drive begins in 3,541-foot-high Globe, an old mining town nestled along Pinal Creek in a shallow valley below the ragged Pinal Mountains. Prospectors, finding silver in nearby hills, set up a mining camp along the creek. Globe, supposedly named for a silver nugget etched with lines that resembled the continents, incorporated in 1880. The silver played out after a few years, but rich copper strikes kept Globe in business. The greatest producer was Old Dominion which yielded a fortune in gold, silver, and copper until its closure during the Great Depression. Besh-ba-gowah Ruins, a Salado Indian site just south of town, stretches along Pinal Creek. Several Forest Service roads climb south from Globe into the cool Pinal Mountains and the 7,812-foot summit of Pinal Peak. Numerous campgrounds and scenic views attract summer visitors to the range.

The U.S. 60 scenic drive begins on the eastern outskirts of Globe. Turn north off U.S. 70 and head northeast. The road rolls by dry, barren mountains for the first few miles, passing over rocky washes lined with mesquite trees. After a few miles, the road turns north up Cammerman Wash toward Richmond Mountain, a broad, round-shouldered peak broken by cliffs. The drive slowly begins to climb up dry arroyos toward a pass between Richmond Mountain and 5,771-foot Chrome Butte. The road crosses over the Apache Group, Precambrian rock formations including quartzite, conglomerate, shale, and limestone. Dark volcanic rocks, intruded into the sedimentary layers over 600 million years ago, forms erosion-resistant caps atop the surrounding mesas.

Past the saddle, the road dips and rolls over pinyon pine and juniper-covered ridges and dry, brushy canyons carved into ancient granite. After a few miles the highway passes once was once the booming town of McMillanville. A rich silver vein that ran for ten miles was discovered here in 1874 by Charlie McMillan and Dore Harris after a night of drinking in Globe. By 1880 almost 2,000 miners lived here, but in 1890 the town population had shrunk to one.

A couple miles past McMillanville, the highway drops into Sevenmile Wash and reaches Jones Water Campground. This pleasant National Forest campground, seventeen miles from Globe, is open year-round and has twelve sites tucked under tall sycamore and oak trees. The blacktop climbs sharply away from the campground and crosses a pass between pointed Rock Springs Butte and 6,106-foot-high Jackson Butte. The south-facing hillsides are studded with stunted juniper and prickly pear cacti. Jackson Butte Picnic Area lies just past the saddle. The small roadside rest area has five picnic tables and restrooms.

After climbing past Timber Camp Mountain, the road, at an elevation of almost 6,000 feet, passes stands of ponderosa pine that lift their rounded crowns above the pygmy juniper forest. The highway begins losing elevation as it follows sedimentary sandstone beds that dip gently to the north and the Salt River Canyon. A side road, Forest Road 304, takes off northwest from the main highway just before it leaves national forest land and drops down to the ghost townsite of Chrysotile. Ash Creek Canyon below was mined extensively for asbestos, which was hauled by long mule trains to the railroad at Globe.

The drive leaves Tonto National Forest twenty-nine miles from Globe and enters San Carlos Apache Reservation. A few miles later the road passes twenty-seven-acre Seneca Lake, a tribal campground, and the abandoned town of Seneca, before entering the Salt River Canyon. The highway, with six-percent grades, drops steeply past cliff bands of basalt and sedimentary rocks. Hieroglyphic Point, an overlook and pulloff partway down the canyon wall, makes an excellent viewpoint. Ancient petroglyphs, pecked into black

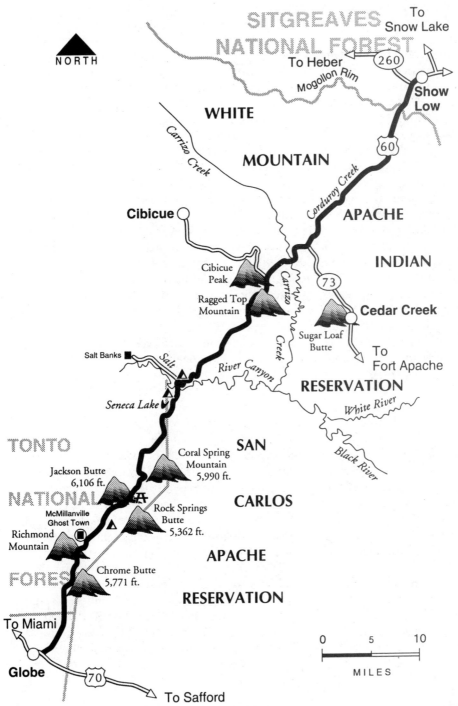

12 U. S. 60: GLOBE TO SHOW LOW

SITGREAVES
NATIONAL FOREST

To Snow Lake

To Heber

Mogollon Rim

260

Show Low

60

NORTH

WHITE

Carrizo Creek

MOUNTAIN

Corduroy Creek

APACHE

Cibicue

INDIAN

Cibicue Peak

73

Ragged Top Mountain

Cedar Creek

Carrizo Creek

Sugar Loaf Butte

To Fort Apache

Salt Banks

Salt

River Canyon

RESERVATION

Seneca Lake

White River

TONTO

SAN

Black River

Coral Spring Mountain 5,990 ft.

Jackson Butte 6,106 ft.

NATIONAL

CARLOS

McMillanville Ghost Town

Rock Springs Butte 5,362 ft.

Richmond Mountain

APACHE

FOREST

Chrome Butte 5,771 ft.

RESERVATION

To Miami

0   5   10

MILES

Globe

70

To Safford

65

boulders by early Indians, scatter along the steep slope below the road. A rough trail leads down to a cliffed overlook almost 2,000 feet above the canyon bottom.

The frothy Salt River, far below the overlook, churns through rocky gates of Apache Group limestone. Above lie layer upon layer of Precambrian and Paleozoic rock formations in shades of cinnamon, rust, and buff that stairstep up to the canyon's north rim. The Salt River, draining 13,000 square miles and formed by the Black and White rivers from snowmelt high on the White Mountains, was called *a'kimult* or "salty river" by the Pima Indians for the water's saline taste. The name was perpetuated by the canyon's first white visitor, Padre Eusebio Francisco Kino who named it Rio Salado or "Salt River" in 1698. The canyon was and still is the heart of Apache country with San Carlos Reservation on its south and the White Mountain Apache Reservation on its north. Apache warriors used the steep, twisting canyon as refuge until General Crook's troops flushed them out in 1873.

Past the overlook the road loops down to the canyon bottom where a girder bridge spans the river. The river plunges over rock benches and boulders creating swirling rapids. A parking area south of the bridge allows access to the cobbled riverbank and picnic tables. A gas station and store sit above the river's north bank. A dirt road heads west on the north side of the bridge to Cibicue Creek and the Salt Banks. The Salt Banks, a sacred Apache area, lie seven miles downriver. The banks are colorful travertine formations deposited by salt springs along the river. Primitive camping is allowed by the river with a permit from the White Mountain Apache tribe. Fishermen catch catfish and small-mouth bass in the Salt River.

The drive climbs abruptly from the canyon bottom, winding past towering crags and steep slopes covered with prickly pear cactus, sotol yucca, and agave. The road, at places a shelf atop 300-foot cliffs, reaches Becker Butte Overlook after four miles. The steep canyon, walled with limestone cliffs, falls away below the viewpoint. The butte is named for Gustav Becker, a pioneer trailbuilder, rancher, and freighter, who pushed the freight route that U.S. 60 now follows from Springerville to Globe.

Past the overlook, the highway quickly leaves the canyon behind and begins rolling over ridges, rounded mountains, and through shallow canyons. Panoramas of the White Mountains to the northeast unfold from the ridgelines. Almost twenty miles from the Salt Canyon, the road follows Carrizo Creek, its banks lined with cottonwoods. Palisades of basalt from old lava flows rim the canyon above. The highway climbs out of the canyon and passes the turnoff to Arizona 73, which heads east into the Apache reservation.

The road heads up cliff-lined Corduroy Creek, then climbs onto benches above the steep canyon rim. Slowly the highway gains elevation, and the forest changes from pinyon pine and juniper to an open ponderosa pine woodland. When the road reaches 6,600 feet on the Mogollon Rim, it enters Sitgreaves National Forest and a few miles later ends in Show Low, an old ranching and lumber town whose name and ownership were decided in a game of cards.

General description: A thirty-mile-long highway that traverses the northern flank of the Pinal Range before dropping into Superior and the Sonoran Desert.

Special attractions: Scenic views, camping, rock climbing, nature study, old mines, cacti, Tonto National Forest, Superior, Boyce Thompson Southwestern Arboretum.

Location: Central Arizona. Florence Junction lies about fifty miles east of Phoenix on U.S. 60.

Drive route number: U.S. Highway 60.

Travel season: Year-round. The road is dry most of the time. Spring rains and occasional snow can make driving hazardous on the upper elevations between Miami and Superior. Summer temperatures are hot.

Camping: One national forest campground borders the highway—Oak Flat. It is four miles east of Superior, open year-round, and has sixteen sites.

Services: All services are available in Globe, Miami, and Superior.

Nearby attractions: Globe, Besh-ba-gowah Ruins, Superstition Wilderness Area, Apache Trail, Roosevelt Lake, Tonto National Park, Pinal-Pioneer Parkway, Pinal Mountains, Lost Dutchman State Park.

For more information: Tonto National Forest, 2324 E. McDowell Road, P.O. Box 5348, Phoenix, AZ 85010, (602) 225-5200; and Rt. 1, Box 33, Globe, AZ 85501, (520) 425-7189. Globe Chamber of Commerce, 1450 N. Broad St., P.O. Box 2539, Globe, AZ 85502, (520) 425-4495.

The drive: The thirty-mile-long section of U.S. 60 between Miami and Florence Junction is one of central Arizona's most magnificent scenic drives. The road, a busy east-west highway, climbs over the northern flank of the Pinal mountains, drops steeply down Queen Canyon to Superior, then crosses into the Sonoran Desert. It continues another fifteen miles across rough desert studded with cacti, dry washes, and volcanic mountains to Florence Junction and the broad outwash plain south of the fabled Superstition Mountains. This drive, coupled with the Apache Trail, makes a good one-day excursion from Phoenix. The drive offers scenic views, passes part of Arizona's rich mining legacy, and allows the opportunity to discover the desert's natural history at the Boyce Thompson Southwestern Arboretum.

The drive is open year-round. Expect hot summer temperatures in the lowlands from Superior to Florence Junction, with daily highs over 100 degrees. Temperatures are cooler along the road section from Miami to Superior, with highs atop the road in the eighties and nineties. March through May is an excellent time to drive the route, with colorful wildflowers carpeting the desert floor. Winters are cool up high, but not cold. Mild temperatures are common in winter along the lower road section.

Dripping Springs Mountain towers over U.S. 60 west of Superior.

The scenic drive begins in Miami, an old mining camp that straddles Bloody Tanks Wash north of the Pinal Mountains. The wash was named after an 1864 battle between Colonel King Woolsey's troops, his Maricopa Indian allies, and a band of Apaches. The two sides had met in peace to exchange gifts, but the whites, on a prearranged signal, pulled their weapons and opened fire on the Apaches. The nineteen Indians shot in the encounter crawled over rocks to the creek, staining its water and banks crimson with blood and giving the wash its tragic name.

Miami, at 3,408 feet, is dominated by massive slag dumps and terraced mine tailings from deep copper strip mines north of the town. The town, named by settlers from Miami, Ohio, was laid out in 1907 and mining of nearby low-grade copper deposits began in earnest by the Miami Copper Company. The town grew overnight, and thousands flocked in to work in the mines and smelter. Employment agencies across America had standing orders for "1,000 men wanted at Miami, Arizona." The copper market slumped in 1931 slowing Miami's economy. It rebounded during World War II and the Korean War, but has fallen on hard times again recently. Over 2 billion pounds of copper have been extracted from the area's mines.

The drive heads west from Miami, climbing sharply up Bloody Tanks

The castellated ramparts of the Ajo Range soar over steep saguaro-and organ pipe-cacti-covered slopes in Organ Pipe Cactus National Monument. The 516-square-mile parkland supports an amazing diversity of life, including over 530 plant species.

Towering saguaros dwarf hikers in Tonto National Monument at the end of the Apache Trail. The saguaro, Arizona's largest cactus, lives over 200 years, grows fifty feet tall, and disperses as many as 40 million seeds in its lifetime.

Left: *The setting sun blazes a golden trail across Patagonia Lake State Park, a popular 265-acre boating and fishing lake off Arizona Highway 82.*

Below: *Vivid blossoms of buckhorn cholla cactus add brushstrokes of color to the Sonoran Desert along the Pinal Pioneer Parkway.*

Massive sandstone buttes, spread out like huge sculptures, tower beyond the North Window in Monument Valley. The valley, a land of startling views and vast

panoramas, is protected by the Navajo Indians as a tribal park. John Ford's famed movie "Stagecoach" was filmed here.

Watered by gentle winter rains, wildflowers spread a riotous blanket of color across the broad Ajo Valley along Organ Pipe Cactus National Monument's Puerto Blanco Drive. The annual flower display, occurring in March and April, includes poppies, lupines, and owl's clover.

A lone bicyclist, framed by cigar-shaped saguaro cacti, climbs the steep western grade of Gates Pass on the Gates Pass Saguaro National Monument Scenic Drive west of Tucson. The rocky Tucson mountains, a haven for wildlife and birds, loom above the road.

Morning light illuminates the Grand Canyon below its South Rim Drive. The canyon, a stunning kaleidoscope of color, form, and light, is over a mile deep, eighteen miles wide, 227 miles long, and documents 2 billion years of the earth's history in its twenty rock layers.

Wash to 4,200 feet on the northern flank of the Pinal Mountains. This range is part of the Central Highlands, a diagonal band of mountain ranges that forms a transition zone between the Colorado Plateau to the north and the Basin and Range desert to the south. Pinal Peak, the range high point at 7,812 feet, lies to the southeast. Scattered across the range are numerous campgrounds, reached by forest roads from Miami and Globe; cool refuges from hot summer temperatures.

As the highway crosses the mountainside, spectacular views unfold north of the strip mines and beyond to the ragged peaks of the Superstition Mountains and the Sierra Anchas. The distinct thumb of 4,553-foot Weaver's Needle punctures the Superstition skyline to the northwest. The ancient granite hillsides along the road are covered with brushy chaparrel.

After a few miles, Devils Canyon Picnic Area lies on the north side of the road. Oak Flat Campground lies a mile farther down, on Forest Road 469, Magma Mine Road, in pretty Oak Flat. Small granite canyons filled with oak trees cover this high undulating benchland. The campground, with sixteen sites, offers shaded picnic tables. Excellent rock climbing and bouldering abounds on the small crags scattered across Oak Flat. The Apaches often camped at Oak Flat, with its abundant firewood, game, and edible plants.

From Oak Flat, the drive drops abruptly down Queen Creek Canyon for four miles to Superior. This spectacular highway section passes beneath sharp ridges, buttresses, and pinnacles of welded tuff that tower above the road. It is a popular climbing area. The highway passes through 1,217-foot-long Queen Creek Tunnel before bending into Superior. Tilted Paleozoic sedimentary rocks edge the mountains around Superior. Most impressive is Apache Leap, a high squarish peak broken by jagged cliffs southeast of the town. The mountain was named after cavalry from nearby Camp Pinal chased a party of Apache warriors across the precipitous mountainside. The troops pursued the Apaches who grudgingly retreated and were finally cornered above a high cliff. Rufusing to surrender or be killed, they plunged off the cliff and died on the rocks below. Pieces of shiny black obsidion, called Apache Tears, are found nearby. Myth says they were shed by the seventy-five Apache braves as they leapt to their deaths.

Superior, like Globe, got its start as a mining town when silver was discovered in the rich Silver King Mine in 1875. Over 6 million dollars in silver were found in the Silver King, making it Arizona's richest silver mine. The town boomed as prospectors scoured the surrounding hills for their fortune. As the area's silver lodes played out, underlying copper deposits were uncovered. In 1910, the Magma Copper Company took over the defunct Silver Queen Mine and found one of Arizona's biggest copper bonanzas. The town was named for the Lake Superior and Arizona Mine, one of the area's largest silver producers. Superior still relies on the mines for its economy. It has all services for travelers.

The drive heads west from Superior along Queen Creek and after three miles reaches the famed Boyce Thompson Southwestern Arboretum in the northern shadow of rugged 4,375-foot-high Picketpost Mountain. The arbo-

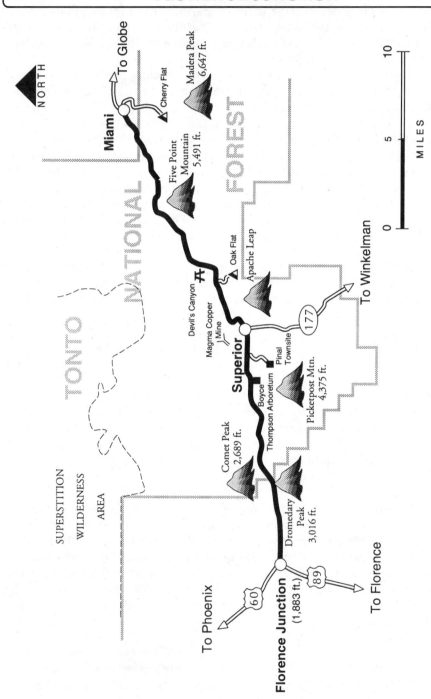

retum was created in 1927 by William Boyce Thompson, the mining magnate who amassed a fortune at the nearby Magma Copper Mine. The arboretum makes an excellent stop, especially in spring when wildflowers, including lupine, firecracker penstemon, fleabane, and Mexican gold-poppy, scatter their colors across the desert. Over 1,200 arid species collected from around the world can be seen here. Several trails loop across the arboretum's grounds, allowing hikers to discover the diversity and beauty of the Sonoran Desert. A visitor center and shaded picnic area lie along Queen Creek. The arboretum is open daily from 8 a.m. to 5 p.m.

Past the arboretum, the highway climbs away from Queen Creek and crosses open slopes covered with stately saguaro cacti, cholla cacti, and octotillos. As the road rolls west it crosses onto a wide bajada or outwash plain. The famed Superstition Mountains stretch their jagged profile across the northern horizon. Tales and legends of lost gold mines, including the Lost Dutchman Mine, permeate this maze of canyons and peaks, but no gold has ever been found in the mountains. The range was formed by massive volcanos that erupted here between 35 and 15 million years ago. The Superstition Wilderness Area spreads across 159,700 acres of the range. Over 180 miles of trail lace the area, attracting hikers, backpackers, and adventurers.

The scenic drive ends at 1,883-foot-high Florence Junction. U.S. 60 continues northwest along the base of the Superstition Mountains for sixteen miles to Apache Junction and the start of the Apache Trail scenic drive. U.S. 89 heads south across open desert and irrigated fields to Florence and the Pinal Pioneer Parkway scenic drive.

14 THE APACHE TRAIL:
Arizona Highway 88

General description: This forty-four-mile paved and gravel road, a National Scenic Byway, traverses the rugged northern fringe of the fabled Superstition Mountains and offers access to three large reservoirs on the Salt River.

Special attractions: Lost Dutchman State Park, Superstition Wilderness Area, Canyon Lake, Tortilla Flat, Fish Creek Hill, Apache Lake, Roosevelt Dam, Tonto National Forest, Salt River, scenic views, photography, hiking, backpacking, camping, cacti.

Location: Central Arizona. The drive begins off U.S. 60 in Apache Junction about thirty miles east of Phoenix and ends at Roosevelt Dam twenty-nine miles northwest of Globe.

Drive route name and number: Apache Trail, Arizona Highway 88.

Travel season: The road is open year-round. Winter, spring, and autumn are great times to travel the trail, with mild temperatures and clear skies. Gentle rain occasionally falls in winter and spring. Summer temperatures are generally hot, often climbing above 100 degrees. Severe afternoon thunderstorms can muddy or wash out sections of the gravel road. The steep, winding road is not recommended for large motorhomes or trailers past Tortilla Flat. **Camping:** Several National Forest campgrounds are scattered along the road: Canyon Lake, forty sites; Tortilla, seventy-seven sites; Apache Lake, twelve sites; Burnt Corral, seventeen sites. Lost Dutchman State Park, five miles from Apache Junction, offers thirty-five sites.

Services: No services are available on the road. Limited services, including a cafe, small hotel, and store, are at Tortilla Flat. Drive the road with a full tank of gas.

Nearby attractions: Phoenix, Four Peaks Wilderness Area, Roosevelt Lake, Tonto National Monument, Boyce Thompson Arboretum, Salt River Canyon Wilderness Area, Globe.

For more information: Tonto National Forest, P.O. Box 5348, Phoenix, AZ 85010, (602) 225-5200. Phoenix Convention & Visitors Bureau, 1 Arizona Center, 400 E. Van Buren, Suite 600, Phoenix, AZ 85004, (602) 254-6500. Apache Junction Chamber of Commerce, P.O. Box 1747, Apache Junction, AZ 85217-1747, (602) 982-3141.

The drive: The forty-four-mile-long Apache Trail meanders across central Arizona's most beautiful piece of real estate. The road dips, rolls, and twists along the northern flank of the rumpled Superstition Mountains northeast of Phoenix. This rugged land is a tangle of precipitious canyons, sharp volcanic peaks, tawny cliffs, undulating mesas, and stately saguaro forests. The drive, traversing a land of raw, pristine beauty, offers unmatched views. The Apache Trail is one of Arizona's best scenic drives. Every traveler needs to put it near the top of their "must do" list. Shortly after its completion in 1911, President Teddy Roosevelt called the road "one of the most spectacular, best-worth-seeing sights in the world."

The road is half-paved and half gravel, with numerous scenic pullouts. Patience is needed when driving the road as it winds through canyons and over mountain ridges. It is not made for high-speed travel. Watch for blind curves, steep grades and drop-offs, and narrow bridges. Large motor homes and trailers should not attempt the gravel road past Tortilla Flat. The road's most spectacular and potentially dangerous section is Fish Creek Hill where the mostly one-lane, cliff-hugging trail drops 800 feet in a mile. The road is often busy, particularly on spring weekends.

The Apache Trail, open year-round, is most spectacular in spring when wildflowers add patches of color to the landscape. Spring weather is generally mild, with highs between sixty and eighty degrees and occasional rainshowers. Winters are pleasant, although it is often cool enough for a sweater atop the road's higher elevations. A dusting of snow falls a few times each winter. Autumn brings clear, hot days. Summers, from May through September, are hot. Daily high temperatures are usually in the 100s and can reach 115 degrees. Carry water for yourself and your car. Violent thunderstorms on July, August, and September afternoons can make the road temporarily impassable or wash out sections.

Saguaros stud a hillside at Tonto National Monument above Lake Roosevelt just off the Apache Trail.

The drive begins in Apache Junction, some thirty miles east of Phoenix, at the intersection of U.S. 60 and Arizona 88. Head northeast on Arizona 88. The paved highway quickly leaves the city behind. After a few miles the road passes the Goldfield Ghost Town. A recreated underground mine here illustrates how miners extracted the precious metal. The true townsite of Goldfield, an 1890s gold town, lies a mile up the highway on the left. Gold was found in the granite Usery and Goldfield mountains.

Five miles from Apache Junction, the drive passes 300-acre Lost Dutchman State Park. This small parkland, with a thirty-five-site campground, lies in the morning shadow of the fabled Superstition Mountains. The range's western ramparts, a jumble of cliffs, buttresses, spires, and peaks, loom over the park. The park offers several hiking trails, including a handicapped-accessible native plant trail.

The park is named for the "dutchman", German prospector Jacob Waltz, who supposedly found a rich gold vein in the Superstitions. He died in 1891 without revealing his mine's exact location and left treasure hunters to search for the mother lode. It's never been found. Geologists say the mountains, the remains of several giant volcanic calderas, are an unlikely place for gold to occur. Waltz, says one theory, more likely concocted his Superstition Mine story to cover up a gold-laundering operation for high-graders or gold thieves at Wickenburg's Vulture Mine. But the myth of the lost mine endures.

Just past the state park, the drive enters 2,960,000-acre Tonto National Forest, one of the nation's largest national forests. The road from here to Roosevelt Dam is designated by the Forest Service as a National Scenic

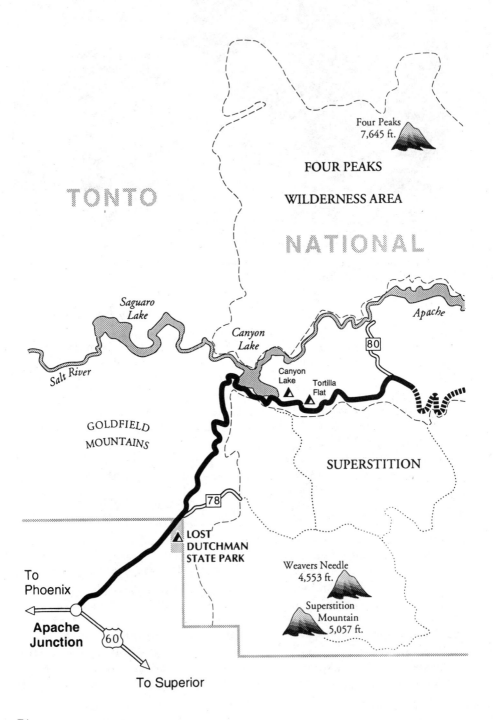

Four Peaks
7,645 ft.

FOUR PEAKS

WILDERNESS AREA

NATIONAL

TONTO

Saguaro
Lake

Canyon
Lake

Apache

80

Salt River

Canyon
Lake

Tortilla
Flat

GOLDFIELD
MOUNTAINS

SUPERSTITION

78

LOST
DUTCHMAN
STATE PARK

To
Phoenix

Weavers Needle
4,553 ft.

Superstition
Mountain
5,057 ft.

Apache
Junction

60

To Superior

14 THE APACHE TRAIL: ARIZONA HIGHWAY 88

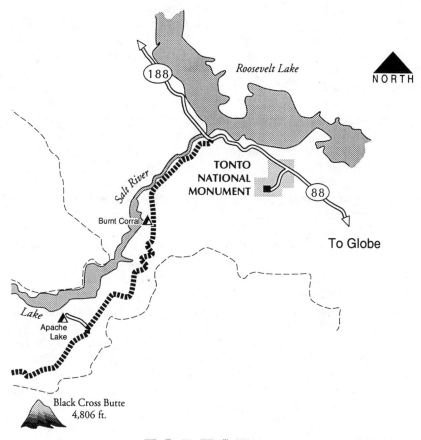

Roosevelt Lake

(188)

NORTH

Salt River

TONTO NATIONAL MONUMENT

(88)

To Globe

Burnt Corral

Lake

Apache Lake

Black Cross Butte
4,806 ft.

FOREST

WILDERNESS

White Mountain
6,100 ft.

AREA

```
0   1   2   3
|---|---|---|
    MILES
```

Byway. A turnoff here onto Forest Road 78 leads 2.5 miles to a main trailhead of the Superstition Wilderness Area. The Dutchman's Trail and Second Water Trail leave from here and climb into the rugged wilderness. Only foot and horse traffic are allowed. Over 180 trail miles lace the Superstition Wilderness.

The drive heads north and passes Needle Vista. The view looks south into the Superstitions to 4,535-foot Weaver's Needle, a landmark for those seeking the Lost Dutchman's gold. The spiked volcanic peak is named for early Arizona trailblazer Pauline Weaver. Past the vista the road winds through steep, rocky hills to Apache Gap. An old Indian trail drops down Willow Creek from the gap to the Salt River.

The road corkscrews down from the gap, passing rough hills studded with tall saguaros. The 7,645-foot-high Four Peaks, centerpiece of 60,700-acre Four Peaks Wilderness Area and the Mazatazl Mountains, towers to the northeast. Canyon Lake Vista Point offers marvelous views of 950-acre, ten-mile-long Canyon Lake. The narrow, cliff-lined lake was formed in 1925 when Mormon Flat Dam backed up the Salt River.

Mormon Flat, Horse Mesa, Stewart Mountain, and Roosevelt dams form a ladder of four lakes that impound the Salt River. The construction of the first dam, Roosevelt Dam, at the confluence of the Salt River and Tonto Creek, was one of Arizona's most momentous events. The dam's construction, part of the Salt River Project, tamed the fickle Salt River, raging one year and dry the next, harnessed the water of Arizona's central mountains, and transformed the desert surrounding Phoenix into a major irrigated agricultural area.

Roosevelt Dam was also responsible for the Apache Trail's existence. The road generally follows an ancient route long used by Indians, including the Apaches, and was a late 1800s horse route called the Tonto Trail. A supply road, needed to build the dam, was marked out along the old path. Work on it began in November, 1903 and finished in 1905. Much of the labor was provided by as many as 400 Apache and Pima Indians, who made roadcuts and laid dry-stone retaining walls. The road was laid out along the land's natural contours to avoid steep grades. After the Apache Trail's completion, twenty-mule teams hauled construction equipment and materials to the dam site at road's end. A stage and freight line later operated along the trail between Phoenix and Globe from 1914 to 1939.

The road winds down from the viewpoint to Canyon Lake. The lake, a popular recreation site, offers boating, fishing, and swimming. The lake is very busy on weekends from spring through mid-summer. It boasts excellent rainbow trout, largemouth bass, catfish, bluegill, crappie, and walleye fishing. Numerous recreation facilities spread along the lake's south shore. Acacia Picnic Area offers forty tables and a good swimming beach. Palo Verde Recreation Site has eight picnic sites and a boat ramp. Boulder Recreation Site has covered picnic tables and a wheelchair-accessible fishing dock. Canyon Lake Marina, operating under a Forest Service concession, has a forty-site camp area, primarily set up for RVs and trailers. Tenters are better off camping at nearby Tortilla Flat. Boulder Trail #103 heads south from the marina up scenic Boulder Canyon for seven miles in the Superstition Wilderness Area.

The Apache Trail drops down Fish Creek Hill below Wild Horse Mesa.

Continuing east, the drive climbs away from Canyon Lake to 1,979-foot Tortilla Vista Point. Great views of azure Canyon Lake and Tortilla Flat unfold from the overlook and nearby ridges. The road drops down to Tortilla Flat. The low mountains and buttes here were given the fanciful name by Major William Emory in 1853 because of their resemblance to stacks of tortillas. Horizontal cracks seam the rock buttresses forming the tortillas. Excellent seventy-seven-site Tortilla Campground sits on the canyon floor. It's open only during the cool season from October to April.

Tortilla Flat, population six, is the only community, if you can call it that, along the drive. This popular stop has a cafe, gift shop, and its own post office. The town, looking properly dilapidated, hosts throngs of weekend tourists who browse for Arizona knick-knacks, watch the dummy outlaw swaying from the "hanging" tree, or sample a jalapeno ice cream cone. It's also a good place to stop and wade in cool Mesquite Creek as it rushes over water-worn boulders.

The Apache Trail splashes through the creek and climbs away from Tortilla Flat. Steep peaks, topped with crags, surround the road. Typical plants of the Sonoran Desert Scrub plant community cover the slopes, including candelabra-shaped saguaro cacti, prickly pears, hedgehog and barrel cacti, cholla cacti, ocotillo, catclaw acacia, mesquite, ironwood, and palo verde. A wide range of animals roam this remote desert enclave. Birds flit among the trees along the creeks and lakes. Hawks, owls, eagles, and vultures soar on sky currents high above the deep canyons. Mammals, while shy and secretive, are sometimes sighted by alert visitors. Coyotes, skunks, javelinas, mountains lions, bobcat, deer, and bighorn sheep all live in the adjoining Superstition Wilderness. The bighorns were reintroduced to the area in 1984.

The road follows Mesquite Creek and climbs onto Mesquite Flat, a broad basin broken by cliffs. The area was once used as a holding place for cattle. The drive slowly climbs to 2,886-foot Horse Mesa Vista, the road's high point. The overlook offers marvelous views of the Superstition country and Four Peaks. The pavement ends here, five miles from Tortilla Flat. The next twenty-two miles to Roosevelt is a graded dirt road that is one-lane in many places and has several one-lane bridges. The road bends south on the mesatop and passes a parking area for Tortilla trailhead. A rough jeep road heads south here to the Superstition boundary. Several seldom-used trails penetrate the wilderness area here.

Fish Creek Hill, the drive's best scenery, lies beyond the trailhead. A parking area lies at the hill's edge. A short trail north leads to Fish Creek Vista, a spectacular viewpoint that looks into the precipitous, cliff-lined canyon below. The area's buff-colored cliffs are composed of welded volcanic ash called tuff. The Superstition Mountains south of the drive were, between 35 and 15 million years ago, an active volcanic field. Massive eruptions spread thick layers of ash across the land. Five major calderas or collapsed volcanos have been identified in the Superstitions.

Fish Creek Hill drops steeply from the mesatop to the canyon bottom. The one-lane road, falling 800 feet in a mile, tightly hugs the canyon wall. Soaring cliffs tower over the road and steep dropoffs fall away from the track. Numerous pullouts allow cars to safely pass each other. It's customary for downhill traffic to yield to uphill traffic. Near the canyon floor tower tall cliffs, festooned in springtime with hanging, spring-fed gardens, called the Walls of Bronze. A one-lane bridge crosses Fish Creek at the hill's bottom. An excellent hike traverses the creek south of the road. Vertical walls pinch down to the trickling creek.

The drive hairpins north along Fish Creek and then east along Lewis and Pranty Creek. It's banks are lined with sycamore, ash, cottonwood, and willow trees that provide welcome shade on hot days. Horse Mesa looms north of the road. Saguaros march up its boulder-strewn slopes and steep cliff bands rim its 4,110-foot high point. After a few miles the drive climbs away from the creek, swings under pointed 4,348-foot Bronco Butte and drops down toward Apache Lake.

Apache Lake Vista Point views this slender, seventeen-mile-long, 2,600-acre lake. The gaudy Painted Cliffs stretch along the mountain wall north of the lake, terminating at flat-topped Goat Mountain. Forest Road 79 drops one mile down from the overlook to Apache Lake Recreation Area. A marina and resort here have a boat ramp, boat rentals, camping supplies, restaurant, motel, and campground.

The road's last ten miles parallel Apache Lake to Roosevelt Dam. It dips through dry arroyos, climbs cactus-covered hillsides, hugs the rocky lakeshore, and gives stupendous views. Burnt Corral Campground, with seventeen shady sites, lies a .5 mile off the drive on the fjord-like lake. Past the campground the road twists along the narrow gorge. Beware of blind corners; keep to the right.

The Apache Trail ends at Roosevelt Dam, the world's largest masonry dam and a National Historic Landmark. The dam, built with quarried stone blocks between 1905 and 1911, stands 280 feet high and stretches 723 feet along its crest. A new concrete dam is being constructed over the old one to mitigate the effects of a possible earthquake. Mushroom-shaped Roosevelt Lake is twenty-three miles long and two miles wide, the largest of the Salt River's four reservoirs. It's a water recreationist's paradise, with fishing, boating, and camping.

Tonto National Monument lies a few miles east of the dam on Arizona 88. This small park protects and preserves the masonry ruins of the ancient Salado people who lived here over 700 years ago. These ancient farmers grew corn, beans, pumpkins, and cotton in irrigated fields along the Salt River. The picturesque ruins, nestled in airy cliff caves that overlook Roosevelt Lake, are accessible via a short self-guided trail.

To return to Phoenix, either redrive the Apache Trail or head south twenty-nine miles on Arizona 88 to Globe. The U.S. 60 scenic drive from Miami to Florence Junction begins here, making an excellent loop drive.

15 U. S. 666
The Coronado Trail

General description: A 123-mile-long paved highway that traverses spectacular mountain country from Springerville to Morenci in east-central Arizona.

Special attractions: Scenic views, camping, hiking, fishing, autumn foliage, copper mines, Blue Range Primitive Area, Bear Wallow Wilderness Area, Escudilla Wilderness Area, wildlife, Apache-Sitgreaves National Forest.

Location: East-central Arizona. The highway, paralleling the Arizona and New Mexico border, travels from Springerville to Morenci.

Drive route number: U.S. Highway 666.

Travel season: Year-round. The road can be temporarily closed due to heavy snows in winter. Be prepared for snow and icy spots along the highway's upper elevations.

Camping: Eight National Forest campgrounds are spread out along the route. Bring drinking water, some are dry.

Services: All services are available in Clifton, Morenci, Alpine, and Springerville. Food and lodging are available at Hannagan Meadow.

Nearby attractions: White Mountains Scenic Byway, Sunrise Ski Area, Lyman Lake State Park, Mogollon Rim, Petrified Forest National Park, Roper Lake State Park, Swift Trail, Casa Malpais Ruins.

For more information: Apache-Sitgreaves National Forest, P.O. Box 640, Springerville, AZ 85938, (520) 333-4301. Round Valley Chamber of Commerce, P.O. Box 31, Springerville, AZ 85938, (520) 333-2123.

The drive: The Coronado Trail twists and turns for 123 miles between Springerville and Morenci in eastern Arizona. The highway, roughly paralleling the Arizona-New Mexico border, traverses a wild, rugged, and scenic section of Arizona's mountain province. The road crosses a wide diversity of elevations, ecosystems, and climates, dropping from high conifer and aspen forests in the north to palm trees and cacti in the southern desert. The drive is named for Franciso Vasquez de Coronado, who four centuries earlier in 1540, crossed this wilderness of peaks and canyons in search of the elusive Seven Cities of Cibola.

The paved highway has numerous scenic pullouts, eight campgrounds, several picnic sites, but few good passing areas. Travelers are strongly advised to slow down and enjoy the winding drive. The highway boasts 460 curves between Morenci and the road's summit just south of Alpine. Little wonder that locals nicknamed the highway the "white-knuckle road." This is not a road to be in a hurry on, but rather a road for leisurely stopping, exploring, and sightseeing. U.S. 666 is also the nation's least traveled federal highway. An Arizona Department of Transportation study found the highway traveler will meet year-round, on the average, an oncoming vehicle once every nineteen minutes. Allow a minimum of four hours to safely negotiate the drive. More if you plan on stopping for the many marvelous views.

Elevations vary drastically along the route, from a low of 3,464 feet at Clifton to a high of 9,400 feet south of Alpine. This 5,000 foot variation in elevation leads to dramatically different climates at both ends of the Coronado Trail. Summer is the best time to travel the road. Expect highs in the seventies up north and the nineties in the south, with daily thunderstorms in July and August. Autumn brings dazzling aspen golds to the high country, while red oaks and yellow cottonwoods splash the lower canyons. Days are generally warm and clear. Winters are cold, especially in the mountains, and heavy snows occasionally close the highway. Alpine recieves over seventy inches of snow in winter. Spring is pleasant, with warm days and snow lingering along the road's upper reaches.

The scenic drive begins in Springerville in far eastern Arizona. Springerville and its adjoining twin city, Eagar, are nestled in a broad grassy valley fourteen miles west of the New Mexico border. The towns are the eastern gateway to

The Coronado Trail winds through abrupt mountains north of Morencei.

the Mogollon Rim and the White Mountains, a broad swath of hilly country that reaches northwest from New Mexico to Flagstaff. Both towns are old ranching communities first settled by Mormon pioneers in the 1870s. Springerville's remoteness made the area a haven for outlaws, including the Butch Cassidy gang, Billy the Kid, and the Clanton clan of Tombstone fame. The Madonna of the Trail, an eighteen-foot, ten-ton granite statue of a pioneer mother with a child in her arms, overlooks Springerville's Main Street and commemorates the westward spirit. Springerville and Eagar received the first traffic lights in all of Apache County in 1988.

The Coronado Trail, U.S. 666, heads south from U.S. 60 on the east side of Springerville. The route crosses a broad valley, before swinging east and climbing up an abrupt juniper and pinyon pine-covered hillside. A pulloff atop the hill offers a great view north of Springerville, the wide valley of the Little Colorado River, and numerous cinder cones that break the rolling plains. Here the highway enters 2,003,552-acre Apache-Sitgreaves National Forest, a recreation wonderland of lakes, mountains, and canyons that flanks the Coronado Trail as it twists southward.

Beyond the overlook, the road drops into a canyon rimmed by basalt cliffs and after a few miles reaches Nelson Reservoir Recreation Site, a thin, one-mile-long, sixty-acre lake that borders the highway. This National Forest area offers a five-site picnic area, restrooms, and a boat ramp. Fishermen catch rainbow, brown, and brook trout here.

The canyon opens into a wide grassy valley shaped by meandering Nutrioso Creek. Five miles past the lake the road passes through Nutrioso, a pleasant town established by Mormon settlers in the 1870s. Nutrioso is a combination of the Spanish words nutria for beaver and oso meaning bear.

Above the highway to the east towers 10,955-foot Escudilla Mountain, Arizona's third highest peak and the centerpiece of 5,220-acre Escudilla Wilderness Area. Escudilla means soup bowl in Spanish—an apt name for an old volcano whose crater resembles a hollowed-out bowl. Steep ridges, cloaked in ponderosa pine and juniper, plunge down to the road, while on the mountain's high escarpment shimmer groves of quaking aspen. A disastrous fire swept across Escudilla's northern slopes in 1951, decimating the conifer forest and allowing the aspen forest to fill in.

Escudilla Wilderness Area is accessible via Forest Road 56, about three miles south of Nutrioso. Two trails leave the road and climb to the mountain summit. Escudilla National Recreation Trail is the best one to hike. It climbs three miles up a well-graded trail from Terry Flat to 10,876-foot Escudilla Lookout. Government Trail climbs a steep two miles from Forest Road 56A to join Escudilla Trail on the summit ridge. Escudilla is well-known for its wildlife. Hikers can see elk, deer, black bear, and wild turkeys. Old Bigfoot, one of Arizona's last grizzly bears, was killed here by a government trapper in the early part of the century.

South of Nutrioso the Coronado Trail climbs up a forested valley, crosses 8,550-foot Alpine Divide, and drops down a narrow canyon. Alpine Divide Campground, with twelve sites nestled in the pines, lies just south of the pass summit. Four miles later the highway enters Alpine, a small, pleasant community in the heart of Arizona's high country. Alpine was originally called Bush Valley for Anderson Bush, its first settler. Later arriving Mormons named it Frisco for the San Francisco River, and then Alpine because of the surrounding mountain peaks. The village is now a base for outdoor recreation—hiking, fishing, hunting, snowmobiling, and cross-country skiing. It has lodging, restaurants, and a golf course. A good side-trip travels east on U.S. 180 to Luna Lake, a popular fishing hole near the New Mexico border. The recreation area has forty campsites.

The thirty-mile-long highway section from Alpine to Blue Vista traverses the eastern flank of the White Mountains and some of the trail's best scenery. The road curves and swings across densely forested hillsides and flower-carpeted meadows. It is especially gorgeous in autumn when the brilliant golds of changing aspens spread through the forest like wildfire. Hannagan Meadow, twenty-three miles south of Alpine, makes a good stopover. There is a rustic lodge here, and Hannagan Campground with five sites. This area offers some of Arizona's very best cross-country skiing.and snowmobiling.

The Coronado Trail climbs to its high point at almost 9,500 feet just south of Hannagan Meadow. Nearby is five-site K.P. Cienega Campground. This makes a great spot to stop for a day and poke around in the nearby canyons and forests. Forest Trail 70 drops east through a lush canyon, past a small waterfall, and into the Blue Range Primitive Area.

Past K.P. Cienega, the route reaches 9,184-foot Blue Vista on the edge of the spectacular Mogollon Rim. The views from this lofty vantage are impressive, the best on the Trail. Mountains spill out below the viewpoint. Ridge upon ridge marches across the land. A confusion of canyons and wooded mountains spreads to the horizon. Haze fills distant valleys, while black thunderstorms trail their dark shadows over the forest. Far to the south lies a blue peak—10,717-foot Mt. Graham and the Pineleno Mountains. Beyond them the keen eye can spot the Chiracahua Mountains. East and far below lie the tangled canyons of the Blue River, and farther east in New Mexico stretch the humpbacked Gila Range.

Past Blue Vista, the highway corkscrews abruptly down the precipitous face of the Mogollon Rim, the upturned, eroded southern edge of the Colorado Plateau. The Rim, one of Arizona's most notable geographic features, runs northwest from here to the western edge of the Grand Canyon. As the road twists down ridgelines and across scalloped mountainsides, it passes Stray Horse Campground with six sites. Further along is 8,153-foot Rose Peak. The parking area is seventeen miles south of Blue Vista. A short .5-mile trail climbs steeply up to a fire lookout. The views from here are outstanding.

The magnificent wild country west of the highway, broken only by a few jeep roads and trails, shelters the historic route of Francisco Vasquez de Coronado. He commanded an exploratory group that included 336 soldiers, Fray Marcos de Niza and four Franciscan padres, and over 700 Indians that worked as herdsmen, servants, and slaves. The 1540 expedition searched for the mythic Seven Cities of Cibola and their golden streets in southern Arizona, the Zuni and Pueblo villages of New Mexico, and on the Great Plains of Kansas. The conquistadores returned to Mexico empty-handed. Coronado's route climbed the rugged ridges of the Gila Mountains west of Clifton and about fifty miles west of today's Coronado Trail. This rough country was the most difficult terrain encountered on the expedition. Coronado wrote, "The horses were so exhausted they could not endure it, and, in this last desert, we lost more than previously. The way is very bad for at least thirty leagues or more through impassable mountains."

As the highway winds south, it drops from the open ponderosa pine forest into a woodland with gambel, white, and gray oaks. Further down, the road crosses grassy Four Bar Mesa and enters a pygmy forest of pinyon pine and juniper. Open grasslands dotted with grazing cattle are scattered among the trees. A couple campgrounds, Upper Juan Miller and Lower Juan Miller, lie just east of the scenic drive on Forest Road 475. Each campground has four sites. Forest Road 475 continues another fifteen miles east to the Blue River.

Past Juan Miller Creek the highway begins climbing steep ridges and passes Greys Peak Campground with seven sites. After a few miles the road twists around Grey Peak, a sharp 7,698-foot mountain just west of the asphalt and edges along a steep mountainside to a lofty lookout point at HL Saddle. Drivers can nearly coast from here to Morenci. Granville Campground, with nine sites, is nestled along shady Chase Creek in a narrow canyon. Two miles past Granville, the highway leaves Apache-Sitgreaves National Forest and switchbacks down a shelf road into rocky Chase Canyon.

Along the way is the ghost townsite of Metcalf, a mining town settled in 1872. In 1870 Robert Metcalf, tracking a band of outlaws in Chase Canyon, spied an outcropping of copper ore. He staked the first claim and began work. Two years later the town boasted a population of 2,000 and by 1878 it shipped tons of gold and copper south along the Coronado Railroad, the first railroad in the Arizona Territory, to smelters in Clifton. Nothing remains today of Metcalf save a few piles of rubble. South of Metcalf the road passes hundreds of abandoned tunnels that probe the once-rich mountainsides. Take care if you hike around. Most of the "glory holes" are disintegrating, overgrown, and treacherous.

Near the bottom of Chase Canyon lies the Morenci Mining District, home to one of the world's largest open pit mines. An observation point on its southwest edge allows spectacular views into the working mine operated by the Phelps-Dodge Corporation. Almost three billion tons of earth and ore has been removed from the pit, enough to make a small mountain.

The Coronado Trail and the scenic drive ends at Morenci, a mining town and smelter. The highway drops an additional 500 feet down to historic Clifton sandwiched between cliffs in the San Francisco River's narrow canyon. The town's name was shortened from Cliff Town to Clifton. The town, one of Arizona's most picturesque communities, was established by propectors in 1872. Since then its population and prosperity has fluctuated with the copper market. Many of Clifton's old buildings have survived. One of the most interesting is the Clifton Cliff Jail hollowed into a cliff face. The blasting work was done in 1881 by Margarito Verala. After finishing the job, he invested his pay in mescal and shot up Hovey's Dance Hall. That night he was the first guest in the jail he built. Clifton has all services, including lodging, restaurants, and shopping. Stop by the Chamber of Commerce on Chase Creek Street for information.

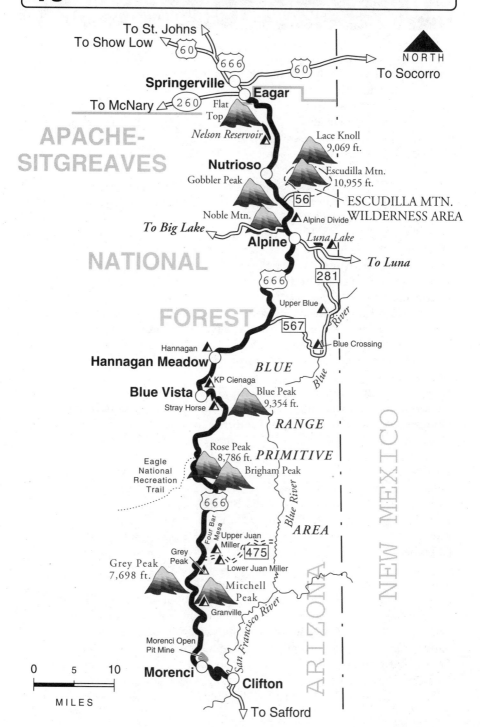

To St. Johns
To Show Low

60

666

60

To Socorro

NORTH

Springerville

Eagar

To McNary 260 Flat Top

Nelson Reservoir

Lace Knoll
9,069 ft.

APACHE-SITGREAVES

Nutrioso

Gobbler Peak

Escudilla Mtn.
10,955 ft.

56

ESCUDILLA MTN.
WILDERNESS AREA

Noble Mtn.

Alpine Divide

To Big Lake

Alpine

Luna Lake

To Luna

NATIONAL

666

281

Upper Blue

River

FOREST

567

Blue Crossing

Hannagan

Hannagan Meadow

BLUE

Blue

KP Cienaga

Blue Vista

Blue Peak
9,354 ft.

Stray Horse

RANGE

Rose Peak
8,786 ft.

PRIMITIVE

Eagle
National
Recreation
Trail

Brigham Peak

Blue River

666

AREA

Four Bar Mesa

Upper Juan Miller

475

Grey
Peak

Grey Peak
7,698 ft.

Lower Juan Miller

Mitchell
Peak

Granville

San Francisco River

Morenci Open
Pit Mine

0   5   10

Morenci

Clifton

MILES

To Safford

NEW MEXICO

ARIZONA

16

U. S. 89A
Oak Creek Canyon

General description: A twenty-seven-mile-long paved highway that drops from Flagstaff through spectacular Oak Creek Canyon to the red rock country at Sedona in central Arizona.

Special attractions: Scenic views, camping, hiking, fishing, swimming, nature study, rock climbing, Coconino National Forest, Oak Creek Canyon Recreation Area, Oak Creek Canyon Natural Area, Slide Rock State Park, ·Oak Creek Vista, Red Rock-Secret Mountain Wilderness Area, West Fork of Oak Creek Canyon.

Location: Central Arizona. Sedona, the southern terminus of Oak Creek Canyon, is 120 miles north of Phoenix, and fifteen miles north of Interstate 17 via Arizona Highway 179. Use exit 298 on I-17. U.S 89A begins off Interstate 40 in Flagstaff, or two miles south of Flagstaff at Exit 337 on Interstate 17.

Drive route number: U.S. Highway 89A.

Travel season: Year-round.

Camping: Five national forest campgrounds—Pine Flat, Cave Spring, Bootlegger, Banjo Bill, and Manzanita—are spread along the canyon road with a total of 173 sites. All campgrounds have restrooms and tables. All but Bootlegger have water. Pine Flat and Cave Spring campgrounds are the only ones with trailer spaces. There are private RV parks and campgrounds in Sedona and Flagstaff.

Services: All services are available in Flagstaff and Sedona.

Nearby attractions: Flagstaff, Museum of Northern Arizona, Sunset Crater Volcano and Wupatki national monuments, Walnut Canyon National Monument, Mogollon Rim, Tuzigoot National Monument, Montezuma Castle National Monument, Ft. Verde State Historic Park, Jerome, Munds Mountain Wilderness Area, Sycamore Canyon Wilderness Area, West Clear Creek Wilderness Area, Wet Beaver Wilderness Area, Schnebly Hill Road, Devil's Bridge.

For more information: Coconino National Forest, Sedona Ranger Station, P.O. Box 300, Sedona, AZ 86336, (520) 282-4119. Sedona-Oak Creek Canyon Chamber of Commerce, P.O. Box 478, Sedona, AZ 86336, (520) 282-7722.

The drive: The twenty-seven-mile-long Oak Creek Canyon scenic drive drops abruptly from the ponderosa pine woodlands near Flagstaff into slender Oak Creek Canyon before ending in the red rock country of Sedona. This spectacular drive, one of Arizona's very best, offers both sweeping views from its upper elevations of the Mogollon Rim and San Francisco Peaks, and intimate glimpses within the canyon of leafy grottos, tumbling Oak Creek, soaring sandstone cliffs, and colorful autumn colors.

The Oak Creek Canyon drive, following U.S. 89A, spans over 2,000 feet

Sandstone buttes loom over U. S. 89 in lower Oak Creek Canyon.

of elevation between Flagstaff and Sedona. Such a dramatic elevation difference in such a short distance creates a jumbled mosaic of climates and an astonishing number of biological communities. The dense forests atop the rim and in the canyon's upper reaches are cool and moist. The scrubby woodland near Sedona is dry and dusty. Cacti, yucca, and chapparal grow on warm, south-facing slopes, while a hundred yards around the bend in shaded alcoves live Douglas fir and ferns. Oak Creek Canyon forms a transition zone between the Colorado Plateau to the north and the Sonoran Desert to the south, with plants from both areas mingling together.

The canyon's elevation variations make markedly different climates along the drive. The upper elevations are cool, with temperatures generally in the seventies or low eighties in summer. Summer temperatures in the canyon are pleasant, with highs only rarely climbing above 100 degrees. The frigid, spring-fed creek is always close by to offer relief on the hot days. Autumn brings cool, clear days and colorful autumn foliage in late October. Winters are cold and snowy.

The drive, following U.S. 89A, begins two miles south of Flagstaff at Exit 337 on Interstate 17. Three miles down the road lies Lindbergh Spring Roadside Park with shaded picnic tables. The first eight miles of highway travel south through a thick ponderosa pine forest that coats the undulating Coconino Plateau. This ponderosa pine forest, the world's largest, stretches across central Arizona from the New Mexico border. The ponderosa pine, the largest conifer in the southern Rocky Mountains, reaches a maximum height

Oak Creek Canyon's rock walls are mirrored in placid Oak Creek along U. S. 89.

of 150 feet with trunks up to four feet in diameter. The pine forests are clean and open, with a sparse understory of plants growing beneath the trees. They have a very complex and efficient root system that leaves scant moisture for competing plants. Fallen pine needles also make the forest soil too acidic for most other plants.

After eight miles, the highway reaches 6,400-foot Oak Creek Vista Point, a spectacular overlook perched on the lip of the Mogollon Rim, the southern edge of the Colorado Plateau, and Oak Creek Canyon. The narrow floor of the canyon lies almost 2,000 feet below the rim. Western novelist Zane Grey described the scene in *Call of the Canyon*: "The very forest-fringed earth seemed to have opened into a deep abyss, ribbed by red rock walls and choked by steep mats of green timber."

A short loop trail circles down from the parking lot to the canyon rim. This is a good place to examine the canyon's geology. The rock formations seen here are the same ones exposed below the rim of the Grand Canyon. The bottommost layer on the canyon's floor is the 1500-foot-thick Supai Formation, a 280-million-year-old deposit of sediments washed from the ancestral Rockies onto a wide floodplain. The thick, cliff-forming Coconino sandstone preserves fields of ancient sand dunes. Streams later deposited white Toroweap sandstone atop the dunes. Above is the Kaibab limestone, laid down in a shallow sea some 225 million years ago. The canyon is rimmed by erosion-resistant lava that flowed from the nearby San Francisco Peaks. Oak Creek Canyon, excavated by time and running water fed by year-round springs, follows an old fault zone southward to Sedona. The west canyon rim is faulted higher than the east.

The drive plunges down from Oak Creek Vista, switchbacking steeply for two miles and 1,500 feet to the canyon floor at Sterling Spring, one of Oak Creek's year-round sources. The upper canyon here is forested with towering ponderosa pine, Douglas fir, quaking aspen, maple, and occasional spruce. Pine Flat Campground, with 58 sites, and Cave Spring Campground, with seventy-eight sites, lie just down the road. Both are pleasant overnight spots with water, tables, restrooms, and RV and trailer sites.

The highway continues down Oak Creek Canyon, winding alongside the creek's sparkling water as it tumbles over worn boulders, between tall sandstone cliffs streaked with desert varnish, and past three more campgrounds, two picnic areas, and two swimming holes. The three campgrounds—Bootlegger, Banjo Bill, and Manzanita—are small and intimate. RVs and trailers will not fit in any of them. They have a total of thirty-seven campsites, with water and restrooms. Halfway and Encinosa picnic grounds have eighteen tables. Both are day-use areas only.

Slide Rock State Park and Grasshopper Swim Area are the two established swimming holes in Oak Creek Canyon. Slide Rock, the most popular area, lies midway through the canyon. The creek dashes through a shallow, slippery trough worn into the bedrock sandstone. Summer bathers cavort in the cool water here on hot summer days, sliding down the algae-slickened sandstone. Slide Rock, a fee area, is open in summer from 8 a.m. to 7 p.m. Further downcanyon is Grasshopper Swim Area. Exit the highway and drop down to a paved parking area. The creek makes a wide bend through a shallow cliff-lined canyon, creating deep, peaceful pools. There are lots of other secret swimming holes scattered along the canyon. Be forewarned that the water can be very cold, especially in early summer.

Oak Creek Canyon is bordered on the west by the Red Rock-Secret Mountain Wilderness Area, a spectacular region of high mesas, cliffs, and deep canyons. Numerous hiking trails explore west from the highway. One of the best is the 5.6-mile-long Wilson Mountain Trail, a National Recreation

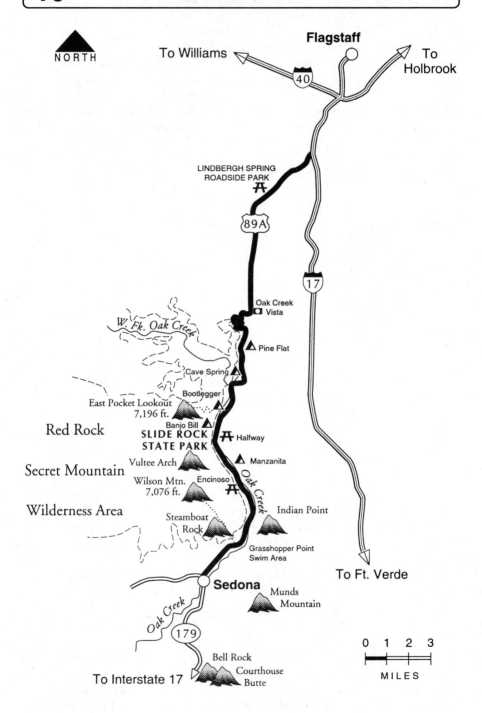

NORTH

To Williams

Flagstaff

To Holbrook

40

LINDBERGH SPRING
ROADSIDE PARK

89A

17

Oak Creek
Vista

W. Fk. Oak Creek

Pine Flat

Cave Spring

Bootlegger

East Pocket Lookout
7,196 ft.

Banjo Bill

Red Rock

**SLIDE ROCK
STATE PARK**

Halfway

Vultee Arch

Secret Mountain

Manzanita

Wilson Mtn.
7,076 ft.

Encinoso

Oak Creek

Wilderness Area

Steamboat
Rock

Indian Point

Grasshopper Point
Swim Area

To Ft. Verde

Sedona

Munds
Mountain

Oak Creek

179

Bell Rock

Courthouse
Butte

To Interstate 17

0 1 2 3

MILES

Trail, that climbs 2,300 feet from the highway's Midgley Bridge to the peak's 7,076-foot summit. Another ascends an easy 2.5 miles up an old cattle trail from Bootlegger Campground to 7,196-foot East Pocket Lookout. More trail information is available from the Coconino National Forest office in Sedona.

The West Fork of Oak Creek is an excellent day hiking area. The trail into this idyllic, unspoiled canyon begins near milepost 385. The deep canyon forms the Oak Creek Canyon Natural Area. The trail follows the creek westward. After three miles the sandstone cliffs pinch down to the creek, requiring the intrepid hiker to wade its shallow water.

As fourteen-mile-long Oak Creek Canyon drops from the pine and fir forest at its head to the arid pinyon pine and juniper woodland at Sedona, the creek is lined with a lush forest of cottonwood, sycamore, alder, box elder, ash, and walnut trees. In the lower, warmer canyon grow catclaw acacia, agave, ocotillo, creosote, cholla cactus, and prickly pear cactus.

The diverse plant communities offer habitat for an equally diverse number of animal species, including elk, mule and white-tail deer, javelina, coyote, bobcat, mountain lion, beaver, ringtail cat, skunk, raccoon, and black bear. Over 275 insect species inhabit the canyon. The stream's cold water provides good trout fishing.

The scenic drive ends at Sedona, an arts colony and resort community set amid the spectacular red rock country of lower Oak Creek Canyon. Numerous other scenic drives and trails explore the area around Sedona. Some of the best include Arizona Highway 179, which travels south fifteen miles from Sedona, past Bell Rock, Courthouse Butte, and the Chapel of the Holy Cross to Interstate 17. The Schnebly Hill Road winds east out of Sedona to the Mogollon Rim and offers unbelievable views of this sculptured land.

17 PERKINSVILLE ROAD

General description: A forty-seven-mile-long road that runs south from Williams across the pine-covered Mogollon Rim, drops into the scenic Verde River Valley, and climbs up an old railroad grade to the old mining camp of Jerome.

Special attractions: Bill Williams Mountain, White Horse Lake, Sycamore Point, Sycamore Wilderness Area, Verde River, Jerome, Prescott National Forest, scenic views, camping, hiking, wildlife, fishing.

Location: Central Arizona. The road runs from Williams on Interstate 40 south to Jerome on U.S. Alt. 89 west of Interstate 17.

Drive route name and numbers: Perkinsville Road, Forest roads 173, 492, 354, and 318.

Travel season: This is a three-season road, generally open from April through October. Snow and mud can block and muddy the dirt sections of the road. Use four-wheel drive only in winter. The upper paved section is open year-round and plowed after snowstorms.

Camping: Four national forest campgrounds lie near the drive. South of Williams are Dogtown Campground (sixty sites), three miles east on Forest Road 140, and White Horse Campground (eighty-five sites), ten miles east on Forest Road 110. Potato Patch (fourteen sites) and Mingus Mountain (twenty-four sites) campgrounds are just south of Jerome in the Black Hills. Primitive camping is permitted in both Kaibab and Prescott National Forests.

Services: All services are available in Jerome and Williams. There are no services along the drive. White Horse Resort, east of the byway, offers RV camping, cabins, a store, fishing tackle, and rental boats.

Nearby attractions: Grand Canyon National Park, San Francisco Peaks, Kaibab National Forest, Oak Creek Canyon, Sedona, Tuzigoot National Monument, Montezuma Castle National Monument, Prescott, Flagstaff, Walnut Canyon National Monument, Sunset Crater and Wupatki national monuments.

For more information: Forest Service Visitor Center, Kaibab National Forest, 200 W. Railroad Ave., Williams, AZ 86046, (520) 635-4061. Prescott National Forest, 344 S. Cortez Street, Prescott, AZ 86303, (520) 445-1762. Williams-Grand Canyon Chamber of Commerce, P.O. Box 235, Williams, AZ 86046, (520) 635-4061.

The drive: The Perkinsville Road travels forty-seven miles of paved and gravel road between Williams and Jerome in central Arizona. The drive drops from the cool, pine-clad Coconino Plateau to the twisting Verde River, before steeply climbing up to the historic mining town of Jerome on the north flank of the Black Hills. The road passes through an unpopulated, empty region of grand views, brushy canyons, rock-rimmed mesas, open coniferous forests, grassy meadows, and spacious skies. The road's first twenty-five miles south of Williams are paved, the remaining twenty-seven are dirt. Allow at least three hours for the drive.

It's best to drive the road from April through the end of October. Temperatures range from cool to hot. Cool weather prevails on the drive's northern reaches around 6,780-foot-high Williams, with summer highs rarely reaching above eighty degrees. Dropping south to the Verde River, at 3,800 feet, the temperatures rise into the nineties. Expect heavy thunderstorms on July and August afternoons. The gravel section of the road becomes muddy and often impassable after rain and snow. Four-wheel-drive vehicles are recommended in winter on the gravel road. The paved section near Williams is open year-round, with several winter recreation sites off the road.

The Perkinsville Road begins in downtown Williams at the intersection of Bill Williams Avenue, the town's main eastbound one-way street, and Fourth Street. Head south on Fourth Street, which turns into Forest Road 173 on entering Kaibab National Forest. Williams, lying astride Interstate 40, bills itself as the "Gateway to the Grand Canyon." The town, founded as a lumber and ranch town on the Atlantic and Pacific Railroad in the early 1880s, is named for Bill Williams Mountain south of town. Bill Williams, a famed early

The Perkinsville Road drops steeply through pinyon pine and juniper forest to the Verde River.

19th century trapper and guide, reportedly spent several seasons here in the 1830s. The 9,264-foot mountain, called *Hue-ga-woo-la* or Bear Mountain by the Havasupai Indians, was named for the mountain man by Captain Lorenzo Sitgreaves who surveyed the region in 1851 with the Corps of Topographical Engineers.

A half-mile after leaving Williams, the paved road passes red sandstone Santa Fe dam and reservoir and winds up narrow Santa Fe Canyon. The small reservoir offers trout fishing. A couple miles south of town is the turnoff to Williams Ski Area, with a 600-vertical-foot slope cut into Bill Williams Mountain's north face. The area also offers marked cross-country ski trails.

Beyond the ski area turnoff the landscape becomes rolling, ponderosa pine-covered hills broken by expansive meadows. Trickling streams lined with tall grass and colorful wildflowers meander alongside the drive. Forest Road 111 leaves the byway almost five miles south of Williams and switchbacks seven miles to the rounded summit of Bill Williams Mountain. This narrow, gravel road, passing groves of white and Douglas firs and copses of quaking aspen, makes a great side trip. George Wharton James described the summit view in 1917: "Imagine standing on a mountain top...and then looking out over a varied panorama, with practically unrestricted vision over a radius of two hundred miles. It is bewildering in its stupendous majesty and uplifting in its impressive glory." All of central Arizona spreads out below the lookout—the Grand Canyon rim and the snowcapped San Francisco Peaks lie to the north; the forested Mogollon Rim, broken by Sycamore Canyon, stretches east; the Verde Valley and Black Hills stretch to the south; and range upon range of mountains march to the hazy western horizon.

The road, for the first ten miles from Williams, crosses a wide, undulating lava plain that covers the under-lying Kaibab limestone on the southern fringe of the Coconino Plateau, a vast plateau that stretches northward to the Grand Canyon. Bill Williams Mountain itself is a small volcano that erupted some 4 million years ago, spewing a sea of lava across the land. Stubby cinder cones dot the plateau north and east of Williams.

Forest Road 110, leading to White Horse Lake and Sycamore Point, leaves the drive eight miles south of Williams. White Horse Lake, with an eighty-five-site Forest Service campground and small lakeside resort, is a thirty-five-acre reservoir that offers catfish, bluegill, and trout fishing. Sycamore Point, seventeen miles southeast of the drive, boasts one of Arizona's most spectacular, yet least known scenic views. This deep, twenty-one-mile-long gash, protected in 55,937-acre Sycamore Canyon Wilderness Area, is a stunning masterpiece of sculpted sandstone. Below the viewpoint lie red rock buttresses that soar over the twisting creek and separate leafy side canyons full of coolness and birdsong.

Vista Point sits along the scenic drive a couple miles beyond the turnoff to Sycamore Point. This overlook views the rest of the country traversed by the Perkinsville Road. Southward lies the Verde Valley and above that Mingus and Woodchute mountains, and the Bradshaw Range near Prescott.

The road begins dropping past Vista Point, steadily losing elevation as it descends toward the Verde Valley. The roadside forest quickly changes from ponderosa pine to a pygmy woodland of juniper and pinyon pine. The remote country the road passes through is rich in wildlife. Large mammals include black bear, elk, mule deer, and mountain lion. The road, dropping down a flat ridgetop, is flanked on the east by cliff-lined Bear Canyon.

A junction is reached twenty-three miles south of Williams. Turn east on Forest Road 492. Shortly after the junction the road turns to dirt and, swinging into Government Canyon, becomes Forest Road 354. The road, bouncing down the dusty canyon, descends quickly to the Verde River. The sparkling, tree-lined river is crossed by a one-lane, steel girder bridge. Broad, grassy valleys surrounded by rolling, juniper-clad hills spread along the drive, now Forest Road 318, south of the river. The area, originally settled by cattleman James Baker in 1876, has long been excellent cow country. Just downriver lies the old Perkins Ranch. The Santa Fe Railroad, putting a spur track through here in 1912, made a station at the ranch and called it Perkinsville.

NORTH

64
40

Williams

Bill
Williams
Ski Area

Bill Williams
Mountain
9,256 ft.

106

Dogtown

140

111

KAIBAB

110

109

NATIONAL

Summit
Mountain

White
Horse Lake

FOREST

McCannon

Bear Canyon

Sycamore Point

PRESCOTT

492

173

To
U. S. 89

492

Canyon

354

NATIONAL

Government

Perkinsville

Sycamore Canyon

Verde River

Verde River

FOREST

318

First View

Clarkdale

Tuzigoot National
Monument

Woodchute Mountain
7,854 ft.

WOODCHUTE
WILDERNESS AREA

BLACK

To
Interstate 17

Jerome

Mingus Mtn.
7,743 ft.

0   5   10

89

MILES   **To**
Prescott

HILLS

The last sixteen miles of road from the river to Jerome follows the old narrow gauge railbed of the United Verde and Pacific Railroad, which ran from Jerome to the Chino Valley. The railroad, built in 1893, twisted and turned for twenty-seven miles earning it the sobriquet "the world's crookedest railroad." The drive climbs south onto the forested flanks of 7,834-foot Woodchute Mountain and corkscrews around the mountain to Jerome. Just past a steep roadcut sits First View, a scenic viewpoint that overlooks the Verde Valley. Beyond the valley unfolds the land just traversed by the road, the Mogollon Rim, the pointed San Francisco Peaks, and red rock-lined Sycamore and Oak Creek Canyons.

The drive's last couple miles twist into Jerome, an old mining town that sprawls across 6,050-foot-high Cleopatra Hill. Jerome, one of Arizona's most picturesque towns, began in 1876 when wealthy financier Eugene Jerome backrolled prospectors to develop the hill's rich copper, silver, and gold deposits. The town flourished, becoming Arizona's third largest city with a population of 15,000. Jerome, called by one New York paper "The wickedest town in the West," reached its heyday in the 1920s with plush hotels, restaurants, saloons, and parlour houses. The city's fortunes plummeted with the stock market crash of 1929 and never fully recovered. The mines and smelter were silenced and the population fell to 5,000. The mines shut down for good in 1953 and Jerome became a ghost town until it was rediscovered.

Today the quaint town still stairsteps up precipitous mountainsides as steep as thirty percent, and attracts visitors who prowl its shop-lined streets and historic sites. The town offers three excellent museums, including the excellent Jerome State Historic Park overlooking the famed Little Daisy Mine.

18 PEARCE FERRY ROAD

General description: A forty-five-mile drive that crosses wide valleys and broad ridges covered with some of Arizona's largest Joshua tree forests and ends at South Cove on the shores of Lake Mead.
Special attractions: Lake Mead National Recreation Area, South Cove, Pearce Ferry, Joshua tree forests, scenic views, camping, hiking.
Location: Northwestern Arizona. The drive begins twenty-seven miles northwest of Kingman on U.S. 93.
Drive route name and number: Mojave County Route 25, Pearce Ferry Road.
Travel season: Year-round. The paved road is usually dry, except for occasional winter rains or summer thunderstorms.
Camping: A small primitive campground lies at Pearce Ferry at road's end on the shore of Lake Mead. Primitive camping is permitted on BLM lands along the drive. Good places are at Grapevine Point and Quartermaster Point east of the drive.

Services: Limited services are available in Dolan Springs and Meadview along the drive. Complete services are found in Kingman.

Nearby attractions: Kingman, Hoover Dam, Oatman, Bullhead City, Grand Canyon National Park, Hualapai Indian Reservation, Peach Springs Canyon, Hualapai Mountain Park, Chloride, Cerbat, Lake Mohave, Las Vegas.

For more information: BLM Kingman Resource Area Office, 2475 Beverly Ave., Kingman, AZ 86401, (520) 757-3161. Kingman Chamber of Commerce, 333 W. Andy Devine Blvd., P.O. Box 1150, Kingman, AZ 86402, (520) 753-6106. Lake Mead National Recreation Area, 601 Nevada Hwy., Boulder City, NV 89005-2426, (702) 293-8990.

The drive: Arizona's northwestern corner is a lonely landscape divided by wide basins and rumpled mountain ranges. It's a dry, desolate land of colorful plateaus, deep canyons, and two large lakes—Lake Mohave and Lake Mead—formed by dams on the Colorado River. Most travelers speed through here on U.S. 93 en route to the neon glitter of Las Vegas. Those who slow down and explore, however, find a land rich in plant and animal life, historic sites, and stunning vistas. The forty-seven-mile Pearce Ferry Road, northwest of Kingman, accesses some of this region's best scenery and offers a diverse backroad tour with Joshua tree forests, a dry lake basin, the Grand Wash Cliffs on the west edge of the Grand Canyon, and the turquoise waters of Lake Mead at road's end. The drive's weather in spring, winter, and fall is generally mild. Temperatures range from fifty to ninety degrees, and the sun shines almost every day. Occasional winter rainstorms slicken the pavement, and a scattering of snow might fall once in a long while. Summers, like the rest of western Arizona, are hot, but not as stifling as the furnace-like temperatures to the west at Lake Mohave and Bullhead City because of the road's higher elevation. Temperatures can climb as high as 110 degrees. The drive makes a good summer morning's excursion from Kingman before the day heats up. Be sure to carry plenty of water.

The Pearce Ferry Road scenic drive, following Mojave County Route 25, begins twenty-seven miles northwest of Kingman on U.S. 93. Hoover Dam lies forty-one miles further up the highway. The paved road runs northeast, creeping slowly up the gentle eastern bajada or sloping apron of the broad Detrital Valley. This intermountain valley, bordered on the west by the Black Mountains and the east by the Cerbat Mountains and the White Hills, is filled with detritus—gravel and sand washed into the desert valley from the surrounding highlands. Homes and occasional Joshua trees scatter along the roadside for the five miles from U.S. 93 to Dolan Springs, a small community spread across the low saddle between the Cerbat Mountains and the White Hills. The town has gas, lodging, RV parks, restaurants, and stores.

The Cerbat Mountains, topped by angular 7,148-foot-high Mt. Tipton, are a rough range of sharply weathered metamorphic rocks like gneiss and schist. Cerbat, meaning "bighorn sheep" in the Coca-Maricopa Indian language, was named in 1854 by Army Lieutenant A.W. Whipple. Numerous old mines and ghost towns dot the range. South of the drive, off U.S. 93, lies the picturesque, old town of Chloride, once the center of this rich mining district. The area's mines, operating from the 1860s to the early 1940s, extracted a fortune in copper, zinc, lead, gold, and silver. The White Hills are a low rolling range composed of thick layers of volcanic ash atop ancient metamorphic bedrock.

Beyond Dolan Springs the drive traverses sloping Table Mountain Plateau, crossing dry washes and passing through thick Joshua tree forests. The road drops steadily down into wide Hualapai Valley, a long north-south trending valley that stretches south to Kingman. Northward the valley narrows and ends in the placid waters of Lake Mead. Red Lake, a dry alkalai pan, shimmers east on the valley bottom. Beyond tower the stratified Grand Wash Cliffs, marking the western boundary of the Colorado Plateau and the Grand Canyon. The stair-stepped cliffs, rising as much as 2,000 feet above the roadway, were uplifted by Grand Wash Fault.

At the bottom of the Hualapai Valley, twenty-two miles from the road's beginning, lies two important road junctions. The Stockton Hill Road runs south through the valley for forty miles to Kingman. Another road leads north up Hualapai Wash to remote Gregg's Hideout, a primitive campsite and boat ramp in Lake Mead National Recreation Area.

The drive climbs northeast from the valley floor and after a couple miles enters a dense Joshua tree forest, one of the finest in the Southwest. The trees, a dominant plant of the higher Mojave Desert ecosystem, spill down the rocky hillsides. The Joshua tree, *Yucca brevifolia*, is a tree yucca, a member of the lily family, that grows as tall as twenty-five feet and lives as long as 300 years. The plant only grows in parts of California, Arizona, Utah, and Nevada. The Joshua forests along the drive are one of only three in Arizona. The tree was named by Mormon colonists who fancied the spiked plant looked like the Biblical Joshua with upraised arms. Explorer John C. Fremont called them "the most repulsive tree in the vegetable kingdom," while Forty-niner William Manly said they were "a brave little tree to live in such a barren country." Joshua trees flowers are pollinated only by *Pronuba synthetica*, a small gray moth, forming a true symbiotic relationship between two very different species of life. Neither can survive without the other's help.

The Joshua tree forests are home to other plants and animals. The area sits on the edge of three of North America's five deserts—the Mojave to the west, the Sonoran to the south, and the Great Basin to the north and east. Plants from all three mingle and mix here. The ubiquitous creosote dots the dry desert floor between the trees, while yellow brittlebush flowers spread color. Cholla cacti and yucca stud the land. Over sixty species of mammals are found here and in nearby Lake Mead National Recreation Area, including mountain lions, bobcats, badgers, ringtail cats, jackrabbits, kangaroo rats, gray and kit foxes, feral burros, and the elusive desert bighorn sheep. The National Park Service estimates as many as 2,000 sheep roam the recreation area. The best time to sight them is on sweltering summer days when they come to the lake to drink. Over 250 bird species and forty-two lizards and snakes inhabit the area.

Six miles from the floor of Hualapai Valley, the road crests Grapevine

A lone Joshua tree overlooks Lake Mead near the end of the Pearce Ferry Road.

Mesa, a high ridge that gently dips north toward Lake Mead. The Grand Wash Cliffs loom along the eastern horizon. Diamond Bar Road cuts east through the cliffs, winds up scenic Grapevine Canyon, and ends sixteen miles later at Quartermaster View Point high above the western Grand Canyon. Primitive camping sites lie along this dirt road.

The drive travels north across Grapevine Mesa, passing more Joshua trees and old mining operations like the King Tut and Lone Jack placer mines. As the road drops northward, the Joshua trees become scarcer, growing only in the moister arroyos. At thirty-six miles the road enters 2,338-square-mile Lake Mead National Recreation Area. Lake Mead, formed by 726-foot-high Hoover Dam, is America's largest man-made lake, offering an 820-mile-long shoreline and 115 miles of cold water from the dam to the lower Grand Canyon. A couple miles past the park boundary is a turnoff to Meadview, a

18 PEARCE FERRY ROAD

NORTH

NEVADA

GRAND

CANYON

LAKE

South
Cove

Pearce
Ferry

MEAD

AREA

NATIONAL

Temple
Bar Marina

Gregg's
Hideout

Meadview

PARK

NATIONAL   RECREATION

To U.S. 93

Golden
Rule Peak
3,862 ft.

Grapevine Mesa

Grand Wash Cliffs

To Quartermaster Point
and Grapevine Canyon

JOSHUA   TREE

Senator
Mountain
5,128 ft.

FOREST

WHITE HILLS

Gold   Basin

ARIZONA

Table Mtn.
Plateau

Table Mtn.

JOSHUA

Stockton Hill Road

TREE

FOREST

Red Lake

Hualapai Valley

To Las Vegas

**Dolan
Spring**

25

Mt. Tipton
7,148 ft.

MOUNTAINS

To Kingman

93

0   5   10

CERBAT

To Kingman

MILES

small resort community with limited services.

A mile past the turn is a spectacular viewpoint that overlooks Lost Basin, Lake Mead, and the rugged mountain ranges that surround it in Arizona and Nevada. An historic marker briefly describes the history of Lost Basin, its gold discoveries, and the Pearce, Scanlon, and Gregg ferries that once crossed the now-submerged Colorado River.

The road, running north, drops steadily down the narrowing mesa and a few miles later enters an abrupt canyon capped by low cliffs. Two miles farther is an important junction. The scenic drive turns west and plunges four miles down an eight-percent grade to South Cove. The drive's lonely end is marked by a boat ramp. Retrace the highway back to U.S. 93. A right turn at the junction winds down a steep dirt road for four miles to Pearce Ferry on the lakeshore. A boat ramp and primitive campsites are found here. This remote corner of Arizona is a great place to camp overnight. Out here on the rocky edge of Lake Mead lies the elemental earth, a remote land full of mystery and magic.

19 U. S. 163
Kayenta to Monument Valley

General description: A twenty-six-mile-long drive that runs north from Kayenta to the Utah border and Monument Valley past volcanic plugs and towering sandstone buttes and cliffs.

Special attractions: Agathlan, Monument Valley Tribal Park, visitor center, scenic views, photography, jeep tours.

Location: Northeastern Arizona on the Navajo Indian Reservation. U.S. 163 heads north from Kayenta to the Utah border and on to Mexican Hat and Moab, Utah.

Drive route number: U.S. Highway 163.

Travel season: Year-round. The highway is dry all year except for occasional summer thunderstorms and winter snows.

Camping: A 100-site campground is south of the visitor center at Monument Valley Tribal Park. A fee is charged. It is open except in winter.

Services: All services are available in Kayenta.

Nearby attractions: Navajo National Monument, Four Corners, Canyon de Chelly National Monument, Mesa Verde National Park, Hovenweep National Monument, Mexican Hat, San Juan River.

For more information: Monument Valley Tribal Park, Box 93, Monument Valley, UT 84536, (801) 727-3231. Goulding's Trading Post, Box 1, Monument Valley, UT 84536, (801) 727-3280.

The drive: Northeastern Arizona is a rough, lonely land with sparse vegetation, sparser water, and one of the world's fiercest temperature ranges.

The Agathlan towers over U. S. 163 north of Kayenta.

It's a land of magnificent panoramas, turquoise skies, and an oxidized rock rainbow of rust, orange, purple, and red ochre. The region, part of the vast Navajo Nation, is composed of, and shaped by, the most basic elements—the storm of sunlight from the cloudless sky; the few intermittent north-flowing tributaries of the San Juan River; and the abundance of bare sandstone eroded into bizarre and unusual spires, buttes, mesas, and canyons. The state's most majestic and surreal sandstone forms are those scattered across Monument Valley, a Navajo tribal park that straddles the Arizona and Utah border.

This scenic drive runs twenty-two miles north up U.S. 163 from Kayenta to the Monument Valley Tribal Park turnoff just across the Utah border and then four miles east to the park's visitor center in Arizona. A fee is charged to enter the tribal park. The paved highway is open year-round and generally dry. Occasional summer thunderstorms and winter snowfalls may slicken the pavement.

Expect summer temperatures in the nineties and low 100s. Nights can be cool. Spring days are generally warm and windy, while fall brings clear skies and crisp but warm days. Winter is a delight in Monument Valley, with snow brightening the long shadows and the invigorating cold air. Summer visitation is the highest, while winter is the low season. Annual rainfall at the valley, at an elevation of 5,500 feet, averages less than nine inches.

The scenic drive begins at the junction of U.S. 160 and U.S. 163 just south of Kayenta and heads north on U.S. 163. Kayenta, a Navajo word meaning "a natural game pit" or "boghole," lies along Laguna Creek in a broad, dusty valley flanked on the south by the forested escarpment of Black Mesa and on the north by upturned Navajo sandstone beds on the edge of the Monument Upwarp. Kayenta was established as a trading post by John and Louisa Wetherill in 1910. Wetherill, along with his brothers in Mancos, Colorado, discovered and named many Anasazi ruins including those on Mesa Verde and at Navajo National Monument. Kayenta offers all services to travelers.

The highway crosses Laguna Creek, a thin watery ribbon in a deep arroyo, just past Kayenta and turns northeast through the Comb Ridge. The ridge, a bending of rock layers on the southern fringe of the Monument Upwarp, trends northeast from Kayenta and lifts its serrated edge of salmon-colored Navajo sandstone all the way to the San Juan River in southern Utah. The Navajo sandstone, featuring steep, cross-bedded layers deposited as sand dunes over 200 million years ago, lies east of the road. The Monument Upwarp, a broad, dome-shaped anticline, reaches from the Comb Ridge north to Canyonlands National Park in Utah.

After the drive climbs through the ridge, it drops onto barren Little Capitan Valley. The Navajo Buttes punctuate the valley east of the road. The buttes are diatremes, black necks of ancient volcanos that scattered across the region during Tertiary times over 15 million years ago. The volcanos themselves have eroded away, leaving only their resistant necks behind. Chaistla Butte rises 400 feet above the flat valley just east of the highway. Further north towers Agathlan, a sharp 6,825-foot-high peak that lifts its summit 1,200 feet above the scenic drive.

Agathlan has long been an outstanding landmark. Early Spanish explorers named it El Capitan, but now it is better known by its Navajo name Agathlan, meaning "piles of wool." The peak's rough surface and the piles of debris surrounding it gave the name. Navajo legend says a race of giants once lived on Agathlan. They scraped hair off animal hides and allowed the wind to blow it about. It clung to plants and killed many animals, so the giants carefully piled up the hair at the peak's base and covered the piles with rocks.

A scenic pull off lies on the west side of Agathlan. Owl Rock, a slender spire of Wingate sandstone atop a cone of colorful Chinle shale, sits west of the road. Past Agathlan the highway follows El Capitan Wash before turning northeast. A massive escarpment walled by rusty Wingate Cliffs marches along the eastern edge of the Shonto Plateau west of the blacktop. Navajo hogans and herds of sheep dot the desolate plain below. After a few miles the famed buttes and spires of Monument Valley come into view to the east. The angular rocks here, composed of De Chelly Sandstone, resemble a silent, stone city. The monuments can even be described in an architectural language, abounding with domes, cupolas, steeples, cathedrals, and sky-scrapers. The landscape is grand. Everywhere the eye looks it finds an ever-changing panorama and an overwhelming grandeur. Novelist Willa Cather described the scene: "From the flat red seas of sand rose great rock mesas, generally Gothic in outline, resembling vast cathedrals. They were not crowded together in disorder, but placed in wide spaces, long vistas between. This plain might once have been an enormous city, all the smaller quarters destroyed by time, only the public buildings left."

A scenic gravel road loops through Monument Valley Tribal Park off U. S. 163.

The monuments are excellent examples of erosion. The DeChelly Sandstone has been completely dissected, leaving only small mesas, buttes, and towers. This is partly due to Monument Valley's close proximity to the San Juan River's deeply incised gorge to the north. The dry tributaries drain north, allowing quick removal of eroded debris. Frost wedging along joints in the sandstone shapes the great monuments. Ice, frozen in cracks and fractures, expands and pushes the rock apart until slabs break off and fall to the talus cone below. Water also weathers the soft Chinle Formation siltstone base, leaving the fractured rock slabs unsupported. Contrary to popular belief, wind has little to do with the formation of the monuments.

The road crosses the sagebrush-covered plain west of Monument Valley and twenty miles from Kayenta leaves Arizona and enters Utah. Just past the stateline, a right turn heads four miles east to the Monument Valley Tribal Park Visitor Center. A turn west at the junction leads two miles to Goulding's Lodge, with sixty-one rooms and unobstructed views of Monument Valley. The lodge, once a trading post established by Harry Goulding in 1923, offers Navajo-led tours of Monument Valley, Mystery Valley, and other off-the-beaten-track places. Goulding was instrumental in opening Monument Valley to the film industry. John Ford's famed movied "Stagecoach" was filmed here. Later features include "The Greatest Story Ever Told" and "Back To The Future III." Also at the road junction are numerous Navajo vendors with small stalls selling jewelry, carvings, and other Navajo crafts.

After a couple miles the paved road reenters Arizona and Monument Valley Tribal Park. The 29,816-acre park, straddling the border, was set aside

U. S. 163: KAYENTA TO MONUMENT VALLEY

19

NORTH

To Mexican Hat

UTAH

Monument Valley Tribal
Park Visitor Center

West Mitten Butte

Monument Pass
5,209 ft.

East Mitten Butte

ARIZONA

Mitchell Butte

Merrick Butte
Elephant Butte

EL CAPITAN

Spearhead Mesa

FLAT

163

MONUMENT

Mystery
Valley

Three Sisters

Totem Pole

Boot
Mesa

WETHERILL MESA

VALLEY

HUNTS MESA

Owl Rock

Agathlan
6,825 ft.

Little Capitan Valley

COMB RIDGE

TYENDE MESA

Chaistla Butte

To
Four
Corners

Laguna

Creek

160

Kayenta
(5,798 ft.)

Church Rock

To Tuba City

0 1 2 3

MILES

by the Navajo Tribal Council in 1958. A roadside station collects user fees at the park entrance. The visitor center has exhibits, an Indian craft shop, and information desk. Ask here for jeep tours that explore the valley with Navajo guides. A 100-site campground sits on the windy knoll south of the Visitor Center.

A rough seventeen-mile dirt track begins at the Visitor Center and swings through the park, passing its many notable features including the Mitten Buttes, Three Sisters, Yei-bi-chai, North Window, and the Totem Pole, a slender 500-foot-high dart that towers over surrounding sand dunes. Passenger cars can drive the road, although care must be taken in loose sand and rocky areas. No hiking or driving off the posted track is allowed.

Monument Valley offers some of Arizona's most magnificent and famous views, and rightly so. It's a place of grandeur and majesty. Walk down from the campground on a summer evening to a rocky viewpoint of the Mitten Buttes. Distant late afternoon thunderstorms drop veils of rain on distant mountains. A breeze cools the heat rising from sun-baked sandstone, and the rosy flush of setting sun suffuses the monuments with a lava-red inner glow. The end of another perfect day in Arizona.

20 ARIZONA 260
Springerville to Hon Dah

General description: A thirty-nine-mile-long highway that climbs over the northern flank of the scenic White Mountains.

Special attractions: Camping, hiking, fishing, boating, cool elevations, autumn colors, skiing, Apache-Sitgreaves National Forest, White Mountain Apache Indian Reservation.

Location: East-central Arizona. The drive follows Arizona Highway 260 from Springerville near the New Mexico border to Hon Dah on the Mogollon Rim.

Drive route number: Arizona Highway 260.

Travel season: Year round. Expect heavy snow and icy conditions in winter.

Camping: Two national forest campgrounds, Rolfe Hoyer and Benny Creek, lie just south of the drive near Greer. There are several campgrounds on the Apache reservation east of McNary, including Bog Creek, Shush Be Zahze Lake, Shush Be Tou Lake, Ditch, and Sheep Cienega. Most campgrounds have water and are open only in summer and fall.

Services: All services are available in Springerville, Eagar, and Show Low. Limited services are in McNary.

Nearby attractions: Coronado Trail, Petrified Forest National Park, Lyman Lake State Park, Mount Baldy Wilderness Area, Kinishba Ruins, Mogollon Rim, Greer Recreation Area.

For more information: Apache-Sitgreaves National Forest, P.O. Box 640, Springerville, AZ 85938, (602) 333-4301. White Mountain Apache, Game and

Fish Dept., P.O. Box 220, Whiteriver, AZ 85941, (602) 338-4385. Round Valley Chamber of Commerce, P.O. Box 31, Springerville, AZ 85938, (520) 333-2123.

The drive: The White Mountains, Arizona's largest range covering over 2,500 square miles, rise abruptly from the Mogollon Rim on the southern edge of the Colorado Plateau in east-central Arizona. The mountains are not sharp, precipitous peaks, but rather high, humpbacked ridges coated with thick forests and broken by wide, grassy valleys. Their forests and excellent fishing attract summer visitors who find a cool refuge from the surrounding deserts. This thirty-nine-mile-long scenic drive follows Arizona Highway 260 from Springerville to Hon Dah. The road, traversing the northern flank of the White Mountains, passes through the Apache-Sitgreaves National Forest and the White Mountain Apache Reservation.

Summer is the best time to visit the White Mountains, with pleasant daily temperatures between fifty and eighty degrees. Nights, especially at the higher elevations, can be cold. Heavy thunderstorms often fall on July and August afternoons. Be prepared if hiking by bringing a raincoat or poncho. Spring and fall are cooler. Highs range from forty to seventy, with below freezing nights. Winters are long and frigid. Snow lies alongside the highway from November through March.

The drive begins in Eagar, Springerville's twin town a couple miles south of U.S. 60. The towns lie in Round Valley, a broad, grassy basin on a bend of the Little Colorado River. Springerville, plugged as the "Gateway to the White Mountains," was founded as an outlaw camp and named for pioneer trader Henry Springer. Some of its more infamous residents included the Clanton gang which operated out of here after being run out of Tombstone. Eagar was founded by the three Eagar brothers, Mormon settlers from Utah, who found rich soil and plentiful irrigation water. They settled upriver from Springerville to avoid moral degradation. Today, both towns are friendly communities that serve as a center for local ranchers and offer all services for travelers.

Arizona Highway 260 heads west from Eagar, traveling across a wide valley beside the sparkling Little Colorado River, its grassy banks lined with bands of black basalt and dotted with grazing cattle. After three miles the road reaches a junction with Arizona Highway 273. This paved road climbs twenty-three miles south to Big Lake and some of Arizona's best trout waters. More trout, mostly rainbows, are caught in this 480-acre lake than any other Arizona lake. Groceries and rental boats are available. Facilities include a paved boat ramp and four national forest campgrounds with 210 campsites.

After a few miles the drive begins climbing away from the river valley on the bald, grassy flank of Antelope Mountain, an inactive cinder cone volcano. Old lava flows and over 200 cinder cones dot the land north of here. The White Mountains themselves were formed by volcanic action, with Mount Baldy, the range high point at 11,590 feet, the central volcano. The range was later sculpted by massive glaciers that perched atop the mountains.

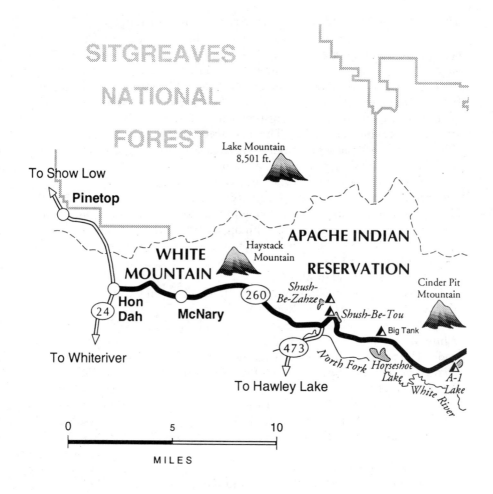

SITGREAVES
NATIONAL
FOREST

Lake Mountain
8,501 ft.

APACHE INDIAN

To Show Low

Pinetop

Haystack
Mountain

WHITE
MOUNTAIN

RESERVATION

Cinder Pit
Mtountain

Shush-
Be-Zahze

260

Hon
Dah

24

McNary

Shush-Be-Tou

Big Tank

To Whiteriver

473

North Fork

Horseshoe
Lake

A-1
Lake

To Hawley Lake

White River

0   5   10

MILES

The road enters Apache-Sitgreaves National Forest after ten miles. Arizona Highway 373 turns south just beyond the forest boundary. This road threads south for five miles to Greer, a small community at the confluence of the east and west forks of the Little Colorado River. Three lakes north of town and the river offer great fishing. Two national forest campgrounds, Benny Creek and Rolfe C. Hoyer, lie along the highway to Greer. Marked cross-country ski trails bring winter visitors to Greer.

Past the Greer turnoff, the drive begins climbing steadily through a thick ponderosa pine forest dotted with quaking aspens. After three miles the road reaches a 9,200-foot-high, rolling cienaga or meadowland flanked by gentle

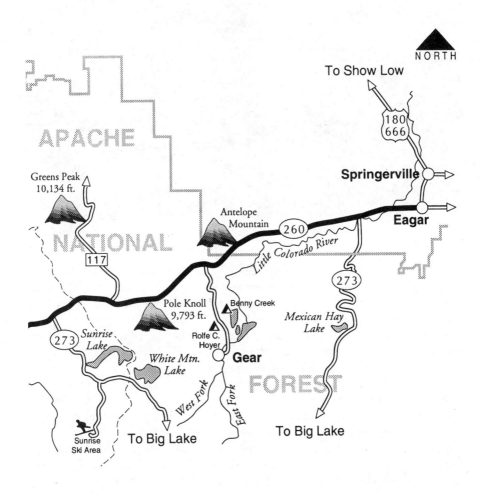

forested ridges. A good hike with spectacular views north across the Colorado Plateau can be found atop 10,134-foot Greens Peak. Turn north on Forest Road 117 and follow it about four miles to the peak's base. To the south towers Mount Baldy and Sunrise Ski Area, its forty-two runs cut onto steep north-facing slopes. The ski season is from November to April. The ski area, Mount Baldy, and several fishing lakes including Sunrise Lake and Lee Valley Reservoir, are accessible from the scenic drive via Forest Road 112 and Arizona Highway 273.

Mt. Baldy, the heart of the White Mountains, straddles the 6,975-acre Mount Baldy Wilderness Area on its north slope and the White Mountain

A stock corral below the White Mountains on Arizona 260.

Apache Reservation. Two campgrounds lie near the foot of Baldy, and two seven-mile-long trails climb the east and west forks of the Little Colorado River to Baldy's summit. The actual summit lies on the Apache reservation and is closed to non-Apaches. Mount Baldy, called *Dzil Ligai* or "White Mountain," is a sacred peak to the Apaches. This holy place is home of the wind and mountain spirits, and the source of life. Tribal members make pilgrimages to the mountain summit to worship.

The drive continues across the high meadowland and soon passes onto the White Mountain Apache Indian Reservation, a 1.6- million-acre reserve that is bordered by the Mogollon Rim on the north and the Salt River on the south. Two miles after entering the reservation, the highway drops into a pine and aspen forest and reaches A-1 Lake, the first of many small fishing ponds that border the road like watery beads. A-1 Lake has a small, four-site campground. Horseshoe Cienega Lake, a 121-acre lake with thirty campsites, a store, and boat rentals, sits on the south side of the road five miles past A-1. As the highway drops west, it passes other lakes with campgrounds—Bog Tank, Shush-Be-Tou, and Shush-Be-Zahze. Hawley Lake lies eight miles south of the highway on Arizona 473.

Finally the road levels out alongside Gooseberry Creek and enters McNary, an old lumber town. The McNary Lumber Company, started by James McNary, built a sawmill and a town here in 1924. By 1950 it boasted a population of 2,000. A fire destroyed the mill in 1979 and it was rebuilt by Eagar. Today the town's population and economic base is slowly dwindling.

The scenic drive ends three miles past McNary at Hon Dah and the highway junction with Arizona route 73, which heads south to Whiteriver and Fort Apache, the heart of the Apache reservation. Northwest along Arizona 260 lies a strip of development in the towns of Pinetop, Lakeside, and Show Low. Hon Dah, eastern gateway to the White Mountains, is named for the Apache word for "welcome."

21 MOUNT LEMMON HIGHWAY

General description: A twenty-five-mile-long paved road that steeply ascends 9,157-foot Mt. Lemmon in the rugged Santa Catalina Mountains north of Tucson.

Special attractions: Scenic views, camping, hiking, picnicking, rock climbing, wildflowers, cacti, Windy Point Vista, San Pedro Vista, Summerhaven, Mt. Lemmon Ski Valley, Pusch Ridge Wilderness Area, Mt. Lemmon.

Location: Southern Arizona. The drive begins at the Coronado National Forest boundary on the Catalina Highway off Tanque Verde Road in northeastern Tucson.

Drive route name and number: Mt. Lemmon Highway or Hitchcock Highway, Forest Road 5.

Travel season: Year-round. The road, climbing to almost 9,000 feet, offers a cool retreat from Tucson's summer heat. The temperature drops about twenty-five degrees from mountain base to top. Warm weather weekends are extremely busy, with traffic limited by the sheriff's department. The road is less busy on weekdays. Spring and fall are excellent times to drive the road, with wildflower and autumn color displays. Winters are snowy atop Mt. Lemmon, with the road occasional closed for plowing.

Camping: Four national forest campgrounds—Molino Basin (forty-nine sites), General Hitchcock (thirteen sites), Rose Canyon (ninety-eight sites), and Spencer Canyon (sixty sites)—line the highway. Showers Point, with three sites, is a group campground by reservation only. Molino Basin, the lowest at 4,500 feet, is the only one open year-round. The others are open seasonally depending on their elevation.

Services: Limited services, including lodging and dining, is available at road's end at Summerhaven. No gasoline is available on the Mt. Lemmon Highway. All services are found in Tucson.

Nearby attractions: Saguaro National Park, Colossal Cave, Tucson, Tucson Mountain Park, Old Tucson, Arizona-Sonora Desert Museum, Catalina State Park, Sabino Canyon, Fort Lowell Museum, San Xavier del Bac Mission, Madera Canyon, Santa Rita Mountains.

For more information: Coronado National Forest, Federal Building, 3000 W. Congress, Tucson, AZ 85701, (520) 670-4552. Camping information: (520) 629-5113. Tucson Convention & Visitors Bureau, 130 S. Scott, Tucson, AZ 85701, (520) 624-1817.

The Mt. Lemmon Highway sweeps by Goose Head Rock just past Windy Point.

The drive: The Mt. Lemmon Highway, one of Arizona's most beautiful scenic drives, steeply ascends the south flank of the Santa Catalina Mountains from the saguaro-studded Sonoran Desert outside Tucson to just below the fir-clad summit of 9,157-foot Mt. Lemmon. The road, passing through five of North America's seven distinct life zones, climbs over 5,300 feet making the drive a telescoped journey that is the biologic equivalent of traveling from Mexico to Canada.

The Santa Catalinas are one of Arizona's "sky islands," mountain ranges that poke up above surrounding desert basins. The ranges that tower over southeastern Arizona—the Santa Catalina, Rincon, Santa Rita, Huachuca, Dragoon, Pinaleno, Galiuro, and Chiricahua mountains—are cool refuges from the lowland heat and diverse communities of plants and animals. Every 1,000 feet traveled upward is like driving 600 miles northward. Temperatures drop as much as thirty degrees between Tucson and Mt. Lemmon, and precipitation dramatically increases. Snowfall at the ski area on Mt. Lemmon averages over 120 inches annually, while Tucson recieves a scant inch every four years. These perceptible climate changes make southern Arizona a biological paradise, harboring an astonishing array of plants, animals, and birds.

The scenic drive is open year-round, although heavy snow can temporarily close the upper road in winter. The road makes an excellent day trip at anytime. Summer is a great time to travel the road. It takes the traveler from Tucson's sauna-like temperatures to shady forests ruffled by cool breezes. The temperatures atop Mt. Lemmon average twenty-five to thirty degrees cooler than Tucson. Expect temperatures in the seventies, with cool nights. Heavy thunderstorms are common in July and August, with moisture-laden clouds building almost every afternoon. Autumn and spring bring pleasant weather. March visitors discover the mountain's climatic variety, driving from wildflower displays on the lower slopes to snow-blanketed forests at road's end.

The paved, two-lane road offers numerous scenic pulloffs and is very narrow on its upper section. Traffic can be heavy on weekends, especially in summer when it is often regulated to avoid over-use. While an average of 900 cars a day use the road, weekday traffic is generally light. Drive carefully, there are many hairpin turns and blind corners.

The Mt. Lemmon Highway, also called the Hitchcock Highway, begins by turning northeast onto the Catalina Highway off Tanque Verde Road in northeastern Tucson. The road angles for five miles across a gently sloping plain south of the mountains, passing suburban developments. The scenic drive starts at about 2,500 feet on the Coronado National Forest boundary at the mountain base about seventeen miles from downtown Tucson.

The road edges east along the rocky lower mountain slopes, past dipping outcrops and buttresses of banded gray Catalina gneiss. A typical Lower Sonoran ecosystem lines the blacktop. Stately stands of giant saguaro cacti tower among boulders, while mesquite and paloverde trees line dry washes. Brittlebush and other flowering plants spread a carpet of color across the mountainside. The first vista, Babat Duag Viewpoint, is reached after 2.5 miles. The Tucson Valley spreads out below. The wild Rincon Mountains, the Catalina's sister range, looms to the southeast.

After three miles the drive swings into Molino Canyon and hugs the west wall. The deep, boulder-strewn canyon falls away below the road to a sparkling creek that rushes over rock benches and pools in deep hollows. Saguaros and ocotillos scatter across the slopes. The Molino Canyon Overlook offers a spectacular view down the canyon and a short hike over to the creek as it drops over a succession of waterfalls. Willow, sycamore, and cottonwood trees grow in sandy soil along the clear stream.

Beyond the overlook, the highway climbs into Molino Basin and passes Molino Campground with forty-nine units. The campground, open all year, makes an excellent winter and spring basecamp to explore the Catalinas and Tucson area. It has no fee or water.

The basin, at 4,200 feet, marks the transition from the desert scrub community below to oak woodlands characterized by gnarled Mexican blue, Emory, and Arizona white oaks. Red-barked manzanita, yucca, and prickly pear cactus spread across the forest floor. Past the campground the drive turns west and rapidly climbs out of the basin toward a low pass that separates it from Bear Canyon. The oaks quickly give way to a dense pinyon pine and juniper forest.

Near the divide lies the site of an abandoned labor camp that housed prisoners who worked on the highway's construction. The road, proposed in the 1920s, was twice turned down by Tucson voters, but got the go-ahead in 1933 when *Tucson Citizen* publisher General Frank Hitchcock persuaded the Federal Bureau of Prisons to lend inmate help to build the road. Some 8,000 prisoners, eighteen years, and almost $1 million later the highway was finished and named the Hitchcock Highway for its advocate at its 1950 dedication.

The drive, after crossing the ridge, turns north and contours shelf-like above Bear Canyon. Further west lies Sabino Canyon's deeply incised trench and dark forested ridges and sharp peaks including 7,850-foot Cathedral Peak. The Santa Catalina Mountains, named by the famed Jesuit priest Padre Eusebio Kino on St. Catherine's Day in 1697, is a swollen blister of granite seamed by precipitous gorges. The mountains are a jumble of steep slopes, aretes, escarpments, buttresses, waterfalls, spires, and cliffs.

The road passes through a cliff-lined gateway into lush Upper Bear Canyon and twists alongside the creek. Again the vegetation and climate change dramatically along with the altitude, now almost 6,000 feet. Towering Chihuahua and Arizona pines, sycamores, alders, and feathery Arizona cypresses cover the creekbed and climb the cool, moist east canyon wall. The canyon's cypress stand is one of Arizona's best. The state's largest cypress grows just below the highway and measures seventy inches in circumference. Pines lift high above the forest floor, some as old as 300 years and six feet thick. Several good hiking trails ramble through the canyon woods. Bear Canyon Picnic Area and General Hitchcock Campground sit in the canyon bottom, making a cool summer retreat. The shady campground, open February through November, offers thirteen sites.

The drive loops out of Bear Canyon, climbing sharply up the canyon's west slope through dense chaparral. Granite pillars, aretes, buttresses, and hoodoos scatter across the mountainside from here to past Windy Point. These crags and spires offer some of Arizona's best rock climbing on their vertical faces. The Beaver Wall below Windy Point boasts some of the mountain's hardest routes, while the stubby spire General Hitchcock above Windy Point's parking lot thrills non-climbers below.

Windy Point, fourteen miles from the drive's start, yields the road's premier vista. The whole Tucson Basin spreads out like a ragged carpet below the lofty 6,400-foot overlook. A patchwork of buildings and roads dissect the valley, while the dark humpbacked Tucson Mountains mark its western edge. The Santa Rita Mountains, topped by pointed 9,453-foot Mt. Wrightson, soar above the southern horizon. Beyond, over seventy miles away, lie hazy ridges and peaks in Mexico. Distant Baboquivari Peak, piercing the sky to the southwest, is the sacred home of I'itoi, the Elder Brother of the Tohono O'odham Indians. A small parking area allows access to the viewpoint and to a National Forest display that details Mt. Lemmon's vegetation zones. The night view from here is stupendous, with a carpet of city lights twinkling in the valley blackness.

The highway swings northeast from Windy Point and runs up a high ridge above Bear Canyon. Geology Vista, .5-mile past Windy Point, briefly interprets the Catalina's geology and offers a great view into the canyon. The road climbs steadily away from the viewpoint and in another mile at an altitude of about 7,000 feet enters a dense pine forest. The five-needled

The Mt. Lemmon Highway edges along the east flank of Bear Canyon.

Arizona pine, the woodland's main tree, is hard to differentiate from its close relative, the three-needled ponderosa pine. The trees, lifting their crowns as high as 100 feet, cast deep shade on the pine needle-covered floor. The mountain's cool forest zone is its summer playground, with numerous picnic and campgrounds, and hiking trails.

After a couple miles of twisting through the forest, the drive passes the turnoff to Rose Canyon Lake, a seven-acre lake stocked with trout. Nearby ninety-eight-site Rose Canyon Campground, open from April to November, makes a pleasant idyll among the butterscotch-scented pines.

San Pedro Vista lies just beyond the lake turn. This spectacular 7,400-foot viewpoint, framed by tall firs, looks north to the broad San Pedro River valley. The dry desert valley below, hemmed in by the Tortilla and Galiuro mountains, runs north to the ragged outline of the fabled Superstition Mountains. Indian Head Rock sits just east of the overlook. Four-mile-long Green Mountain Trail leaves the vista, spirals around Green Mountain and drops down to General Hitchcock Campground. The walk is all downhill from the viewpoint.

The scenic drive bends northwest here and rolls another seven miles to the paved road's end at Summerhaven. Palisade Ranger Station sits a few miles up the road from San Pedro Vista. Exhibits here illustrate the Catalina's ecological diversity. Two hiking trails begin at the station. The Mt. Bigelow Trail hikes 1.5 miles to the summit of 8,550-foot Mt. Bigelow. The Butterfly Trail winds almost six miles northwest to Soldier Camp.

Past the ranger station, the road quickly climbs over 8,000 feet and the forest, a mixture of white and Douglas firs and pines, resembles that of southern Canada. Picnic and campgrounds line this road section. Secluded Spencer Canyon Campground offers sixty wooded sites. Bear Wallow is well-known for the 150 bird species that frequent its trickling spring. Other wildlife that roams the Catalinas include both whitetail and mule deer, peccary, coyote, fox, ring-tailed cat, mountain lion, bobcat, turkeys, and a small black bear population. The highway, bringing hordes of visitors to relatively fragile ecosystems, impacts the mountain's wildlife and plant communities.

Soldier Camp, a summer cabin area a mile beyond Spencer Canyon, was a popular summer campspot for cavalry troops stationed in hot Fort Lowell in Tucson in the 1870s. The soldiers, after chasing Apache bands across the searing desert, rode up here and spent a week or two recuperating in the cool woods. Later visitors were miners who prospected across the Santa Catalinas for gold, silver, and copper in the 1880s. Claims were staked and roads were built, but little of value was extracted from Lemmon's flanks.

A lost gold mine tale, however, haunts the Catalinas' rocky western slope. A wealthy vein, found by Indian hunters in 1698, was supposedly worked by Padre Escalante of Mission San Xavier del Bac. He hired Indians who mined and smelted the gold, which was stored in a cliff-side tunnel barred with a solid iron door. Apaches attacked the Indian laborers and obliterated all traces of the mine, leaving only a legend for weekend prospectors to pursue.

As the road drops northwest following the range crest, the San Pedro Valley and distant sierras are glimpsed through the forest canopy. Inspiration Rock and Loma Linda picnic areas lie past Bear Wallow Picnic Ground. Another road descends a mile to Summerhaven, a rustic village set along wooded Sabino Creek. Lodging and dining are available here. The road rambles down Sabino Creek another mile to end at Marshall Gulch Picnic Area. The four-mile Aspen Loop Trail begins here, climbing through a aspen, pine, and fir forests to Marshall Saddle.

A paved spur road just before Summerhaven leads two miles to Mt. Lemmon Ski Valley, the southernmost ski area in the United States. The 250-acre area, with sixteen runs, receives as much as 110 inches of snow and is open from December through March.

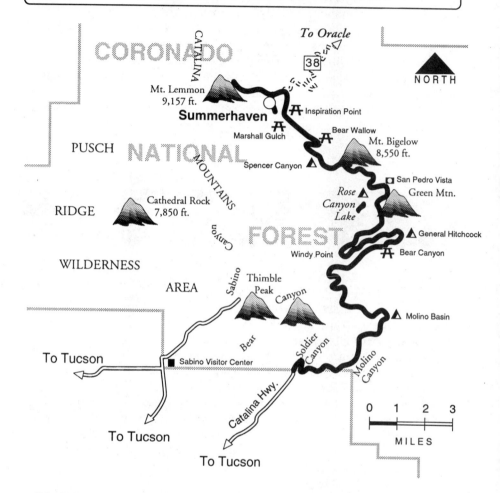

Mt. Lemmon, queen peak of the Catalinas, is climbed from the ski area. An unmarked one-mile-long trail ascends through a quiet forest to the range's rooftop. The mountain is named for Sarah Lemmon, wife of botanist John Gill Lemmon. The pair arrived in Tucson in March of 1881 and decided to explore the botanical diversity of the surrounding ranges. After failing to scale the dangerous, rugged peak, they contacted rancher and miner Emerson O. Stratton on the mountain's north slope. He agreed to guide them through the range. After reaching the summit Stratton christened the peak Mt. Lemmon in honor of Sara Lemmon, the first white woman to reach the 9,157-foot-high point. The Lemmons explored the Santa Catalinas and other ranges, finding over 100 new plant species growing on these isolated Arizona sky islands.

Dirt Forest Road 38 leaves the scenic drive near the ski area and switchbacks north twenty miles to Oracle in the San Pedro Valley. The road, losing almost 5,000 feet, was completed in 1917. Peppersauce Campground, shaded by towering sycamores, lies in the northern foothills of the Catalinas along the road. Other scenic areas to explore in the range include the Santa Catalina Natural Area and its wilderness of rocks southwest of Summerhaven and the rugged 56,933-acre Pusch Ridge Wilderness Area that encompasses the entire western part of the massif.

Come to the Catalinas and drive this spectacular scenic drive, one of the most beautiful and diverse roads in Arizona, but remember to walk lightly and leave little trace of your passing. Mt. Lemmon serves not only as an enclave of wildness and beauty, but as a playground for a major metropolitan area. The highway corridor up this lovely sky island needs to be loved, but not loved to death.

22 GATES PASS
Saguaro National Park Drive

General description: A twenty-two-mile-long paved and gravel scenic drive that traverses Gates Pass and Tucson Mountain Park, passes the famed Arizona-Sonora Desert Museum, and explores the spectacular saguaro forests of Saguaro National Park.

Special attractions: Saguaro National Park, saguaro cacti, Red Hills Information Center, hiking, wildlife observation, nature study, camping, picnicking, Arizona-Sonora Desert Museum, Old Tucson, Gates Pass.

Location: West of Tucson. The scenic drive, making an open loop, connects with Interstate 10 at Exit 248. Go west on Ina Road for six miles to the monument boundary. The southern access is via Speedway Boulevard at Exit 257. Go west nine miles to Tucson Mountain Park boundary.

Drive route names: Gates Pass Boulevard, Kinney Road, Bajada Loop Drive, Golden Gate Road, and Picture Rocks Road.

Travel season: Year-round.

Camping: Gilbert Ray Campground, administered by Tucson Mountain Park, lies a mile off the scenic drive just north of Old Tucson. The campground, open all year, offers 130 tent and RV sites in a scenic setting.

Services: All services in Tucson.

Nearby attractions: Tucson Botanical Gardens, Fort Lowell Museum, Reid Park and Zoo, Saguaro National Park East, Mission San Xavier del Bac, Pima Air Museum, Santa Catalina Mountains, Mt. Lemmon Scenic Drive, Catalina State Park, Sabino Canyon, Colossal Cave, Kitt Peak National Observatory.

For more information: Saguaro National Park, 3693 South Old Spanish Trail, Tucson, AZ 85730-5699, east: (520) 733-5153, west: (520) 733-5158. Tucson Convention & Visitor's Bureau, 130 S. Scott, Tucson, AZ 85701, (520) 624-1817.

Sunrise over the Tucson Mountains from the Gates Pass-Saguaro National Park Scenic Drive.

The drive: The twenty-two-mile-long Gates Pass-Saguaro National Park scenic drive traverses the western slope of the Tucson Mountains making an open loop west of Interstate 10 and Tucson. The spectacular road passes through a dense saguaro forest that covers the sloping bajadas or outwash plains below the Tucson Mountains, a rumpled range that separates Tucson and the Santa Cruz River Valley from the broad Avra Valley to the west. The drive lies entirely within Tucson Mountain Park and the Tucson Mountain District of Saguaro National Park.

Spring is perhaps the most pleasant time to drive the route and visit the park. April highs average eighty degrees with lows of fifty. March is slightly cooler, with highs generally in the seventies. Summers are hot, but not as hot as Phoenix. Average June, July, and August temperatures hover just below 100 degrees. Almost half the area's annual precipitation falls in violent cloudbursts in July and August. This rainy season, locally called the monsoon, begins when moisture is pumped into the Southwest from the Atlantic Ocean and the Gulf of Mexico by strong high pressure cells. Autumns are warm and dry, with long periods of clear days. Winter offers ideal weather with daytime highs in the sixties and an occasional rare snowfall that blankets the desert in a brief white mantle.

The scenic drive begins at the eastern boundary of Tucson Mountain Park, a Pima County parkland, almost ten miles west of Exit 257 on Interstate 10. Head west on Speedway Boulevard which turns into Gates Pass Boulevard.

Past the park boundary, the narrow, paved road twists up a canyon to Gates Pass. Recreational vehicles or cars pulling trailers are not allowed on this road section to Old Tucson. A parking area just north of the pass makes a good stop. From rocky overlooks, great views unfold of the pass, the mountains, and stately saguaros marching up the steep slopes. A good hiking trail climbs north from here into the Tucson Mountains.

The road turns south at the pass and hugs the mountain edge. After a half-mile the drive swings around a hairpin turn and heads northwest across a sloping bajada. Bajadas are gentle slopes below desert mountains that form when alluvial fans join together at canyon mouths. Here, as in Arizona's other desert mountains, runoff from torrential thunderstorms quickly drops its burden as the water sinks into the ground. The heaviest boulders and cobbles are deposited near canyon mouths, while the finer silt and sand are swept out into surrounding basins. The mountain bases are hidden under thousands of feet of gravel and sand, including as much as 7,000 feet in the Tucson Basin. Several pulloffs along the road allow visitors to stop, picnic, and hike in the desert.

After another mile Gates Pass Boulevard reaches a junction with Kinney Road. A left turn leads south to Old Tucson, a movie set that recreates a 19th century wild West town with dusty streets, plank sidewalks, and weathered buildings. Arizona Highway 86 lies five miles south. The scenic drive turns north at the junction. Gilbert Ray Campground, run by Pima County Parks, lies a half-mile off the drive on McCain Loop Road. The scenic campground, open year-round, boasts 130 tent and RV sites scattered among saguaros and paloverdes. The campground, one of the best near Tucson, makes a great basecamp for exploring the region.

The acclaimed Arizona-Sonora Desert Museum lies just over a mile up the scenic drive from the campground. The museum, considered among the world's ten best zoos, exhibits the flora, fauna, and natural history of the Sonoran Desert, a 120,000-square-mile desert that encompasses southern Arizona, extreme southeastern California, and most of Baja California and Sonora in Mexico. The museum displays over 200 live animal species, including many rare rattlesnakes, various scorpions and spiders, desert bighorn sheep, coyotes, peccaries, mountain lions, ocelots, jaguars, beavers, and otters, as well as bizarre desert plants like the elephant tree and boojum. A huge walk-through aviary is alive with myriad species of birds. An underground replica of a desert cave and earth science exhibits detail the region's geological history. Allow at least a half-day to explore this fascinating zoo. King Canyon Trail heads northeast up King Canyon, site of the only permanent spring in the Tucson Mountains, from a parking area just across the road from the museum. The canyon is a good place to spot wildlife.

The drive turns into Saguaro National Park West a mile past the desert museum. Red Hills Information Center, a short distance up the road, acquaints visitors with the park. The center's paved Cactus Garden Trail identifies various plants and their uses.

Two units, one east of Tucson on the Rincon Mountains and one west of Tucson, comprise Saguaro National Park. The parkland, established in

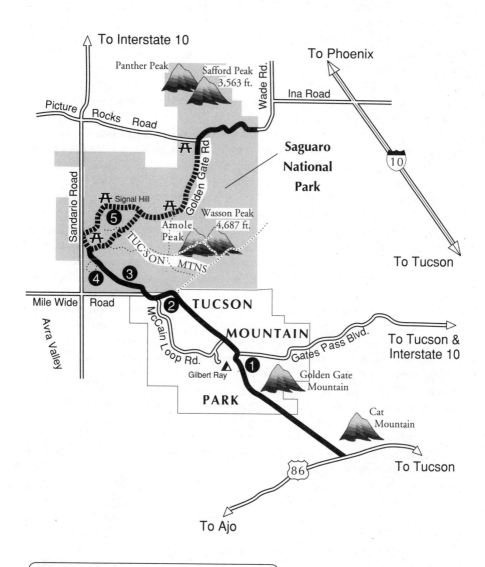

To Interstate 10

To Phoenix

Panther Peak

Safford Peak
3,563 ft.

Wade Rd.

Ina Road

Picture Rocks Road

Saguaro
National
Park

10

Sandario Road

Signal Hill

Golden Gate Rd.

Wasson Peak
4,687 ft.

5 BAJADA LOOP DRIVE

Amole Peak

TUCSON MTNS

To Tucson

4 **3**

Mile Wide Road

2

TUCSON

Avra Valley

McCain Loop Rd.

MOUNTAIN

Gates Pass Blvd.

To Tucson &
Interstate 10

Gilbert Ray

1

Golden Gate
Mountain

PARK

Cat
Mountain

86

To Tucson

To Ajo

1 OLD TUCSON
2 ARIZONA-SONORA DESERT MUSEUM
3 RED HILLS INFORMATION CENTER
4 DESERT DISCOVERY NATURE TRAIL
5 BAJADA LOOP DRIVE

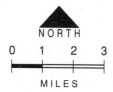

NORTH

0   1   2   3

MILES

1933, protects some of Arizona's finest stands of saguaros along with almost untouched patches of pristine Sonoran Desert. Urban sprawl from Tucson has encroached on the park, leaving it increasingly as an isolated sanctuary of wildness.

The road runs northwest, passing a waterhole with a wildlife viewpoint and the half-mile Desert Discovery Nature Trail. The drive continues by turning onto the gravel Bajada Loop Drive and climbing into a magnificent saguaro forest in the mountains. The Lower Sonoran Life Zone, particularly the paloverde-saguaro plant community, dominates the park. The mountaintops, like 4,687-foot Wasson Peak, tower 2,000 feet above the saguaro-studded bajadas. A relict oak grove, a remainder from wetter times, tucks onto Wasson Peak's north slope.

After passing Sus Picnicground and the Hugh Norris trailhead, the drive becomes a narrow, one-way road for a mile. The Hugh Norris Trail is a great hike that climbs onto a high, rocky ridge and ends atop Wasson Peak, the highest point in the Tucson Mountains.

The Valley View Overlook Trail, on the one-way section, offers an excellent 1.5-mile round-trip introduction to the park's namesake. Candelabra-like saguaro cacti are scattered across the rock-studded ridges and pebbly soil alongside the trail. Saguaros, the mightiest of desert plants, astound the imagination simply through their sheer size. The largest, having lived as long as 200 years, can reach heights of fifty feet and weigh as much as eight tons. Mature saguaros, over the course of a century of bearing fruit, produce in excess of 40 million seeds. Perhaps four or five of these seeds live to maturity. The cacti are very slow growing. A seedling is .25 inch high at one year, and they do not grow arms until they are seventy-five years old.

Other cacti seen in the park include teddy-bear cholla, chain cholla, prickly-pear, hedgehog, and fishhook barrel. Trees, usually found along washes and arroyos, include mesquite, catclaw acacia, ironwood, and paloverde, the Arizona state tree. Spring brings showy wildflower displays to the Tucson Mountains. Brilliant yellow brittlebush are among the first perennial flowers to bloom. Other flowers seen are lupine, desert marigold, and bladderpod. A wide variety of animals range across the park, including desert tortoise, rattlesnakes, horned lizards, Gila monsters, javelinas, coyotes, and jackrabbits. Gila woodpeckers, elk owls, and gilded flickers nest in holes excavated in saguaros. The drive continues another mile to an intersection with Golden Gate Road. A left turn leads down a dirt road 2.5 miles to the Bajada Loop Road start. Ancient Indian petroglyphs decorate rounded boulders near Signal Hill Picnic Area along the road. The drive turns right and winds along a two-way gravel road for about five miles to paved Picture Rocks Road. Turn east and follow the road as it dips and curves below a high, volcanic escarpment topped by ragged 3,563-foot Safford Peak. After a couple miles the drive climbs through a notched pass and leaves the national park. This is the end of the scenic drive. Continue east on Ina Road six miles to Exit 248 on Interstate 10.

General description: A winding thirty-five-mile-long road that climbs steeply up the southern flank of 10,717-foot-high Mount Graham to scenic Riggs Lake.

Special attractions: Scenic views, camping, picnicking, fishing, hiking, backpacking, photography, wildflowers, fall colors, Riggs Lake, Mt. Graham, Snow Flat.

Location: Southeastern Arizona. The road begins seven miles south of Safford off U.S. 666 or twenty-eight miles north of Exit 2 on Interstate 10.

Drive route number and name: Arizona Highway 366, The Swift Trail.

Travel season: Summer and fall. The upper reaches of the trail are closed by heavy snow from November into May. Check with the Coronado National Forest office in Safford for information on road closure.

Camping: Five national forest campgrounds with a total of seventy-seven campsites are scattered along the route.

Services: No services are available along the Swift Trail. All services, including lodging, restaurants, gas, and food, are available in Safford.

Nearby attractions: Safford, Willcox, Chirichua National Monument, Fort Bowie National Historic Site, Roper Lake State Park, Clifton, Coronado Trail, Aravaipa Canyon, San Carlos Lake, Galiuro Wilderness Area, Santa Teresa Wilderness Area.

For more information: Coronado National Forest, Safford Ranger District, P.O. Box 709, Safford, AZ 85548. (520) 428-4150. Safford-Graham County Chamber of Commerce, 1111 Thatcher Blvd., Safford, AZ 85546, (520) 428-2511.

The drive: Southeastern Arizona is a land of broad outwash valleys flanked by towering mountain ranges. The mountains dominate this basin-and-range topography. Their rocky, forested peaks loom like giant monuments above the dusty desert floor. Their coolness beckons travelers weary of the dry winds that sweep across the sandy bajadas. The Pinaleno Mountains, the highest range in southern Arizona, lords over Safford and the wide valley sculpted by the Gila River, southern Arizona's longest river. The range's high point, 10,717-foot Mt. Graham, is Arizona's fourth highest peak and the highest in southern Arizona. Mt. Graham also rises 7,000 feet above Safford and the desert—the single greatest vertical rise of any Arizona mountain.

The thirty-five-mile-long Swift Trail, one of Arizona's best scenic drives, weaves and loops its way up the eastern and southern flanks of Mt. Graham, passing from cactus, creosote, and ocotillo-clad hillsides to forests of aspen, spruce, and fir. The drive, climbing higher than any other road in southern Arizona, passes through five of North America's seven life zones, encompassing a wide diversity of plant communities and climates. A drive up the Swift

*The Swift Trail, Arizona 366, switchbacks steeply up Mt. Graham in the
Pinaleno Mountains.*

Trail is like taking a telescoped journey from Mexico to Alaska. The trip takes
a minimum of five hours, allow more time to leisurely stop and explore along
the road.

The road is generally open from May through November. Heavy snow on
the Mt. Graham's upper elevations closes the road in winter. Check with the
Coronado National Forest office in Safford for road conditions and closures.
Because of the dramatic elevation gain, temperatures drop about thirty
degrees from mountain base to mountaintop. If it is in the 100s in the Gila
Valley, expect the cool seventies on the road's upper heights. Nights, even
in summer, can be chilly. Be prepared by bringing warm clothes. Heavy
thunderstorms are daily occurrences in July and August when monsoon
moisture sweeps north into Arizona. The road's high point is 9,300 feet.

The Swift Trail, with twenty-nine paved miles and the remainder gravel, begins seven miles south of Safford on U.S. 666. Turn southwest on Arizona Highway 366 and ascend a gently sloping bajada studded with creosote, mesquite, and acacia trees toward the looming Pinaleno Mountains. The Apache Indians, who settled in the valleys below the mountains in the sixteenth century, lent their word *pinal* for "deer" to the range. Pinaleno is a Spanish derivation of the word. The Mogollon and Hohokam people built large communities and cultivated arable land along the Gila River, watering their corn, beans, and squash with runoff from the mountains, in the centuries prior to the coming of the Apaches.

The road, after passing a Federal prison, climbs straight toward the ragged mountains. Five miles later the trail enters Coronado National Forest, a 1,780,196-acre forest that scatters across twelve mountain units in southern Arizona. The overlook here is a good stop. Yuccas, century plants, ocotillos, and prickly pear cacti cover the rocky hillsides around the road.

The Swift Trail is named for Theodore Swift, a Forest Service supervisor of the Pinaleno range from 1910 to 1923. His dream of a road into the wild range became a reality when the late 1800s wagon route to Columbine west of Mt. Graham was completed as a roadway in 1931. The Pinaleno Mountains were originally protected as the Mt. Graham Forest Reserve in 1902. In 1908 it became part of Crook National Forest, and in 1953 was incorporated in Coronado National Forest.

Past the overlook, the Swift Trail begins its serious climbing. The road loops and switchbacks upwards. Noon Creek Picnic Area, with sixteen sites, is reached at seven miles. The area got its name back in pioneer days. Families, traveling by horse and buggy, could leave Safford at sunrise and reach this idyllic lunch spot among the oaks and alligator junipers by noon. After another two miles the road passes another picnic area. Here a small creek rushes through a lush forest. Spiraling upward the road enters a Chiricahua and ponderosa pine forest and after another couple miles reaches 6,700-foot-high Arcadia Campground with eighteen campsites and drinking water. Higher still is Turkey Flat, site of several summer cabins nestled among the trees.

Ladybug Saddle, at 8,508 feet, is reached after seventeen miles of steady climbing. A short trail climbs from the pull-off here to the craggy summit of Ladybug Peak. Every summer hordes of ladybugs swarm among the rocks and trees atop the peak. The view from Ladybug Peak is magnificent. Southern Arizona unfolds below this lofty viewpoint. Northeast lie Safford and the Gila River, and beyond on the horizon's rim some ninety miles off stretch the hazy White Mountains. Range upon range of sky islands—the Chirichuas, Galiuros, Dragoons, Santa Ritas, Rincons, and Catalinas—punctuate wide, windswept basins to the south. On a clear day, a sharp eye can spot the abrupt needle of Baboquivari Peak 130 miles away.

From the saddle the road turns onto the south flank of the range and wends in and out of steep, shallow canyons. This road section offers exceptional views. Three miles later a narrow, one-mile-long road heads west from the Swift Trail and drops down to Snow Flat. A bucolic lake and meadow make

CORONADO

P I N A L E N O

NATIONAL

Clark Peak

CHESLEY
FLAT

Webb Peak
10,086 ft.

Mt. Graham
10,720 ft.

*Riggs
Lake*

△

RIGGS
FLAT

Soldier
Creek

△

Hospital
Flat

△

Shannon

△

SNOW
FLAT

Swift

0   1   2   3

MILES

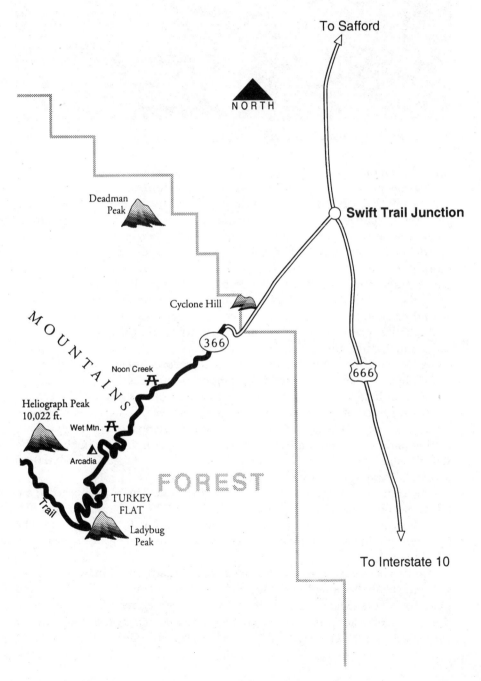

To Safford

NORTH

Swift Trail Junction

Deadman
Peak

Cyclone Hill

366

Noon Creek

M O U N T A I N S

Heliograph Peak
10,022 ft.

Wet Mtn.

Arcadia

FOREST

Trail

TURKEY
FLAT

Ladybug
Peak

666

To Interstate 10

Riggs Lake, at the end of the Swift Trail, offers trout fishing.

this an ideal picnic spot. Primitive camping is also permitted.

The topographic and climatic diversity of the Pinaleno Mountains' 200 square miles offers home to a variety of wildlife. Javelinas, black-tailed jackrabbits, kangaroo rats, and rattlesnakes are found in the dry lower elevations. Both mule and whitetail deer are often seen browsing in roadside meadows. Coyote, bobcat, mountain lion, turkey, and four species of skunk roam the area's wilderness. The Pinalenos have one of Arizona's largest concentrations of black bears. Campers are advised to keep food, ice chests, and cooking utensils stowed safely in their car to avoid unnecessary contact with the bears.

As the last great ice sheets retreated 12,000 years ago, southern Arizona had a much different environment than today. With more moisture and a cooler climate, pinyon pine and juniper forests spread across the low basins while dense fir forests cloaked ice-capped mountains like Mt. Graham. Slowly the climate warmed and dried, leaving the basins sere and dusty. The forests survived atop the isolated mountain ranges. As the forests became isolated, so too did plants and animals. On the Pinalenos several evolved into distinct species, including the wild daisy Rusby's mountain fleabane, the white-bellied vole, the Mt. Graham pocket gopher, and the Mt. Graham red squirrel. These species live here and nowhere else.

The endangered squirrel is currently threatened by a proposed seven telescope observatory atop Mt. Graham. The 300 squirrels inhabit old-growth trees, many of which would be cut down for the observatory. The squirrels' plight has brought lawsuits from environmental groups seeking to halt the project.

A mile past Snow Flat, another spur road turns right to Shannon Campground. Nestled among the spruce and fir are ten campsites. This is a good place for hikers to stay. The best trail follows a rutted road two miles up to the summit of historic 10,028-foot Heliograph Peak. During the 1886 military campaign against Geronimo and his Apaches, Brigader General Nelson Miles built a mirrored, sun-reflecting signal tower, or heliograph, to communicate with his soldiers spread all over southeastern Arizona.

Beyond Shannon the road drops down to grassy Hospital Flat and its twelve-site campground. This meadow is carpeted with wildflowers in summer. A summer hospital was built here during the Apache wars for wounded soldiers to recuperate in the cool mountain air rather than in stuffy Ft. Grant on the southwest flank of the Pinalenos. The fort is now a state prison.

The pavement ends as the road leaves Hospital Flat. The narrow dirt track twists and turns through a forest corridor. Tall fir and spruce trees line the road. The trail crosses Grant and Moonshine creeks. Both streams are home to the endangered Gila trout, an Arizona native. Six miles later the road passes Columbine, a Forest Service work center. Just past here a side road and trail leads to icy Ash Creek, a good place to angle for trout. A mile past Columbine is Soldier Creek Campground, the highest point on the Swift Trail at 9,300 feet. The eleven-site campground has water and restrooms.

The road, skirting the shaggy southern escarpment of the Pinalenos, dips and rolls another five miles to Riggs Lake. Chesley Flat lies halfway along the route. This large meadow is named for Abner and Sarah Chesley, who met and were married on Mt. Graham in 1883. They lived in a cabin here in the 1890s. Wild turkeys and deer often roam this broad, sloping meadow in the early evening.

Riggs Lake, the drive's end, is the most popular fishing and camping spot on the mountain. This small eleven-acre reservoir, at 8,600 feet, nestles in a hollow surrounded by fir and pine trees. A lush understory of ferns, flowers, and grass clots the forest floor. Built in 1957, the lake provides excellent fishing for rainbow trout. The nearby campground has twenty-four sites, water, and restrooms. The road continues another rough two miles past Riggs Lake to a dead-end at Clark Peak.

24 ARIZONA HIGHWAY 186
Willcox to Chiricahua National Monument

General description: A forty-two-mile-long road that swings along the southern flank of the Dos Cabezas Mountains before climbing up Bonita Canyon to scenic Massai Point in Chiricahua National Monument.

Special attractions: Chiricahua National Monument, scenic views, hiking, birdwatching, camping, nature study, Dos Cabezas, Fort Bowie National Historic Site.

Location: Southeastern Arizona. The drive begins in Willcox off Interstate 10 and runs southeast to Chiricahua National Monument.

Drive route numbers and name: Arizona highways 186 and 181. Bonita Canyon Drive.

Travel season: The drive is open year-round, however, snow may temporarily close the road in the national monument. Expect hot weather in summer.

Camping: Chiricahua National Monument's twenty-six-site Bonita Canyon Campground is open year-round .5 mile north of the visitor center. There is camping in Pinery Canyon in Coronado National Forest south of the monument, including Rustler Park, Sunny Flat, and Idlewild.

Services: All services are available in Willcox. No food, lodging, or gasoline is available in the monument.

Nearby attractions: Coronado National Forest, Portal, Cave Creek, Bisbee, Tombstone, Cochise Stronghold, Aravaipa Creek, Mount Graham.

For more information: Chiricahua National Monument, Dos Cabezas Route, Box 6500, Willcox, AZ 85643, (520) 824-3560.

The drive: Southeastern Arizona is a dry land punctuated by tall mountain ranges that loom over broad, dusty basins like islands in the sky. This forty-two-mile-long scenic drive, following Arizona highways 186 and 181, traverses the northeastern edge of the broad Sulphur Springs Valley along the western fringe of two sky islands, the Dos Cabezas and Chiricahua mountains, in the state's extreme southeastern corner. Gorgeous views line the drive—rugged peaks, the wide valley and its alkaline playa, grasslands dotted with grazing cattle, and Chiricahua National Monument, the drive's best scenery, at its very end.

The drive, above 4,000 feet, offers generally mild weather year-round. Winter days are pleasant, with occasional snowfalls in the national monument. Snow may close Bonita Canyon Drive. Spring and autumn are warm, with daily temperatures between fifty and eighty. Summers can be hot. Expect highs in the nineties in the lower elevations. Cooler temperatures prevail atop the Chiricahuas. Most of the area's yearly precipitation falls in violent thunderstorms in July and August and in winter snowstorms atop the mountains.

Willcox, a rural community astride Interstate 10, marks the beginning of the drive. The town, named for Arizona army commander General Orlando B. Willcox, began in 1880 as a camp for construction crews on the Southern Pacific Railroad and quickly became a supply and shipping center for huge cattle ranches that sprawled across southeastern Arizona. Willcox, at 4,167 feet, continues to be a center for ranching and agriculture. Artisan water, trapped in deep, porous gravel layers, is used to irrigate cotton fields and orchards in the surrounding valleys. Turn east from downtown Willcox on Arizona Highway 186 to start the scenic drive.

The paved highway heads southeast after leaving Willcox, crossing sandy hummocks on the eastern edge of Willcox Playa, a National Natural Landmark and the lowest part of Sulpher Springs Valley. Vegetated dunes and gravel terraces along the road and lower mountainsides trace the ancient shoreline of Lake Cochise, a twenty-mile-long lake that drained south into Mexico and formed during Pleistocene ice ages when the climate was much wetter. The lake, as deep as fifty feet and covering over fifty square miles, dried up about 12,000 years ago as the area's climate warmed. Today the valley has no outlet, and after heavy summer thunderstorms the playa, filled

Bouldering near Massai Point in Chiricahua National Monument, Arizona 186 Drive.

with run-off, glistens with a new inches-deep lake that eventually evaporates leaving a dusty white alkali crust. When water does cover the lakebed, it teems with protozoans, algae, fairy shrimps, and myriad bird species including avocets, killdeers, and sandpipers. As many as 10,000 sandhill cranes winter on the playa and surrounding wetlands.

After six miles the highway swings east and begins climbing a wide bajada or outwash plain toward the ragged outline of the Dos Cabezas Mountains. Desert plants thrive on the bajada and the lower mountain flanks, including sotol yucca, creosote, agave, thick clusters of prickly pear cacti on the hot south-facing slopes, and twisted mesquite trees along dry arroyos. The Dos Cabezas Mountains, named by some early Spanish passerby for the two rocky heads atop the highest peak, are a roughly carved range of steeply tilted sedimentary layers and ancient granite and schist.

After fourteen miles the road enters the almost deserted town of Dos Cabezas. In the late 1800s the town prospered as gold and silver poured out of surrounding mines. The crumbling village of adobe ruins and tin-roofed houses, now home to a handful of residents, once boasted a newspaper, saloons, churches, and hotels. A small museum, open irregular hours, houses artifacts from nearby Fort Bowie and other area sites. A few miles beyond Dos Cabezas, the drive leaves the mountains and heads southeast across a sloping grassland, broken by shallow arroyos and rolling hillsides. Grazing cattle and windmills dot the pastoral scene. Eastward towers the long north-south ridge of the Chiricahua Mountains, a fault block range that reaches 9,795 feet atop Chiricahua Peak. The range, mantled with a dark brooding forest, stretches across the horizon like cardboard cut-out scenery.

Fort Bowie National Historic Site lies a few miles north of the highway on a spur dirt road. The turnoff is twenty-two miles from Willcox. The site, one of Arizona's best historical parks, is reached by a 1.5-mile-long footpath just north of Apache Pass. The fort, now sun-baked adobe ruins, was established in 1862 to protect settlers, travelers, and stage and mail traffic on the Butterfield Stagecoach line. The fort was an important post during the war with the Chiricahua Apaches and their chiefs Cochise and Geronimo until the late 1880s. The fort was abandoned in 1894. The site, operated by the National Park Service, preserves the fort ruins, the Battle of Apache Pass site, the post cemetery, and part of the Old Butterfield Overland Trail. Many of the cemetery graves read "Unknown. Killed by Indians."

The drive travels southeast over a grassy bajada, dips across tree-lined Pinery Creek, before turning east on Arizona 181. The highway runs four miles to the abrupt base of the Chiricahua Mountains and the entrance to Chiricahua National Monument. A right turn here on Forest Road 42 leads southeast up Pinery Canyon, past good camping areas, over 7,600-foot Onion Saddle, and drops down through spectacular Cave Creek Canyon to Portal. This rough, narrow road, closed by winter snows, is an excellent drive.

The scenic drive swings north around Erickson Ridge, named for early settlers Neil and Emma Erickson, and enters Chiricahua National Monu-ment. The monument, established in 1924, protects seventeen square miles of the Chiricahua Mountains, one of Arizona's most unique and remote mountain ranges. Five of North America's seven life zones ranging from the desert scrub of the Upper Sonoran to climax fir and pine forests in the Canadian zone spread over the small parkland's rugged terrain. The range's plants and animals more closely resemble the highlands of Mexico's Sierra Madre than surrounding ranges.

The road, passing spreading sycamore trees and the Faraway Ranch, runs 1.5 miles to the park's visitor center. Here, numerous displays detail the monument's natural history, history, and geology. The visitor center parking lot is also the lower trailhead for the Rhyolite Canyon Trail. The drive turns north here and passes the park's shady twenty-six-site campground after a .5-mile.

The road, lined with a dense mixed forest, climbs north and east four miles up Bonita Canyon. The monument boasts a diverse variety of trees, including seven oak species, six pine species, Arizona cypress, alligator juniper, Arizona madrone, and many shrubs, cacti, and yuccas. The startling changes in elevation, terrain, and habitats allows for an equally wide array of animals and birds. Mammals include black bear, coyote, mountain lion, bobcat, peccary, coati, ringtail, deer, and four skunk species. Seven rattle-

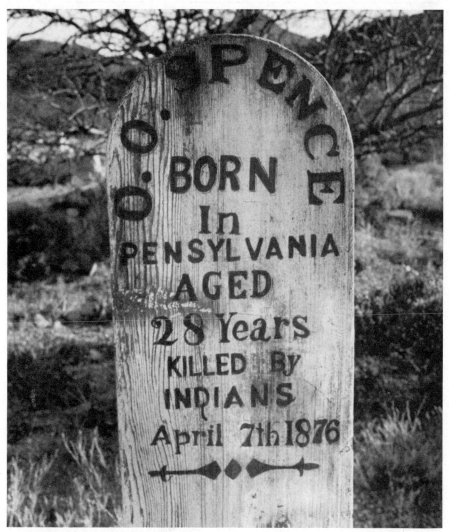

A soldier's grave at Fort Bowie National Historic Site, a reminder of the violence of Arizona in the 1870s.

snake species, coral snakes, and twenty-four other snakes roam the canyons and cliffs. The range shelters an extraordinary number of birds, including rare Mexican species like the elegant trogon and the thick-billed parrot.

Above Bonita Canyon the drive turns south onto a shelf road and climbs four miles to the road's end at 6,870-foot Massai Point. Lofty views of the monument and the Chiricahua Mountains spread out from the viewpoint. This area, called the Wonderland of Rocks, is best explored by some of the monument's twenty miles of trail. The 3.5-mile Echo Canyon Trail makes a scenic loop past soaring pinnacles, forests full of birdsong, and trickling creeks. The fantastic rock sculptures here are the result of violent volcanic

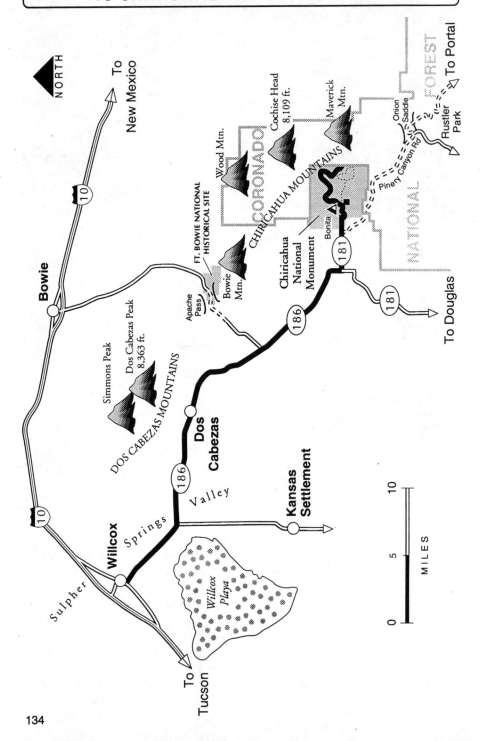

NORTH

To New Mexico

To Portal

FOREST

Cochise Head
8,109 ft.

Maverick Mtn.

Onion Saddle

Rustler Park

Wood Mtn.

CORONADO

Pinery Canyon Rd

CHIRICAHUA MOUNTAINS

NATIONAL

FT. BOWIE NATIONAL HISTORICAL SITE

Bowie

10

Bonita

Apache Pass

Chiricahua National Monument

Bowie Mtn.

181

Simmons Peak

Dos Cabezas Peak
8,363 ft.

DOS CABEZAS MOUNTAINS

186

To Douglas

181

Dos Cabezas

186

Kansas Settlement

10

Willcox

Springs

Valley

Sulpher

Willcox Playa

To Tucson

10

5

0

MILES

134

Dos Cabezas Peak rises beyond an abandoned adobe house in Dos Cabezas. Arizona 186 Drive.

eruptions 25 million years ago. Over 2,000 feet of hot ash from eight eruptions piled up and fused into rhyolite. Wind, water, ice, and time weathered the rock along cracks into the bizarre jumble of spires, buttresses, gargoyles, and castles seen from Massai Point. Return to Willcox via the same route or, conditions permitting, drive over the Pinery Canyon Road to Portal.

25 ARIZONA 83 & 82
Interstate 10 to Nogales

General description: A forty-five-mile-long paved drive that skirts the eastern edge of the Santa Rita Mountains, crosses the rolling Sonoita Plains, follows Sonoita Creek, and drops down to Nogales and the Mexican border.
Special attractions: Santa Rita Mountains, Coronado National Forest, Patagonia-Sonoita Creek Sanctuary, Patagonia Lake State Park, Museum of the Horse, Nogales.
Location: Southern Arizona. The drive begins at Exit 281 on Interstate 10 just east of Tucson and runs south to Nogales on the Mexican border. Also accessible from Interstate 19 in Nogales.
Drive route numbers: Arizona Highways 83 and 82.
Travel season: Year-round.
Camping: Patagonia Lake State Park offers 105 first-come, first-served campsites, ten with hookups, restrooms, and showers.
Services: All services in Nogales, Patagonia, and Sonoita.
Nearby attractions: Madera Canyon, Pena Blanca Lake, Tumacacori National Monument, Tubac Presidio State Historic Park, Tucson, Saguaro

National Park, Arizona-Sonora Desert Museum, Colossal Cave, Coronado National Memorial, Tombstone, Mexico.

For more information: Coronado National Forest, Federal Building, 300 W. Congress, Tucson, AZ 85701, (520) 670-4552. Nogales Chamber of Commerce, Kino Park, Nogales, AZ 85621, (520) 287-3685.

The drive: The Patagonia-Sonoita Scenic Road, following Arizona Highway 83, sweeps south over undulating grasslands east of the Santa Rita Mountains to the old ranch town of Sonoita. The drive swings southwest on Arizona 82, passing Patagonia and following tree-lined Sonoita Creek before rolling down to the Santa Cruz River and Nogales, gateway to old Mexico. This forty-five-mile road trip, combined with Interstate 19, makes a great loop drive from Tucson.

The paved highway, open year-round, lies above 4,000 feet except for a lower section just south of Interstate 10. The elevation makes summer temperatures pleasant, with highs seldom climbing above 100 degrees. Heavy thunder-storms, fueled by monsoon moisture, build up over the Santa Rita Mountains almost every July and August afternoon. Autumn is pretty along the route, particularly when Sonoita Creek's many deciduous trees change color. Winters are generally pleasant with warm days and cool nights.

Arizona Highway 83, the first leg of the scenic drive, begins at Exit 281 on Interstate 10 about twenty miles east of Tucson. The road heads south across a wide sloping bajada or outwash plain densely covered with ocotillo, prickly pear cactus, mesquite and palo verde trees, sotol yucca, and barrel cactus.

After five miles the highway enters Davidson Canyon, an arid canyon coated with scrubby brush named for O. Davidson, an Indian agent at Tubac. The canyon separates the Empire Mountains on the east from the lofty Santa Rita Mountains, topped by pointed 9,453-foot Mt. Wrightson, on the west. An early road followed the canyon in the 1860s and 1870s connecting Tucson with forts Crittenden and Buchanan near today's Sonoita. Apaches often attacked army convoys that traveled the route. One of the worst atrocities occurred in 1872 when two soldiers were separated from their escort party and set upon by an Apache war party. One was immediately killed, while the other, Corporal Joe Black, was abducted. Black, in view of his companions, was tied to a tree, set afire, and murdered by over 100 knife and lance wounds.

Continuing up the canyon, the road enters Coronado National Forest and the foothills on the eastern slope of the Santa Rita Mountains. Clumps of juniper scatter among rounded grassy ridges and shallow canyons along the roadside. After a few miles the highway turns southeast and rolls onto the undulating Sonoita Plain, a rich grassland that has long been one of America's finest ranchlands. The open range, mostly above 4,000 feet, stretches eastward from the Santa Ritas to the Whetstone and Dragoon mountains.

The plain, watered by seventeen inches of annual precipitation, is an old Pleistocene, red-earth land that was deposited by heavy run-off from surrounding mountain ranges during moist ice age cycles. The gravel deposits are as thick as 5,000 feet. The ancient plain was once populated by vast herds of ancestral horses, camels, and other large mammals.

A motorboat swings across Patagonia Lake off the Arizona 82/83 Scenic Drive.

Erosion by oak-lined streams, including Sonoita, Cienega, and Babocamari creeks, have cut into the fertile plain leaving wide swaths of grassland seamed by shallow valleys.

The drive runs across this plain for almost ten miles to Sonoita, offering tableaus reminiscent of eastern Montana or Wyoming—trickling creeks riffling over gravel bars, tall grass rippling in a summer breeze, and cattle grazing under a vault of turquoise sky. It's an immense land of faraway views with a pastoral beauty unlike any other Arizona drive.

The Arizona 83 segment of the scenic drive ends at Sonoita, and the drive continues southwest on Arizona 82. Sonoita, from the Pagago word *sonot* meaning "place where corn will grow," was founded as a stop on the New Mexico and Arizona railroad line from Nogales to Benson in 1882. The railroad hauled Arizona cattle and ore to the Mexican seaport of Guaymas. Earlier the area was the site of Indian villages, a 1701 Jesuit mission, and the San Ignacio del Babocomari Spanish land grant.

Heading southwest on Arizona 82, the drive runs down a wide picturesque valley carved by Sonoita Creek. A historic marker, three miles west of Sonoita, commemorates U.S. Army Fort Buchanan and Fort Crittenden. All of southern Arizona from the Gila River south to today's border with Mexico was purchased by the Gadsden Treaty in 1854 for $10 million. For two years after the treaty Mexican troops protected both American and Mexican settlers in the area around Nogales. Fort Buchanan, established in March of 1856 by Major Enoch Steen and named for President James Buchanan, protected miners, settlers, and ranchers populating the newly acquired land from Apache depredations. The area's history recounts many stories of brutal murders at the hands of the Apaches. The fort was closed during the Civil War, and then rebuilt as Fort Crittenden on a nearby hill in 1867 before being totally abandoned in 1872.

The drive enters Patagonia nine miles later. Patagonia, named for the Spanish term for the local Indians *patagon* meaning "big foot," sits amidst some of Arizona's best rangeland. The Stradling Museum of the Horse houses an interesting collection of wagons and carriages, saddles, bridles, paintings, bronzes, and other artifacts that traces the history of horses. Patagonia is also the gateway to the Patagonia Mountains, a small rough sierra enclosed by Coronado National Forest and studded with numerous silver, copper, and lead mines and ghost towns. A gravel forest road climbs south from Patagonia into the mountains, offering scenic views of the Sonoita Valley and Santa Rita Mountains, and passing the historic towns of Harshaw, Washington Camp, Duquesne, and the famed Mowry Mine which produced over $1.5 million in silver and lead in the 1860s.

The Patagonia-Sonoita Creek Sanctuary, beginning in Patagonia and following Sonoita Creek west along the scenic drive, preserves 312 acres of southern Arizona's best riparian ecosystem. Riparian zones, especially in arid or semi-arid country such as this, are among the most species-rich habitats. This is no exception. Trees shade the creek's bottomland, making a twisting corridor lined with Fremont cottonwood, oak, velvet ash, and sycamore trees. Grassy hillsides above the creek are green with mesquite, mountain mahogany, alligator juniper, and white oak. Animals thrive here, including peccary, white-tailed deer, coyote, fox, coati, and skunk.

It's the birds, however, that visitors flock to see. The sanctuary, lying a scant twenty miles north of Mexico, attracts an astounding number and variety of birds—almost 300 species—from both the Rocky Mountains and Mexico's Sierra Madres. Birds seen include the gray hawk, meadowlark, cardinal, pygmy nuthatch, rose-throated becard, several hummingbird species, and the colorful elegant trogon from Mexico. The sanctuary, preserved and operated by The Nature Conservancy, is reached via Fourth and Pennsylvania avenues in Patagonia.

The highway leaves Patagonia in a broad valley which narrows down to a cliffed canyon within a couple miles. The cliffs, colored in smoldering hues of red and orange, are mostly tuff and breccia tossed out by a nearby volcano and later tilted, faulted, and eroded by Sonoita Creek which drops steeply west from here to the Santa Cruz River north of Nogales. This road section also passes through the San Jose de Sonoita, the smallest Spanish land grant given in Arizona. The 8,000-acre grant was bought by Tubac rancher Leon Herraras in 1821 for $105. The Telles Family Shrine, with a statue of the Virgin Mary, candles, and offerings, lies mid-way through the canyon.

Below ragged Sanford Butte, the drive turns south, crosses Mary Kane and Three R canyons, and climbs up rounded grass and oak-covered ridges to the turnoff to Patagonia Lake State Park. The 265-acre lake, lying four miles north of Arizona 82, was formed when Sonoita Creek was dammed in 1968.

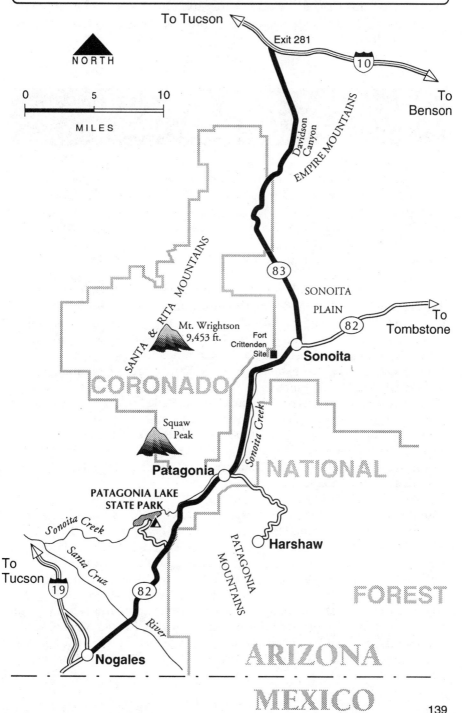

25   ARIZONA 83 & 82 INTERSTATE 10 TO NOGALES

To Tucson

Exit 281

10

To Benson

NORTH

0   5   10

MILES

Davidson Canyon

EMPIRE MOUNTAINS

83

SONOITA PLAIN

82

To Tombstone

SANTA & RITA MOUNTAINS

Mt. Wrightson 9,453 ft.

Fort Crittenden Site

Sonoita

CORONADO

Squaw Peak

Sonoita Creek

Patagonia

NATIONAL

PATAGONIA LAKE STATE PARK

Sonoita Creek

Harshaw

PATAGONIA MOUNTAINS

To Tucson

19

Santa Cruz

82

FOREST

River

Nogales

ARIZONA

MEXICO

The lake, at 3,750-feet, offers moderate temperatures, boating, waterskiing, 105 campsites, showers, a swimming beach, and good fishing for bass, crappie, bluegill, and catfish in summer and trout in winter.

For the last few miles the highway rolls over ridges and valleys, crosses the braided Santa Cruz River, and climbs up Proto Canyon before dropping into Nogales. The international town, an entrance to Mexico, offers complete services to travelers.

26 U. S. 89
Pinal Pioneer Parkway

General description: A forty-two-mile, two-lane highway that crosses a broad, almost untouched section of Sonoran Desert between Oracle Junction and Florence.

Special attractions: Tom Mix Monument, saguaro forests, picnic areas, scenic views, nature study.

Location: South-central Arizona. U.S. 89 makes a pleasant drive between Phoenix and Tucson.

Drive route number and name: U.S. 89, Pinal Pioneer Parkway.

Travel season: Year-round. Expect hot summer temperatures.

Camping: No campgrounds are along the highway. Primitive camping is permitted on adjoining public lands. Catalina State Park, with fifty campsites, lies about nine miles south of Oracle Junction off U.S. 89.

Services: All services are available in Tucson and Florence. Limited services are available in Oracle Junction.

Nearby attractions: Tucson, Saguaro National Park, Mt. Lemmon, Coronado National Forest, Arizona-Sonora Desert Museum, Picacho Peak State Park, McFarland State Historic Park, Casa Grande Ruins National Monument, Superstition Mountains.

For more information: Pinal County Visitor Center, 912 Pinal St., P.O. Box 967, Florence, AZ 85232, (520) 868-4331.

The drive: The Pinal Pioneer Parkway, following U.S. 89, traverses forty-two miles of high Sonoran Desert on the old highway between Tucson and Phoenix. Most travelers today speed up Interstate 10, a quicker but duller trip. This drive offers not only a slower pace than the interstate, but lots of pulloffs to admire the desert's beauty and diversity. The parkway, running between Oracle Junction and Florence, was established in 1961 by the Arizona Highway Department as a scenic drive through a relatively untouched swath of desert. The department acquired 1,000-foot-wide scenic easements on federal and state lands along the road to create a highway nature preserve. The drive, without the usual highway clutter, makes a great

The Tom Mix Memorial, alongside the Pinal-Pioneer Parkway, remembers the cowboy actor who was killed nearby.

introduction to the Sonoran Desert's unique and bizarre plant communities along with great views of the Santa Catalina and Picacho mountain ranges.

Expect generally pleasant temperatures when driving the parkway in spring, winter, and fall. Days are warm, with occasional spring and winter showers. Summer highs are hot, often over 100 degrees, although the drive's higher elevations make it somewhat cooler than Phoenix and Tucson. Torrential cloudbursts build up almost daily during the summer rainy season in July and August. They are usually short-lived and refreshing.

The scenic drive begins at the junction of U.S. 89 and Arizona 77 in 3,312-foot-high Oracle Junction, twenty-seven miles north of Tucson. The highway, following U.S. 89, rolls northwest from Oracle Junction. Florence, the drive's end, lies forty-two miles ahead, while Phoenix is 107 miles. Catalina State Park, about nine miles south of Oracle Junction, spreads across fifty acres at the base of the looming Santa Catalina Mountains. The park, with fifty campsites, offers hiking, picnicking, horseback riding, and nature study. It is the only established public campground near the scenic drive.

For the first five miles the highway rises steadily to the drive's 3,600-foot high point atop Falcon Divide. The drive, from here to its terminus in Florence, crosses a high, slanting plain of sand and gravel deposited during moister Pleistocene times. The plain, almost 2,000 feet higher than the Gila River at Florence, is protected from erosion by surrounding mountain ranges.

Underlying the gravel deposits is a pediment of granite bedrock that extends south from the Tortilla Mountains northeast of the road. These low mountains and other roadside ranges, including the Tortolita and Picacho mountains to the south, are composed of ancient, erosion-resistant Precambrian granite. The gravel plain, between Oracle Junction and Tucson, is deeply dissected by Canada del Oro, Rillito, and the Santa Cruz River, leaving an elevation difference of 1,000 feet.

The Pinal Pioneer Parkway makes accessible to the traveler one of the best examples of the upper Sonoran Desert ecosystem. The drive's higher elevations, correspondingly greater rainfall, and porous gravel soils conspire to make the roadside desert a veritable garden. In March and April, if winter rains were generous, a ribbon of wildflower colors line the blacktop. Spikes of blue lupine, clumps of yellow brittlebush and desert marigolds, mallows, desert verbena, and wavering orange masses of California poppies streak the land. Green grasses and a second flower show come in late summer after thunderstorms have watered the desert.

The most notable plants along the parkway are the myriad species of cacti, with the elegant saguaro the star attraction. Botanists say cacti are one of the youngest plant families to evolve, beginning some 20,000 years ago in the West Indies. Cacti are a uniquely New World plant, spreading from northern Canada to the tip of South America. They range in size from the mighty saguaro and cardon to tiny pincushion species. Cacti are classified as "water-savers," plants that adapt to water shortages by storing moisture from rainfall for use in drought. Saguaros can absorb hundreds of gallons of water from a single rain, stashing it in their accordion-pleated trunks for as long as a year. Other cacti adaptations include shallow, widespread root systems and needle-sharp spines to shade the plant, diffuse dessicating winds, and ward off thirsty animals.

Tall saguaros dot the desert along the drive, expecially the lower northern parkway section. Other cacti seen include the chain cholla with its hanging "chains" of fruit, buckhorn cholla, teddy-bear cholla, prickly pear, and various barrel cacti including hedgehog and fishhook. April to June brings the cacti flowers, the desert's most beautiful blossoms. The delicate flowers bloom in a spectrum of exotic colors—gold, purple, red, lavender, and white. The fragile, waxy white saguaro flowers, the Arizona state flower, open at night and usually last less than a day.

Other plants seen along the drive, particularly the moister washes, include catclaw acacia, paloverde, ironwood, creosote, and ocotillo. Ocotillos are among the stranger and more distinctive plants of the Sonoran Desert. The ocotillo, consisting of numerous thorny stems, is generally leafless. After rain, however, the plant sprouts a crop of small leaves along its stems before shedding them when moisture becomes scarce. Bright red flowers adorn the stem-tips in spring.

Desert highlands dominate the view along the drive. The Tortilla Mountains, topped by 5,587-foot Black Mountain, spread across the northeastern horizon. The Central Highlands, a transitional zone of mountains separating

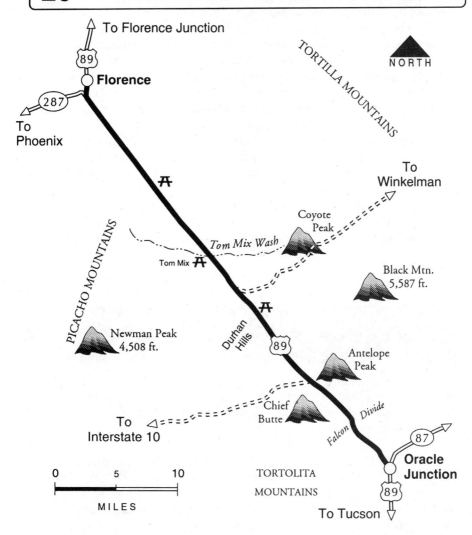

the Colorado Plateau from the southern desert, loom beyond them. The fabled Superstition Mountains present a hazy, ragged profile to the north. South of the asphalt lie the Tortolita Mountains, an immense granite blister that towers over the desert shrub north of Oracle Junction, and the hump-backed Picacho Mountains. Picacho Peak, site of Arizona's only Civil War battle in 1862, lifts its rocky brow above Interstate 10 at the range's southern end.

Three roadside rest areas are scattered along the highway, with ramadas and picnic tables. One, twenty-five miles north of Oracle Junction, has a memorial that honors cowboy movie actor Tom Mix who was killed here on October 12, 1940 when his yellow Cord automobile swerved off a highway detour and crashed into what is now called Tom Mix Wash. An iron outline of Mix's riderless horse Tony sits atop the stone memorial. The plaque says "In memory of Tom Mix, whose spirit left his body on this spot." A short trail loops out into the cactus-studded desert at this rest area.

After thirty miles the drive leaves the official state-designated Pinal Pioneer Parkway and runs another twelve miles northeast to historic Florence. On clear days Squaw Peak and Camelback Mountain, over fifty miles away in Phoenix, poke above the flat Gila River valley. Conical Poston Butte, named for early Arizona settler, miner, Indian agent, and Congressman Charles Poston, rises above the drive's end at Florence. Poston became a sun worshipper while traveling in India, and after returning to Florence in 1878 he built a road to the butte's summit where he constructed a temple to the sun with a continuously burning fire. A few months later the fire went out and the whole affair became known as Poston's Folly. Poston is buried atop the hill.

Florence, one of Arizona's oldest Anglo settlements, was settled in 1866. The town's well-preserved Main Street looks just like it did in the late 1800s. McFarland State Historical Park protects the town's ornate Victorian-style 1891 courthouse. Inside exhibits detail Florence's colorful history.

27 THE RIM ROAD
Forest Road 300

General description: A spectacular forty-two-mile-long gravel U.S. Forest road that follows the lofty Mogollon Rim in central Arizona.

Special attractions: Camping, fishing, hiking, scenic views, photography, historic sites, General Crook National Recreation Trail.

Location: Central Arizona. The Rim Road traverses the Mogollon Rim between Arizona Highways 260 and 87 north of Payson. Western access is twenty-seven miles north of Payson on Arizona 260. Eastern access is thirty-two miles northeast of Payson and twenty-two miles southwest of Heber on Arizona 260.

Drive route name and number: The Rim Road, Forest Service Road 300.

Travel season: May through October. Snow and mud close the road to vehicles in winter and spring. Snowmobiles and cross-country skiers use the road in winter.

Camping: Several campgrounds line the Rim Road or are a few miles off it, including Kehl Springs, Rocky Point, Knoll Lake, Bear Canyon Lake, Rim, and Sink Hole campgrounds. Primitive camping is allowed along the road if campers are well away from the road.

Services: No services along the drive. All services are available in Heber and Payson.

The vista from Hi-View Point on the Rim Road is one of Arizona's best views.

Nearby attractions: Payson, Tonto Natural Bridge, Fort Verde State Historic Park, Montezuma Castle National Monument, Fort Apache Indian Reservation, Mazatzal Wilderness Area, Zane Grey Lodge, Strawberry, Tonto Basin.

For more information: Apache-Sitgreaves National Forest, P.O. Box 640, Springerville, AZ 85938, (520) 333-4301. Coconino National Forest, 2323 E. Greenlaw Lane, Flagstaff, AZ 86001, (520) 527-3600.

The drive: The Rim Road follows the lofty Mogollon Rim for forty-two twisting miles, dipping in and out of shallow side canyons, passing through lush ponderosa pine forest, and stopping atop high cliffs that offer marvelous views. The drive, Forest Road 300, is paved for its first three miles to Woods Canyon Lake and gravel for the remainder. The road traverses the old General Crook Trail, a military road that linked Camp Verde and Fort Apache during the Apache wars. Sweeping views unfold along the route of the broad Tonto Basin, the Mazatzal Mountains, and Camelback Mountain in Phoenix eighty-five miles to the southwest. On clear days the discerning eye can identify the hazy ridges of the Santa Catalina Mountains near Tucson almost 150 miles away. The Mogollon Rim is exactly that—the southern rim of the Colorado Plateau. The rim, one of Arizona's largest geographic features, runs west and then northwest as a high escarpment from the White Mountains near the New Mexico border to Williams, a distance of over 200 miles. The

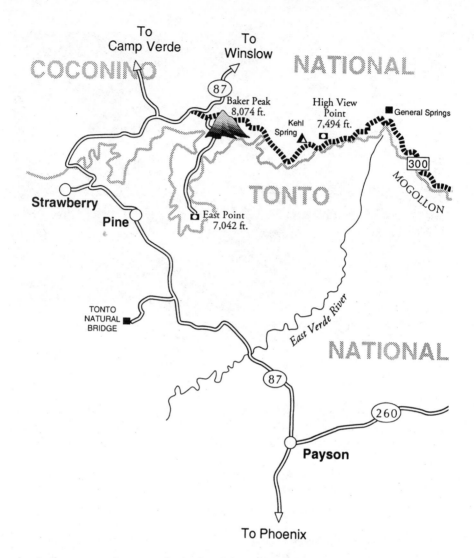

rim is the scarp of a great fault that lifted the plateau above the land to the south. Elevations along the Rim Road average 7,600 feet and reach over 7,900 feet on Promontory Butte. The rim also divides the plateau ecosystems to the north from the basin and range desert to the south.

Summer and autumn are the best times to travel the Rim Road. The road is generally open from May through October, depending on when the snow and mud dry up and when the first snow falls. Summers, compared to the southern lowlands around Phoenix, are pleasant. Expect highs along the rim in the seventies and eighties, with nights in the forties. The rim forces moisture-laden clouds to rise and precipitate. Daily thunderstorms are common in summer. Autumn days are clear and warm. Nights can be frosty, particularly by October. Heavy snowfall and mud closes the road to all but snowmobiles in winter and spring. Allow four to six hours to travel the route.

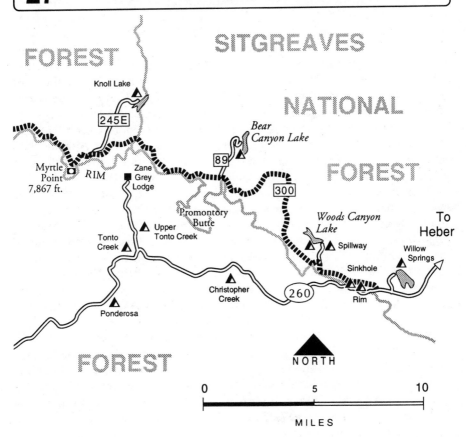

The Rim Road, Forest Road 300, begins on Arizona Highway 260, twenty-two miles southwest of Heber and thirty-two miles northeast of Payson. Turn west and follow the paved road through a dense ponderosa pine forest for three miles. Rim and Sink Hole campgrounds, with thirty-four sites each, lie alongside the road. The Rim Lakes Vista Trail begins in Rim Campground and winds along the cliffed rim for a couple miles. The trail offers intimate views of the rim and the Tonto Basin below.

The road becomes gravel after another mile. A paved spur turns north here and travels a mile to Woods Canyon Lake, a popular trout fishing and camping spot for Arizonans escaping summer's heat. Two campgrounds, Aspen and Spillway, have a total of 149 campsites in the forest and along the lakeshore. A store offers groceries and boat rentals. Rocky Point Picnic Area sits on the south shore.

The drive swings north through an open ponderosa woodland. After a few miles it begins working its way west, dipping through shallow ravines. The first views of the Mogollon Rim are reached opposite 7,914-foot Promontory Butte. Sandstone cliffs and steep slopes matted with timber fall away from the rocky rim. The road continues west, following the rim and offering glimpses of the Tonto Basin. Bear Canyon Lake, three miles north on Forest Road 89, has a primitive campground and good fishing. Eight miles further west is Forest Road 295E, the turnoff to seventy-seven-acre Knoll Lake. This pretty lake, impounded by a dam, nestles in Leonard Canyon. The scenic National Forest campground has forty-two sites, water, and restrooms.

The Rim Road follows or parallels the General George Crook National Recreation Trail, an old military road that connected Fort Apache with Prescott and Fort Verde. The road, some 220 miles long, proved crucial to ending the bloody Apache Wars. General Crook, one of the United States' most effective Indian fighters, and his men scouted the route in 1871 along the Mogollon Rim, an Apache stronghold, and built the road in 1872. The road was used for twenty-two years, although after the railroad reached Holbrook in 1882 it became less traveled. The Rim Road was constructed atop the Crook Trail in 1928. Interest in General Crook and his road revived the trail in the 1970s, with 135 miles of trail marked. White Vs on trees and rock cairns mark the route. Today the trail, designated a National Recreation Trail, serves hikers, historians, and horseback riders. A trail guide provides maps and historical data for hikers.

The Highline Trail, another National Recreation Trail, traverses the base of the Mogollon Rim below the Rim Road for fifty miles between Pine and Arizona 260. This trail follows pioneer paths through lush forests, over sparkling streams, and past historic sites like author Zane Grey's mountain lodge.

The road, threading along the rim, passes numerous overlooks including 7,867-foot Myrtle Point and 7,775-foot Burnt Point. Much of the pine forest along the central portion of the drive was decimated by fires in the late 1980s, leaving blackened tree skeletons.

Nine miles west of the turnoff to Knoll Lake is the head of General Springs Canyon, lowest point along the Rim Road. Springs in the steep canyon, dropping south, form the headwaters of the East Verde River. An historic marker here commemorates the Battle of Big Dry Wash fought between the U.S. Cavalry and a band of sixty Apaches on July 17, 1882. The battle, fought at a site seven miles north of General Springs, marked the end of the Apache Campaign. It was the final battle fought between the Apaches and Army troops in Arizona. A year later, in 1883, the Mineral Belt Railroad attempted to tunnel through the rim for a proposed railroad between Globe and Flagstaff. A trail leads down to the failed tunnel project.

The road, hugging the rimrock, continues west and after a few miles reaches Hi-View Point, the most spectacular overlook on the Mogollon Rim. The forested Tonto Basin spreads out below the rimrock. Steep slopes littered with buff-colored crags drop away. Beyond lies Payson in a forest clearing, and further south tower the Four Peaks in the Mazatzal Wilderness Area.

Alert visitors can spot some of the wildlife, including elk, deer, turkeys, black bear, coyote, and mountain lion, that inhabit the rim forest.

Past Hi-View, the road climbs away from the rim and threads through a thick, lush forest of pine, fir, and spruce. A dense understory of ferns and grass thrives beneath the trees. Kehl Springs Campground, with eight shaded campsites, sits alongside the road. A fifty-year-old pioneer split rail fence surrounds the campground. It makes a peaceful place to camp while exploring the rim country.

Heading west, the road winds through the forest and after a few miles climbs over the flank of 8,074-foot Baker Butte before dropping down to Arizona Highway 87. Payson, via Strawberry and Pine, lies twenty-seven miles south and almost 3,000 feet lower. Tonto Natural Bridge, a 183-foot-high travertine span, sits west of the highway near Pine.

28 PUERTO BLANCO & AJO MOUNTAIN DRIVE
Organ Pipe Cactus National Monument

General description: The twenty-one-mile Ajo Mountain Drive and the fifty-three-mile Puerto Blanco Drive, both gravel roads, make scenic loops through the remote and beautiful backcountry of Organ Pipe Cactus National Monument.

Special attractions: Scenic views, photography, wildflowers, wildlife, nature study, birdwatching, picnicking, organ pipe cacti, senita cacti, hiking, backcountry camping and backpacking, Senita Basin, Quitobaquito Spring, Estes Canyon, Ajo Range, natural arch, Camino del Diablo.

Location: Southwestern Arizona. Both drives begin near the monument visitor center on Arizona Highway 85 about thirty-two miles south of Ajo. The drives lie about 150 miles from both Phoenix and Tucson.

Drive route names: Puerto Blanco Drive, Ajo Mountain Drive.

Travel season: The drives are open year-round, although heavy thunderstorms may wash out and close the roads in summer. Be advised that summer temperatures often climb into the 100s. Carry sufficient water for your needs. Early morning is the best time to travel the roads in summer. Motor homes over twenty-five feet long and trailers are not allowed on either drive. Smaller motor homes may also have trouble with sharp curves and rough road sections. Visitors should call ahead to check on the condition of roads. They are easily damaged by rainstorms and often closed for repairs.

Camping: The monument campground, with 208 tent and RV sites, is open year-round on a first-come, first-served basis. The campground is a mile south of the visitor center. A small primitive campground sits at the mouth of Alamo Canyon off AZ 85 north of the visitor center. Backcountry camping is permitted in the monument. Ask at the visitor center for more information

and permits. Private campgrounds are found in Lukeville, Why, and Ajo.
Services: No services are available on either road. Complete services are found at Lukeville, Why, and Ajo. Make sure you have sufficient gas before driving the Puerto Blanco loop.
Nearby attractions: Sonoyta, Pinacate Lava Fields, Puerto Penasco, Sea of Cortez, Cabeza Prieta National Wildlife Refuge, Ajo, Tohono O'odham Indian Reservation, Painted Rocks State Park, Baboquivari Peak.
For more information: Organ Pipe Cactus National Monument, Route 1, Box 100, Ajo, AZ 85321, (520) 387-6849.

The drive: Organ Pipe Cactus National Monument, sprawling across 516 square miles of southern Arizona along the Mexican border, preserves one of the last great expanses of pristine Sonoran Desert in the United States. The monument belies the image of deserts as being dead and inhospitable environments. The monument fits every definition of a desert with its hot climate and scant nine inches of annual precipitation, yet this dry land supports an amazingly rich flora and fauna including over 500 plant species from delicate flowers to giant saguaros. Organ Pipe supports this diversity of life and a unique blend of five different plant communities because two subdivisions—the Lower Colorado Subdivision and the Arizona Upland Subdivision—of the Sonoran Desert merge here.

Two of Arizona's best scenic drives—the twenty-one-mile Ajo Mountain Drive and the fifty-three-mile Puerto Blanco Drive—explore this spacious parkland of craggy mountains, abrupt canyons, sweeping bajadas, and some of America's rarest and most unusual plants. The graded dirt drives, both one-way for extended sections, twist through the scenic desert and stop at overlooks, picnic areas, and points of interest. A National Park Service guide, keyed to numbered roadside posts, is available at the monument's visitor center for each drive. The narrow, winding road is not recommended for trailers or motor homes over twenty-five feet long.

The scenic drives are open year-round. October through April offers the monument's most pleasant weather, with warm, dry days between sixty and eighty degrees and occasional light rainshowers. January highs average sixty-seven degrees. Intense heat is the norm between May and September. Daily highs regularly climb over 100 degrees. July, the hottest month, averages twenty-five days over 100 degrees. The monument's highest recorded temperature, 116 degrees, was set in July, 1958. July, August, and September also bring the rainy season. Torrential thunderstorms, fueled by the hot days and Pacific moisture, drop a considerable portion of the area's annual 8.7 inches of rainfall. Be aware of flash flooding and possible road washouts when driving the roads during and after storms.

The fifty-three-mile-long Puerto Blanco Drive, beginning just west of the visitor center off Arizona Highway 85, makes a loop through the monument's southwest sector. The road swings around the northern flank of the Puerto Blanco Mountains, follows a broad wash to historic Quitobaquito Springs, parallels the U.S.-Mexico border to route 85 just north of Lukeville, and heads

The rugged Diablo Range looms over the Ajo Mountain Drive in Organ Pipe Cactus National Monument.

north up the paved highway to the road's start. The road is one-way for twenty-two miles from the visitor center to a junction a couple miles north of Quitobaquito Springs.

The drive heads northwest from the visitor center, crossing a wide bajada or outwash plain that gently slopes northward. The road swings around 2,615-foot Twin Peaks, its dark rounded summits lifting high above the road. Heading northwest, the drive tilts, dips, and winds through sandy arroyos and across stony areas of desert pavement. The wide gravel bajada, formed by heavy runoff depositing sand and gravel from surrounding mountains at their base, forms the monument's most species-rich ecosystem—the mixed scrub community. A large and diverse number of plants live here. Dominant plants include the palo verde, the yellow-blossumed brittlebush, ocotillo, and a variety of cacti including saguaro, organ pipe, and cholla.

The drive's first ten miles offer an excellent wildflower extravaganza in March and April. Springtime can bring a riot of color to the cooler, north-facing bajada after sufficient gentle, nourishing winter rains. Masses of lavender lupine grow in roadside gardens; carpets of orange poppies nod in warm afternoon breezes; rich-pink owl clover spreads among prickly pear cacti; and brittlebushes liven the dry hillsides with swatches of gold. Later, when temperatures warm, the cacti burst forth with blossoms. The saguaro and organ pipe begin blooming in mid-May. The palo verde, Arizona's state tree, also becomes a mass of yellow flowers in May.

Pinkley Peak, at 3,145 feet the highest summit in the Puerto Blanco Mountains, towers west and south of the drive as it swings around the range. The peak is named for Frank Pinkley, the superintendent of the southwestern national monuments between 1924 and 1939. Mt. Pinkley and the northern Puerto Blanco Mountains are predominantly volcanic in origin. Massive eruptions during Tertiary times some 14 to 22 million years ago deposited thick layers of hardened volcanic ash or tuff and lava flows. The alternating layers of yellowish tuff and dark lava gives Mt. Pinkley its layered-cake look. Older granite, gneiss, and schist compose the southern part of the range. Block-faulting along north-south trending faultlines uplifted the range above the surrounding basins which are actually fault troughs filled with debris washed from the mountains.

As the road turns around the north flank of the range, marvelous views of the broad Valley of the Ajo and the towering Ajo Range unfold to the north and east. Sharp, rocky peaks stud the landscape along the road. After eleven miles the road crosses a shallow gap through the range.

Past the gap the road rolls west over a broken bajada. The road generally parallels Aguajita Wash, a dry arroyo that runs southwest from the pass to the Rio Sonoyta in Mexico. Palo Verde, ironwood, and mesquite trees line sandy wash floors that drain west from the mountains to Aguajita Wash.

The drive offers good views northward to the Bates Mountains and 3,197-foot Kino Peak, its butte-shaped high point. The mountains, named after early prospector W. Bates, are, like the Ajo and Puerto Blanco ranges, fault-block sierras layered with volcanic tuff and lava flows. The mountains are capped with erosion-resistant basaltic lava. Kino Peak is named for Padre Eusebio Kino, a Jesuit priest who traversed the area while establishing a chain of missions in the Southwest in the late 1600s. He founded the Mission of San Marcel in what is now the Mexican border town of Sonoyta in 1698.

The Bates Mountains harbor the monument's wildest country. The remote range is accessed from the scenic drive via an ancient Indian trail that runs from Quitobaquito Springs northward. It's not a trail easily found or followed. In fact, hiking to the Bates Mountains is almost entirely cross-country. The trail was possibly used as long ago as 9,000 years by early paleo-hunters. The Hohokam walked the trail from A.D. 150 to 1450 on shell and food gathering trips to the Sea of Cortez. The O'odham Indians followed the trail in historic times.

The parking area for the Golden Bell Mine is reached seven miles from the gap. Prospector Charlie Bell operated the mine in the 1930s, finding small quantities of gold and silver. Other mines, including the Victoria, Martinez,

Lost Cabin, Milton, and Baker mines, were worked in the mineralized southern reaches of the Puerto Blanco and Sonoyta mountains. The Victoria, the richest mine, produced only about $125,000 in gold and silver in the late 1800s. Take care when walking around any of the monument's mines. Uncovered prospect holes and cisterns riddle the hillsides.

Bonita Well sits 1.5 miles past the mine. An old stock corral and watering trough, shaded by scrubby trees, sits alongside the road. The well was dug in the 1930s by rancher Robert Gray as a stock tank. A unique trap-gate allowed thirsty cattle to enter the corral. The gate would shut after the cow entered, trapping it in the pen. A small picnic area sits across the road from the now-dry well.

The drive runs southwest and after a few more miles reaches a junction and the end of the one-way segment. A right turn heads north up a four-wheel-drive track to Growler Valley and Bates Well in the remote northwest sector of the monument. A left turn goes south two miles to Quitobaquito Springs.

Quitobaquito, probably meaning "little many springs" in the O'odham language, is a true desert oasis. Because plentiful water flows from springs and seeps here, the oasis has long been a popular stopover. Early Indians watered here; Spanish explorers paused at its refreshing pools; and the California-bound Forty Niners stopped at the lovely oasis for one long, last drink before trekking across the dreaded El Camino del Diablo, the Devil's Highway, which led to the Yuma Crossing of the Colorado River.

The oasis, a large pool about sixty yards across, sits just north of the Mexican border. Bullrushes and willows thickly line its banks. Cottonwoods, including one giant leaning over its west bank, lift their graceful limbs above the still water. Myriad bird species, lured by the area's water, insects, and shelter, flock to the pond. Birds seen include the phainopepla, Gila woodpecker, vermilion flycatcher, house finch, killdeer, ducks, and heron. Also living here is the rare desert pupfish, a small minnow that can survive water temperatures over 100 degrees. The pond is filled by a spring of eighty-degree water that gushes out of a fault in the granite hillside to the north.

The drive runs eastward from Quitobaquito paralleling a barbed wire fence that marks the boundary between the United States and Mexico. The road runs through a saltbush plant community on an alkaline, sandy floodplain. A spur road leads 4.5 miles north to Senita Basin. This shallow valley, lying between the Puerto Blanco and Sonoyta mountains, is home to some of the monument's rarest plants. This dry area is one of the few places in the United States where the senita cacti can be found. This yellow-green cactus looks much like an organ pipe with long stems growing up from the plant's base. At the stem's end are long, whiskery spines that resemble an old man's beard and give the cactus its Spanish name senita meaning "old one." Stunted elephant trees, more common to Baja California, also grow in the basin. A small picnic area lies at the road's end.

The road runs east from the Senita Basin turnoff and climbs through a saguaro forest in the Sonoyta Mountains. A few miles later it ends at paved Arizona route 85. To the south sits Lukeville on the border, and beyond is

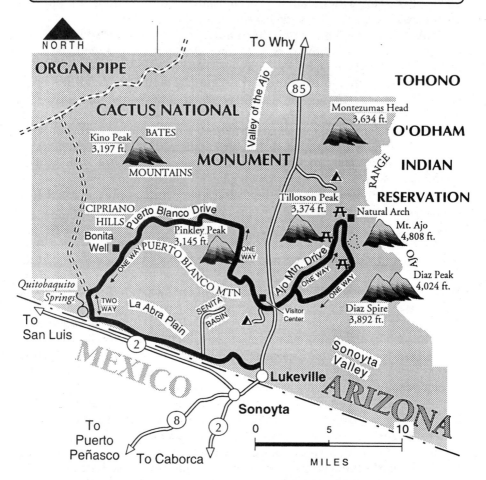

Sonoyta and Mexico. The monument visitor center lies five miles northward.

The graded dirt Ajo Mountain Drive, beginning east of the Visitor Center, loops for twenty-one miles through the Diablo Mountains and beneath the soaring Ajo Range. The road, one-way for seventeen miles, traverses rugged country with deep canyons, steep rock ribs, cactus-studded mountainsides, and spectacular views.

The road bounces northeast for two miles before becoming one-way. A mixed scrub community of brittlebush, bursage, and palo verde scatters across low volcanic hills that flank the roadside. The broad bajada sloping away from the Diablo Mountains is covered with tall cigar and candelabra-shaped saguaros, chain and teddy-bear cholla cacti, creosote, saltbush, and palo verdes. After a few miles the road passes Diablo Canyon Picnic Area,

154

with a couple ramada-covered tables, before climbing the western skirt of the Diablo Mountains.

A good overlook is reached in the saddle between 3,374-foot Tillotson Peak to the west and the craggy bulk of the Diablo range. The scenic view to the south encompasses the wide Sonoyta Valley and the rugged outline of the Cubabi Mountains in northern Mexico. Tillotson Peak is a short but steep hike from here. Head west across its eastern slopes to the final rocky pyramid.

The drive continues northeast, dipping in and out of canyons and climbing over gravel ridges. Organ pipe cacti line the road and ascend nearby dry, hot south-facing slopes. The cacti, growing mainly within the national monument in the United States, is characterized by numerous long, slender stems that reach a maximum height of about ten feet.

After a few miles the road swings below the towering escarpment of the Ajo Mountains. At the road's northernmost point, a natural arch ninety feet wide and thirty-six feet high sits on an eroded rock fin high above the road and Arch Canyon. The Ajo Range, like the Puerto Blanco Mountains, was formed by alternating episodes of violent volcanic eruptions some 14 to 20 million years ago that deposited the light-colored tuff or compressed ash and lava flows that seeped across the surface and formed thick layers of andesite and rhyolite. Erosion-resistant lava rocks cap the range's prominent summits, including 4,808-foot Mt. Ajo, the monument's highest peak.

The drive turns south at Arch Canyon and runs along the western edge of the craggy Ajo Range. Boulder Canyon slices deeply into the abrupt mountain wall, its sides flanked by soaring cliffs and ramparts. Further south the road drops into narrow Estes Canyon and reaches a picnic area and the trailhead for the Estes Canyon-Bull Pasture Trail.

This excellent trail makes up a four-mile loop up Estes Canyon and Bull Pasture, a high, open ampitheater used by early ranchers as a cattle wintering area. Mount Ajo's summit is reached from the Bull Pasture. Ask at the visitor center for a route description. Be sure to carry adaquate water when hiking.

The range, with a diversity of plants, high rainfall, and cool temperatures is home to many wildlife species. Bobcats, grey foxes, badgers, javelinas, coyotes, whitetail deer, and skunks roam the area. The elusive and shy desert bighorn sheep lives atop the rugged mountains. Gila monsters and western diamondback rattlesnakes both inhabit the monument, particularly in the lower elevations. Be careful when hiking where you put your hands and feet, and carry a flashlight at night to avoid stepping on a snake.

The road heads south down widening Estes Canyon and swings around the southern edge of the Diablo Mountains. Marvelous views of 4,024-foot Diaz Peak and 3,892-foot Diaz Spire are seen southeast of here. Both are named for Melchior Diaz who explored the region in 1540. The drive runs southwest, passing dense stands of cacti, to Teddybear Pass. Deceptive-looking teddybear cholla thrive on the hot hillsides along the road. The cholla's soft, fuzzy joints readily break off when brushed against, embedding their sharp spines in their new host. The road, continuing west, rejoins the two-way section and shortly afterwards lies paved Arizona Highway 85 and the drive's end.

U. S. 95
Yuma to Quartzsite

General description: An eighty-mile-long highway that runs north from Yuma across the barren desert of western Arizona to Quartzsite.

Special attractions: Yuma, Kofa Mountains, Palm Canyon, Kofa National Wildlife Refuge, Castle Dome Mountains, primitive camping, hiking, wildlife observation.

Location: Southwestern Arizona. The drive follows U.S. 95 from Yuma north to Quartzsite on Interstate 10.

Drive route number: U.S. Highway 95.

Travel season: Year-round. This part of Arizona offers extremely mild winters. Expect very hot summer temperatures. Carry plenty of water and don't venture off the highway on to the Kofa's backroads without letting someone know your whereabouts.

Camping: Camping is available at the Imperial Dam area, Martinez Lake, and at the BLM's La Posa Recreational Area just south of Quartzsite. Several primitive campgrounds scatter across the Kofa National Wildlife Refuge. The easiest to reach is below Palm Canyon nine miles east of U.S. 95. Many private RV parks are in both Quartzsite and Yuma.

Services: All services in Yuma and Quartzsite.

Nearby attractions: Imperial National Wildlife Refuge, Cibola National Wildlife Refuge, Cabeza Prieta National Wildlife Refuge, Camino del Diablo, San Luis, Mexico, Algodones Sand Dunes, Yuma Territorial Prison.

For more information: Yuma County Chamber of Commerce, 377 S. Main St., Yuma, AZ 85364, (520) 782-2567. Kofa National Wildlife Refuge, P.O. Box 6290, Yuma, AZ 85364, (520) 783-7861.

The drive: The U.S. 95 scenic drive runs north for eighty miles from Yuma and the Colorado River to Quartzsite through one of Arizona's harshest but most beautiful desert landscapes. It's a land of extreme temperatures, dazzling sunlight, wide creosote-studded basins, and jagged mountains that lift rocky ramparts high above the desert floor. It's also a land of peace and solitude. Stop and walk away from the highway and stillness surrounds you. The silence is broken only by the wind's rustle in an ironwood tree, the song of a rock wren among the cholla cacti, and a chorus of coyotes echoing up a dry wash.

The drive, open year-round, offers pleasant weather in fall, winter, and spring. Expect temperatures between sixty and eighty in winter and as high as 100 in late spring or early fall. Light rains gently water the land in winter. Summer, of course, is another matter. Daily highs are almost always over 100 degrees and often climb above 110 degrees. Yuma, at the drive's beginning, boasts an all-time high of 123 degrees in 1950. If you do drive the road in summer be sure to carry sufficient water for yourself and your car. Five

The ragged battlements of the Kofa Mountains rise above teddy-bear cholla cacti off U. S. 95.

gallons is not too much. The highway is frequently traveled so aid comes quickly. If you, however, drive any of the Kofa backroads be sure to make adequate preparations. Carry water and supplies, let someone know your planned route and timetable, and stay with the vehicle in the event of a breakdown.

The scenic drive begins in Yuma, one of Arizona's oldest towns. The area was originally inhabited by the Quechan Indians, who grew corn, beans, and melons on the river flood plain, and built large communal dwellings that housed as many as 100 Indians. The Spanish first visited here in 1540, almost seventy years before Jamestown was settled. They called the Indians the Yumas or "sons of the leader." The Spanish, who established a mission here on the trade route from Sonora to California, found that the river crossing at the confluence of the Colorado and Gila rivers was the easiest on the lower Colorado. American mountain men traversed the region in the early 1800s in search of beaver pelts. The Yuma Crossing was later used by Colonel Stephen Kearny's troops in the Mexican War to pass into California. The 1849 gold rush brought a cascade of Forty-Niners through the sweltering desert to

Yuma. Fort Yuma was built above the river to protect the crossing from Indian attacks in 1851, and three years later Colorado City, which became Yuma, was established. Today Yuma, the center of a rich agricultural region, offers a wealth of things to do. Best known are the Yuma Territorial Prison State Historic Park and boating and fishing on the Colorado River.

The scenic drive follows U.S. 95 east on 16th Street from Interstate 8's Exit 2. The highway runs through the broad South Gila Valley, past irrigated farms and orchards, for just over nine miles before swinging north around the foot of the Gila Mountains. The road crosses the shallow Gila River after four more miles. The Gila, southern Arizona's longest river, rises high in western New Mexico's Gila Mountains and braids across Arizona through Phoenix to its confluence with the Colorado River at Yuma.

A few miles east of the river bridge lies the old townsite of Gila City. Arizona's first gold rush occurred here in 1858 after gold placers were discovered along the river. Soon the town, full of gold-fevered prospectors, boasted a populace of 1,200 people. One wrote, "There was everything in Gila City within a few months but a church and a jail." By 1864, after surpassing $2 million in gold, the lode played out and the town emptied, leaving, according to one wag, "three chimneys and a coyote."

Past the river the highway swings north along Castle Dome Wash and climbs onto the broad Castle Dome Plain. This broad basin, covered with scattered ocotillo, saltbush, and creosote, is part of the U.S. Army's Yuma Proving Ground. Travel off the highway is restricted. The area was established in 1942 as a training ground for General George Patton's north African troops.

Imperial Dam, the first in a long ladder of dams that block the Colorado River, lies five miles west of U.S. 95 almost twenty miles out from Yuma. Water from this impoundment is funneled west through a series of canals to California's fertile Imperial Valley. Three miles up the highway another spur road leads ten miles west to Martinez Lake. Camping is available at private RV campgrounds here. Imperial and Cibola national wildlife refuges border the Colorado River northward for about forty miles. Both areas protect lush riparian and dry desert habitats. A wide variety of birds winter here, including sandhill cranes and thousands of Canada geese. Camping is prohibited in the refuges, although visitors can hike, boat, birdwatch, and fish.

The drive runs arrow-straight across the plain. The hazy Castle Dome Mountains, a remote and rugged desert range in the Kofa National Wildlife Refuge, stretches along the northeast horizon. Castle Dome Peak, a 3,793-foot fortress of gaunt volcanic rock, is the range high point.

The Castle Dome and Kofa mountains to the north are embraced by the Kofa National Game Refuge, a huge swath of desert land east of the highway that protects herds of desert bighorn sheep. This rugged 660,000-acre enclave, established in 1936, is one of the bighorn's last refuges. In other parts of the Southwest it is being slowly squeezed toward extinction by loss of habitat, competition with range cattle, and trophy hunting. Between 800 and 1,000 bighorns roam the preserve.

Further north the highway rolls through low, barren hills on the north end

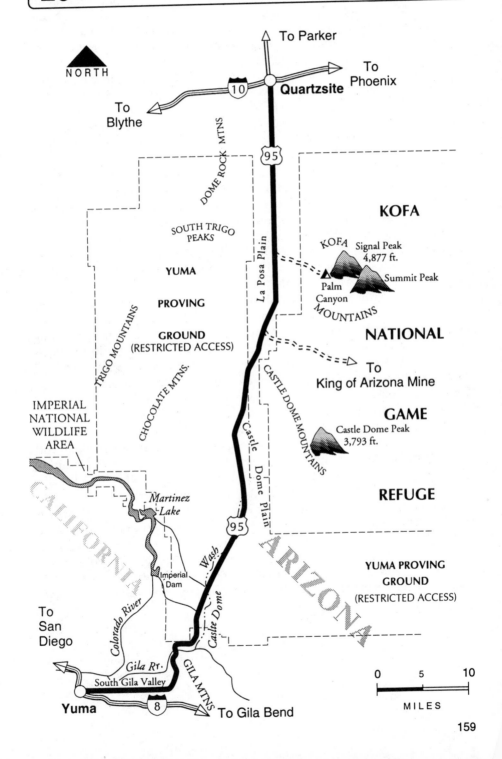

NORTH

To Parker

To Phoenix

Quartzsite

To Blythe

DOME ROCK MTNS

10

95

KOFA

SOUTH TRIGO PEAKS

KOFA

Signal Peak 4,877 ft.

Summit Peak

YUMA

La Posa Plain

Palm Canyon

PROVING

MOUNTAINS

NATIONAL

GROUND (RESTRICTED ACCESS)

To King of Arizona Mine

TRIGO MOUNTAINS

CHOCOLATE MTNS.

CASTLE DOME MOUNTAINS

GAME

Castle Dome Peak 3,793 ft.

IMPERIAL NATIONAL WILDLIFE AREA

REFUGE

CALIFORNIA

Martinez Lake

Castle Dome Plain

95

YUMA PROVING GROUND (RESTRICTED ACCESS)

ARIZONA

Wash

Colorado River

Imperial Dam

Castle Dome

To San Diego

Gila Rr.

GILA MTNS.

South Gila Valley

Yuma

8

To Gila Bend

0   5   10

MILES

of the Castle Dome Mountains and enters La Posa Plain, a wide basin flanked by the Dome Rock Mountains on the west and the Kofa Mountains on the east. The site of Stone Cabin lies about fifty-three miles north of Yuma on the plain's southern edge. Stone Cabin was once a stopover on the stage and freight route between Ehrenberg on the Colorado River and Yuma. Most of the highway follows the old road that was once used by twenty-mule-teams that hauled ore from the mountains.

A rough road heads east from Stone Cabin and hooks twenty-two miles into the Kofa's southern canyons where some of the area's most productive mines operated, including the Rob Roy, North Star, and the fabulously wealthy King of Arizona. The King of Arizona mine, discovered by prospector Charles Eichelberger in 1896, yielded $3.5 million in gold before the lode worked out in 1910.

The King of Arizona also lent its name to the mountains north of the mine. The acronym Kofa derives from the "K of A" label stamped on all the mine's property. Mapmakers applied the name to the mountains, replacing its previous moniker, the S.H. Mountains. In the 1860s, soldiers and prospectors gave the range the impolite name after noticing the slant-roofed, squarish rock formations atop the peaks resembled the era's outhouses. When women came into the area, the name was abbreviated to its initials S.H., which, they were told, stood for Short Horn.

The Kofas form a long, jagged skyline of buttes, towers, buttresses, ramparts, castles, and pinnacles east of the highway. The massive cliffs, volcanic in origin, are composed of andesite and welded tuff. The forbidding range, topped by 4,877-foot Signal Peak, is known not only for its bighorns but the stately groves of rare wild palm trees that grow in a few secluded canyons. The palms, *Washingtonia filifera*, once thrived in the far Southwest. Changing climates, however, forced the palm into isolated groves in northern Baja, the California desert, and the Kofas.

The Kofa's most accessible grove grows in the narrow defile of Palm Canyon on the range's west face. Turn east on graded Palm Canyon Road and travel nine miles over the stony desert to a parking area and primitive campground. A trail threads up into the green canyon where hikers can marvel at these graceful relics of a wetter, vanished world.

Past the Palm Canyon turn the highway runs straight north up the plain for eighteen miles to 875-foot-high Quartzsite and the drive's end at Interstate 10. Rocky ranges—the Dome Rock, Plomosa, and New Water mountains— lift their serrated ridges beyond the road. Quartzsite is a well-known snowbird destination with as many as 20,000 RVers putting down winter roots. It hosts one of the nation's largest rock and mineral shows and attracts rockhounds for ten days every February.

ABOUT THE AUTHOR

   Stewart M. Green is a freelance photographer and writer living in Colorado Springs, Colorado. His photographs appear in many national publications. He is the author and photographer of *Pikes Peaks Country: The Complete Guide*, *Back Country Byways*, *Scenic Driving California*, *Scenic Driving Colorado*, and *Rock Climbing Colorado*. He is currently working on *Scenic Driving New England* and *Rock Climbing Utah*, both for Falcon Press.

SCENIC DRIVING GUIDES

Scenic Driving Alaska and the Yukon
Scenic Driving Arizona
Scenic Driving the Beartooth Highway
Scenic Driving California
Scenic Driving Colorado
Scenic Driving Florida
Scenic Driving Georgia
Scenic Driving Hawaii
Scenic Driving Idaho
Scenic Driving Michigan
Scenic Driving Minnesota
Scenic Driving Montana
Scenic Driving New England
Scenic Driving New Mexico
Scenic Driving North Carolina
Scenic Driving Oregon
Scenic Driving the Ozarks
Scenic Driving Pennsylvania
Scenic Driving Texas
Scenic Driving Utah
Scenic Driving Washington
Scenic Driving Wisconsin
Scenic Driving Wyoming
Scenic Driving Yellowstone and
  the Grand Teton National Parks
Scenic Byways East
Scenic Byways Far West
Scenic Byways Rocky Mountains
Back Country Byways

HISTORIC TRAIL GUIDES

Traveling California's Gold Rush Country
Traveling the Lewis & Clark Trail
Traveling the Oregon Trail
Traveler's Guide to the Pony Express Trail

WILDLIFE VIEWING GUIDES

Alaska Wildlife Viewing Guide
Arizona Wildlife Viewing Guide
California Wildlife Viewing Guide
Colorado Wildlife Viewing Guide
Florida Wildlife Viewing Guide
Indiana Wildlife Vewing Guide
Iowa Wildlife Viewing Guide
Kentucky Wildlife Viewing Guide
Massachusetts Wildlife Viewing Guide
Montana Wildlife Viewing Guide
Nebraska Wildlife Viewing Guide
Nevada Wildlife Viewing Guide
New Hampshire Wildlife Viewing Guide
New Jersey Wildlife Viewing Guide
New Mexico Wildlife Viewing Guide
New York Wildlife Viewing Guide
North Carolina Wildlife Viewing Guide
North Dakota Wildlife Viewing Guide
Ohio Wildlife Viewing Guide
Oregon Wildlife Viewing Guide
Puerto Rico & the Virgin Islands
  Wildlife Viewing Guide
Tennessee Wildlife Viewing Guide
Texas Wildlife Viewing Guide
Utah Wildlife Viewing Guide
Vermont Wildlife Viewing Guide
Virginia Wildlife Viewing Guide
Washington Wildlife Viewing Guide
West Virginia Wildlife Viewing Guide
Wisconsin Wildlife Viewing Guide

FALCON GUIDES® Leading the Way

FIELD GUIDES

Bitterroot: Montana State Flower
Canyon Country Wildflowers
Central Rocky Mountains
  Wildflowers
Great Lakes Berry Book
New England Berry Book
Ozark Wildflowers
Pacific Northwest Berry Book
Plants of Arizona
Rare Plants of Colorado
Rocky Mountain Berry Book
Scats & Tracks of the Pacific
  Coast States
Scats & Tracks of the
  Rocky Mountains
Southern Rocky Mountain
  Wildflowers
Tallgrass Prairie Wildflowers
Western Trees
Wildflowers of Southwestern
  Utah
Willow Bark and Rosehips

FISHING GUIDES

Fishing Alaska
Fishing the Beartooths
Fishing Florida
Fishing Glacier National Park
Fishing Maine
Fishing Montana
Fishing Wyoming
Fishing Yellowstone
  National Park

ROCKHOUNDING GUIDES

Rockhounding Arizona
Rockhounding California
Rockhounding Colorado
Rockhounding Montana
Rockhounding Nevada
Rockhound's Guide to New
  Mexico
Rockhounding Texas
Rockhounding Utah
Rockhounding Wyoming

MORE GUIDEBOOKS

Backcountry Horseman's
  Guide to Washington
Camping California's
  National Forests
Exploring Canyonlands &
  Arches National Parks
Exploring Hawaii's Parklands
Exploring Mount Helena
Exploring Southern California
  Beaches
Recreation Guide to WA
  National Forests
Touring California & Nevada
  Hot Springs
Touring Colorado Hot Springs
Touring Montana & Wyoming
  Hot Springs
Trail Riding Western
  Montana
Wild Country Companion
Wilderness Directory
Wild Montana
Wild Utah

BIRDING GUIDES

Birding Minnesota
Birding Montana
Birding Northern California
Birding Texas
Birding Utah

PADDLING GUIDES

Floater's Guide to Colorado
Paddling Minnesota
Paddling Montana
Paddling Okefenokee
Paddling Oregon
Paddling Yellowstone & Grand
  Teton National Parks

HOW-TO GUIDES

Avalanche Aware
Backpacking Tips
Bear Aware
Desert Hiking Tips
Hiking with Dogs
Leave No Trace
Mountain Lion Alert
Reading Weather
Route Finding
Using GPS
Wilderness First Aid
Wilderness Survival

WALKING

Walking Colorado Springs
Walking Denver
Walking Portland
Walking St. Louis
Walking Virginia Beach

■ *To order any of these books, check with your local bookseller
or call FALCON® at* **1-800-582-2665**.
Visit us on the world wide web at:
www.FalconOutdoors.com

FALCON®

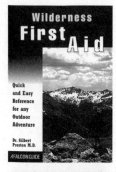
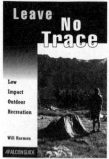